RAISING KIDS

TRAINING DOGS
AND LIVING THE LIFE YOU DARE TO LEAD

BY SALLY MUNN

Published in the United States

Copyright © 2024 by Sally Munn. All rights reserved.

Library of Congress Cataloging-in-Publication Data:

Print ISBN: 979-8-9927503-0-0
eBook ISBN: 979-8-9927503-1-7

First Edition

For **Nate, Jack, and Avery**

You've exceeded all my expectations

and to

Patrick, *who encouraged me to write this book.*

Thank you for your unwavering friendship and support over the decades.

We installed a pool in 2005 when Avery was 2 years old, Jack was 4 ½ and Nate 7. Every year, during our first swim, we took our muscle shot picture.

Our last picture was in 2021.

TABLE OF CONTENTS

INTRODUCTION 1

BUILDING A BUDGET AND FINANCIAL PLANNING 13

SELECTING YOUR VALUES 27

    VALUE 1: CONSISTENCY AND EXPECTATIONS 31

    VALUE 2: HONESTY AND TRANSPARENCY 61

    VALUE 3: EMPATHY 83

    VALUE 4: CONSEQUENCES AND RESPONSIBILITY 105

    VALUE 5: DELAYED GRATIFICATION, PLUS UNDERSTANDING
    MONEY AND CREDIT 125

    VALUE 6: STRATEGIC THINKING 143

    VALUE 7: FAMILY ADVENTURES & TRADITIONS 153

VALUES SUMMARY 177

TEENS 183

INDEX OF STRATEGIES 201

APPENDICES 203

SAMPLE BUDGET 205

EVALUATING EXPENSES 209

SAVINGS STRATEGIES AND USING CREDIT 213

PAYING FOR COLLEGE 217

DAYCARE 229

DAYCARE AGREEMENT 239

DAYCARE PROVIDER INFORMATION 243

INSEMINATION 245

WILLS AND LIFE INSURANCE 257

FOOTNOTES AND ACKNOWLEDGEMENTS 261

ABOUT THE AUTHOR 263

INTRODUCTION

People become parents for many reasons. Sometimes it's planned, other times not. Whatever the circumstances that brought us here, we're all parents. If you're already a parent feeling a bit overwhelmed or a parent feeling daunted by a sense of responsibility but not sure how to move forward, I believe this book can help you develop actions and strategies to feel more confident and in control. Whether you're a soon to be first time parent, or are already a parent, stepparent, or adoptive parent, this book can help clarify your thoughts and provide strategies to help you coordinate with you partner and succeed in raising well-balanced, well-mannered, confident kids.

I approached parenting in a vastly different way than most people. When I was 33 years old, I'd exhausted all efforts to find a suitable partner and have kids "the right" way, so I elected to conceive my kids via artificial insemination – using the same anonymous donor for all three of my children. For those of you considering single parenting, same sex parenting or co-parenting in a platonic relationship, I've added sections in the Appendix that provide practical information about tactical matters regarding insemination as wells as ways to think and communicate about your non-traditional family.

The decision to have my kids on my own was a long, arduous path. I still believe in the value and strength of the two-parent family. I had hoped to follow the traditional path, but in the pre-internet age, finding a compatible partner after finishing college and buying a house in suburbia was challenging. I explored every opportunity not to do it on my own, however given the multiple broken relationships of my parents, I also knew how critical it was to have the right partner. I believed it was better to have no partner than the wrong one or a bad one. I believe that committing to a life partner is critical, so unable to find a partner for this journey, I chose insemination. My primary reasons included safety, ensuring my children would be genetic siblings and avoiding the risk of anyone ever claiming a right to try to take my child(ren) away from me.

While my parents were good people, from solid families, they married straight out of high school because my mother was pregnant with my older sister. I arrived a little over a year after my older sister was born and was followed by two younger siblings. My parents were kids raising kids and while I have many fond memories from a childhood filled with cousins and overnight visits with grandparents, my parents' marriage ended after 13 years in a very ugly divorce, which was followed by years of fighting. The ramifications of my parents' actions scarred our family connections in ways that are still apparent today. This history helped push me towards solo parenting rather than trying to partner with someone I didn't consider a potential life partner.

When I decided to become a parent, I was committed to creating a stable, loving environment for my child(ren). Before going any further, I want you to stop and ask yourself two basic questions:

1. Why do you want to become a parent?   (or why did you become a parent?)

2. What do you think are the qualities and characteristics of a good parent?

For me, becoming a parent felt like a mission, almost a calling, something I felt compelled to do. I believed raising good children would make the world a better place. Perhaps it was egotistical, but I felt I was smart and capable, had good genes, and a solid moral compass. I believed I could be a great role model for my kids. As a parent, I wanted to share my knowledge and experiences with my child(ren). To me, parenting is all about giving to your child(ren); teaching them how to be good people and creating experiences, the environments, and the opportunities so they can thrive and achieve their potential. Perhaps that sounds a bit corny, but a similar motivation led me to join the Peace Corps after college. I wanted to help others, broaden my own perspectives, and make a positive contribution to the world - one person, one group or one community at a time.

I share my motives because I think it's vital for you to look inside yourself and understand why you want to be a parent, what your goals are and how you see yourself in your role as a parent.

- Is it about legacy?

- About how the thought of being a mom or dad makes you feel?

- Are you looking for something to love?

- Are you indifferent, but your partner or family expects you to have children?

- Or you never really gave it much thought, but just always assumed you'd have a family?

- Other?

Good kids or bad kids don't just happen. All of us are the product of our environment, our experiences, our choices, and the people who impacted our lives. As parents, you have the ability to be the most important people in shaping your child(ren). By bringing a thoughtful approach to parenting, and modeling and teaching your kids your fundamental values, I believe that your children have a better chance of becoming responsible, confident, caring, and independent young adults.

When I decided to become a single parent, I tried to think about everything being a parent would entail. First and foremost, I needed to ensure that I could afford a child. Before trying to become pregnant, I set aside my deep, burning desire to become a mom, ignored my ticking biological clock and prepared a financial budget to ensure that I would be financially able to support a child. I knew that kids cost a lot of money. I believed I owed it to my child and myself to ensure that I would have the financial capacity to support him or her. As a single parent, not working wasn't an option, so my budget also needed to include all the additional costs related to babies and kids including daycare expenses to cover the hours I needed to work. Each time I considered trying to conceive another child, I first updated my budget.

I have two sections in this book about building and updating a budget. In the first section, I've provided a high level overview of budgeting, discuss the difference between wants and needs and other financial considerations. The other more detailed budgeting section is in the Appendix. Parenting is demanding enough without the added pressures and challenges of not having enough money. Building your budget enables you to understand your spending priorities and financial capacity. The details in your budget can be highly insightful and may help you identify spending you can reduce or eliminate to improve your financial situation – whether you become a parent or not. Unless you or your partner are planning to take on a side gig or a second job to generate more income, building a budget is fundamentally about honestly understanding your "must have" expenses, your discretionary expenses and how much money is left over.

I suggest you read the chapter on budgeting and when you're ready to build your budget, use the tools and info in the Appendix. Or if you prefer, I'm sure you can find countless books and podcasts on the topic, so take advantage of whatever resources work best for you. But please do it. As a parent, or soon to be parent, I think it is imperative that you understand your financial situation.

Once I'd addressed the question of money, I thought about my plan for parenting. In addition to logistics like balancing daycare and work, I thought about how I'd teach my child(ren) values, goals, and good behavior. It may sound odd, but I believe that teaching babies and toddlers is not too different from training puppies and dogs. Specifically, give them lots of attention and love, try not to let them get overstimulated or stressed, use simple, consistent words, maintain a predictable schedule, encourage good behavior, and promptly address negative behavior. I also thought about discipline and the kinds of environment and experiences I wanted to create for my child(ren). I thought about gender, sports, and ways to protect my child(ren) from over commercialization. Honestly, I likely overthought it, but the process helped me feel calm, in control and prepared. By asking myself and thinking about those things, I was able to develop plans and tactical strategies that helped make me a better, more thoughtful parent.

While I had family in the area, my family wasn't supportive of my choice to build a family on my own. In fact, when I shared the exciting news that I was pregnant with my oldest, Nate, my dad's first comment was, "Just get married. Marry the gas station attendant. But marry someone." Faced with such underwhelming support, I always strove to have both a primary and a back-up plan so I could respond proactively to the unexpected. Rightly or wrongly, I always had the impression that my family was waiting to see me fail. Waiting to say, "I told you so." I knew that failing wasn't an option; not only because of my pride, but more importantly, because my child(ren) would be counting on me. Therefore, I thought about potential scenarios, the logistics of work family balance and identified the values, principles and strategies that would become the foundation of my parenting. The result is this book.

I believe that parenting can be vastly more effective for you and your kids if you have a firm understanding of your values and guiding principles. If you are parenting with a partner, I would strongly encourage you to discuss and define your goals and principles together. To create the best environment for your child(ren), you and your partner must have alignment in your goals. If you don't have agreement, you invite conflict in your relationship and confusion for your children. As the kids grow and mature, you may need to recalibrate and refine your principles to address their changing needs. Always do this together with your partner.

Having goals and guiding principles is like a road map. They help keep you on the right path when emotions or stresses are high, when your reserves are low, or when an unexpected situation creates a crisis. We each make millions of decisions in our lifetimes: what career to pursue, where to live, what to eat, what to wear, what to do next weekend. Make a bad decision, no worries, make another one. But when you decide to become a parent, it's a lifetime commitment. There's no option to send your kid to a shelter like he or she's a bad puppy. You're in it for the long game, no exit options. Increase your odds of success by knowing your guiding principles, thinking about things in advance and periodically evaluating how you're doing and determine what you need to do differently.

The objective of this book is to discuss the processes and strategies that I used and the values I chose with the aim of helping you to develop and define your own values and your own guiding principles. The more you're able to consciously understand what's important to you as a parent and what you want to teach your children, the greater the likelihood that you'll provide your child(ren) with the environment and guidance to flourish. I've also incorporated strategies – tactical solutions - throughout the book that I found helpful in teaching my children and keeping our daily lives on track.

Finally, regardless of the values and guiding principles you embrace, as you navigate your role as a parent, I would encourage you to consider the following:

1. **Your kids are not your friends**. You are their parent. Be their parent. Once your children are in their 20's or older, and are financially independent and emotionally mature, your relationship can shift toward a relationship of equals, of friends; but not before.

2. **At some point(s) in their lives, your child(ren) will profess to hate you and mean it**. I'll also highlight that at times, you will not like your kids very much either. But they're your kids. Focus on the end game and never say or do anything in anger or frustration that you or

they will regret. When you're faced with a challenge that feels overwhelming, lean into your values, cool your emotions, and decide what decisions or actions would address the issue(s) at hand. Try to set aside your emotional reactions and find a course of action that is true to the values you're trying to teach and model. If necessary, step away if necessary to regain your equilibrium. Then, get back in the game. Your kids need you and are counting on you even as they rail against you.

3. **Your kids are not your confidants or advisors**. You need to protect your child(ren), nurture them, guide them and give them age-appropriate information and feedback throughout their lives. If you need to share information about things in your life that could have a negative impact on your family, don't burden your child(ren) with too many details. I was laid off unexpectedly three times in my life. I was terrified, but each time, I assured my kids that everything would be ok. I assured them that I had savings in the bank and that I would work hard to land another job. Which I did, each time, because I had to.

If you and your partner are having difficulties in your relationship, it's ok if your kids are aware, but do NOT use your children as tools to hurt each other or drag them into your problems. Don't overshare. You're the adults. If you and/or your partner have challenges that leave you feeling overwhelmed or lost, reach out to a friend, a colleague, a family member, a neighbor, a counselor . . . but not your kids. Let your kids be kids. Reassure your child(ren) so they know they're safe and loved. Make sure your child(ren) knows that no matter what, both you and your partner love them. Remember, while failure is not an option, seeking help is always an option. Even at the lowest points in my life, there was always someone willing to lend a helping hand if I just asked for it. I try to pay that forward for others. Never feel ashamed to ask for help.

4. **Your kids owe you nothing**. Your child(ren) didn't ask to be born. Whether you planned to be a parent or not, at some point you decided to have them and raise them. Until your kids reach financial and emotional maturity and independence, your job is to provide the support they need to survive and thrive. That does NOT mean giving them everything they want. It means adhering to your values and guiding principles with the aim of working yourself out of a job so that your kids become independent, caring, capable, responsible adults.

I will also add that this does NOT mean going into debt to put them through college. Each of my kids earned at least one bachelor's degree and graduated college debt free. Neither they nor I took on debt. I made an agreement with my kids regarding college and have a section in the Appendix detailing the parameters and saving strategies I used to enable me to pay for their college educations with savings. I was also clear that I would only cover costs for their bachelor's degrees. Their masters' degrees are being paid in whole or part through employer programs, with my kids covering the balance from their own earnings and/or savings.

5. **Don't let your kids wear you down.** When they're little, the primary challenge as a parent is maintaining physical energy and stamina. By the time they're 3 or 4, you need emotional and physical strength plus stamina, endurance. The teen years are a throwback to the "terrible" 2's and 3's when the world revolved around them. I've included a section just about teens as it's such a huge change for your child(ren) and for the dynamics of your relationship.

   At any stage of your child(ren)'s life, if you're feeling overwhelmed, take a step back and take a few deep breaths. Don't be afraid to ask someone to watch your kids for 30 minutes or half a day, or whatever time you need to get yourself back together. It's a sign of strength that you know when you're at your wit's end. Take a break, come back strong. Your kids need you.

6. **Be kind to yourself.** As a parent, especially if you're a working parent, you'll be pulled in many directions. Be sure you take the time to address your own needs. If you're on this journey with a partner, find ways to support each other and nurture your relationship. You can't effectively care for your kids if you're not well or are emotionally or physically worn down.

   I want to stress the importance of being kind to yourself. I've always been highly motivated and driven. Our house is located in a neighborhood that had quite a few stay-at-home moms when I became a parent. They were my friends, however, before I had kids, I often wondered how it was that these ladies never seemed to find the time to complete all the tasks and projects that they said they wanted to do. As I contemplated my first maternity leave, I anticipated using some of my time to paint the garage and complete other minor household improvements. By the second week after bringing Nate home, my goals were reduced to just being able to take a shower each day.

Don't underestimate the <u>massive</u> life change of becoming a parent. Despite all my planning and preparation, I felt incompetent, incapable and both emotionally and physically drained. Ask for help, accept help at least until you find your new equilibrium. Becoming a parent is a life changing adjustment.

I want to share two quick examples of how new parents can over stress themselves. Before I became a parent, I had read both *What to Expect When You're Expecting* and *What to Expect Your First Year* by Heidi Murkoff and Sharon Mazel. The first time I got ready to bathe Nate, I tried to remember all the guidance the maternity nurses had given me and suddenly felt overwhelmed. I knew there were 15 or more steps in the process. I called a friend who was already a mom. Her advice was, "Start at the top, work your way down, clean the private parts last." So simple. Why was I stressed out?

Another time in the first few weeks of being a parent, I was likewise freaking out about something immaterial that I didn't know how to address. I dashed over to my neighbor's house, banged on her back door and asked Donna for her advice on whatever issue I was wigging out about. Donna told me, "Trust your instincts." To which I yelled, "If I had any instincts, I wouldn't be standing here! Just tell me what to do!" Not my proudest moment, but those experiences are reflective of how overwhelming even the most basic, simple tasks can seem as you're figuring out your new normal.

It took me roughly a month or so to successfully implement a daily schedule that kept me both sane and rested while reinforcing Nate's natural circadian wake/sleep/eat cycles. Once we got into a good rhythm, life became much better. Some days were giant steps forward, others a baby step or two backwards, but the trend was good, and I was gaining confidence in my parenting abilities.

The way I think about being kind to yourself is to be a little selfish. Ensuring I got my daily shower during maternity leave was my way of doing something just for me. Not only did it clean my body, but it also made me feel better about myself – mentally, spiritually, and physically. If you have a partner, watch out for each other, and support each other. Being kind to yourself enables you to be a better, healthier person and a better parent.

As you progress on your journey to nurture, protect and cherish your child(ren), I hope this book helps you to fill your parenting toolbox with ideas, skills, and strategies to remain true to your values and guiding principles and be the best parent you can be. When the unexpected arises, your principles and values help cool your emotions and clear your thoughts so you can identify and focus on the best outcome to aim for. Then you just need to figure out the tactical steps to address the specific circumstances of the situation at hand.

As you approach parenting, never forget that while you and your partner hopefully agree on your values and principles, each of you have different personalities, perspectives, talents, styles, experiences, thoughts, and ideas that can benefit your kids. I encourage each of you to give of yourself, connect with your kids, listen to their ideas, and answer their questions . . . those are key steps in establishing a genuine relationship. It's how we build stability, love, and trust. Turn off the tv, put down the device, spend time holding the baby, play on the floor with your toddler, read with your kids, be available to your teen. Ask questions and <u>listen</u> to what they say. When your kids talk about something that's bothering them, ask if they want your advice or just want to talk. If your child(ren) does want your help, be sure to ask questions, try not to be judgmental, understand the situation and help generate potential ideas and solutions for them to consider.

At this writing, my kids are all in their 20's. Looking back to the beginning and reviewing all the intervening years, I've sought to identify and articulate the principles and strategies that helped me to create the environment and structure that supported my kids growing into amazing young adults. That said, in no way do I wish to minimize the hard work, talent, and effort each of my kids has put forth in all aspects of their lives. As their mom, I'd suggest that I created the stage and the background. While I played many of the supporting roles; they wrote their own scripts.

My kids and I have shared many great times and a few rough times. I lost daycare providers without warning and as mentioned, was laid off three separate times during my career. Those experiences made me realize the fragility of the world I'd created, and how our lives could potentially become derailed by factors beyond my control. As a parent, you need to be prepared for those types of situations and keep a level head even when you're afraid. My strategy was to always maintain a solid understanding of our changing budget over time, stay true to my guiding principles, and always save aggressively for a rainy day. When the unexpected occurred, I did whatever it took to get through the current emergency, always knowing that failure wasn't an option. As a single, working parent, I privately shed many tears of frustration and occasionally felt near crippling fear. It wasn't always pretty, but I wouldn't have missed this journey called parenting for anything.

Parenting is work, hard work. It will challenge and test you in ways that you cannot imagine. It's an unpaid position, which is costly in terms of money, emotion, energy, and time. That said, it truly can be the best, most satisfying job in the world. I'm a much better person for being a parent. Many of the lessons, values, and guiding principles I taught my kids became a foundational part of who they've become and strengthened those values in me, making me more tolerant, understanding and forgiving. My hope is that by sharing my thoughts, strategies, and our experiences, you too can be a better, more effective parent.

Never forget that as a parent, you have the ability to make this world a better place - one child at a time. Be strong, be brave and enjoy. It's not a cliché, it's the truth - they grow up so fast.

Being able to laugh at yourself shows your kids that you're human

Experience the world through the eyes of a child.

Set your ego aside and just do whatever needs to be done.

Everyone thinks their kids are the best – and they're right!

Life really is simple when you know what's important.

BUILDING A BUDGET
AND FINANCIAL
PLANNING

I came to parenting in a very deliberate way using artificial insemination. Because I took a non-traditional path and was doing it alone, I wanted to ensure that I was financially prepared for this major life change.

Before trying to become pregnant, the first thing I did was to create a financial spreadsheet, a budget, to ensure I could afford to support a child while still maintaining cushion for the unexpected. I encourage everyone to do this. Don't be intimidated, it's not difficult and is a good activity regardless of whether you plan to have a child, are hoping to buy a house or just want to have a better understanding of where your money goes. But if you're contemplating having a child(ren), it's a must. Make sure your budget will cover both the expected and unexpected costs.

A budget is essentially just a listing of all your income or earnings (after taxes and deductions) minus all your expenses. Creating a budget gives you the chance to really understand how much you're spending and potentially identify expenses that can be reduced or eliminated. While all of us would like to make more money, realistically, you likely have more control over reducing your spending. To do that you need to take the time to drill down into the details to see where your money is going.

Expenses include all the things that you have to spend money on like housing, utilities, and food as well as all the things you choose to spend money on like entertainment, eating out, buying a book or new shirt. When creating a budget, you want to capture everything you spend money on. Whether it's a cup of coffee, the rent, or gasoline for the car, try to account for all your spending.

If your budget is tight and you want to try to find a way to make affording a child work, I'd encourage you to look through the "Evaluating Expenses" portion of the Budgeting section in the Appendices for ideas. I tried to generate suggestions and prompts to really encourage you to dig deep and examine areas where you may be able to make modest changes to your spending and generate real, material savings. Truly, a bunch of small changes can add up to meaningful dollars to help improve your financial situation. Success is really about awareness and sticking to your priorities.

I always carry cash in my wallet, but I learned early in my adult life that I had a hard time keeping track of cash spending. I would think that I had $50-75 in my wallet and the next thing I knew I had only $12 and couldn't recall where the rest had gone. I lived alone, so no one was stealing it, I just wasn't paying close attention when I spent cash. I still have that problem. So I shifted as much of my spending as possible to paying with checks or with credit cards (always paying them off monthly) so I could track my spending. I also made sure that I saved all my receipts and balanced both my checkbook and credit card statement every month. While the balancing process took a little time each month, it helped me to get very intimate with my spending. Not only did I know what everything cost, but I knew where all my money went. It also gave me the chance to reconsider purchases. For example I might realize that the new sweater I'd just bought cost roughly the same amount as a week's worth of groceries. Maybe I should just return the sweater? I had many other sweaters that were just fine. By being more conscious of my spending, I essentially carried my budget around in my head. In addition, by learning and knowing my budget, I was able to start changing my behavior, changing my spending and make better financial choices.

I grew up in a blue collar family, lower middle class. We had enough but not much extra. I wore hand-me-downs from family friends, neighbors and sadly, even clothes that my mother made. We received gifts for birthdays and Christmas, but my siblings and I grew up without a lot of extra stuff. My parents divorced while I was 11-12 years old in a drawn out awful manner. My mother divorced for the second time while I was a sophomore in college. During a phone call to tell me about her second impending break-up, my mother informed me that I was on my own financially going forward and I'd have no further financial support from her for college or anything else. I was 19 ½ years old at the time, had no income and little savings.

At that time, I already had over $13 thousand in student loans and no income. At the end of the semester, I transferred from an IN university in a rural area to a Chicago university. I went to Chicago and found a job and an apartment the same day. I worked full time during the day and in the fall, I started attending college full time at night. I didn't use my employer's tuition reimbursement plan because at the time, the plan required employees to stay for a minimum of five years post-graduation. Employees who left prior to five years had to pay the money back on a pro rata basis. I refused to indenture myself for five years and instead scraped by living paycheck-to-paycheck.

While I lived in Chicago and was pursuing my bachelor's degree, I was earning roughly $25 thousand (pre-tax) each year and college cost about 25-30% of what it does now. I counted on every penny I earned and managed to pay for school out of my earnings, i.e., no additional debt. However, money was scary tight. I learned not to be hungry at lunchtime because I couldn't afford $2 a day to buy the subsidized lunch at my employer's cafeteria. The bank frowned on people bringing in their own food and did not have refrigerators for employees. However, I learned how to live on my own, how to squeeze the last cent out of dollar and still survive, thrive, and have fun in the big city despite being essentially broke all the time.

Just before I graduated college with my bachelor's degree, I worked on a school project with a gal who had applied and been accepted to join the Peace Corps and was leaving for her assignment in Africa after graduation. I thought that was the coolest idea and inspired by her, I applied to the Peace Corps too. Another part of my consideration for applying was that student loan debt payments and interest would be frozen while I was a Peace Corps Volunteer. While I could share many amazing stories about my Peace Corps experiences overseas, what's relevant to budgeting was learning about how people in a third world county earned and spent their money and the daily reminders of the stark contrast between wants and needs. After graduation, I got a two year assignment to the Dominican Republic at a time when no cruise ships stopped there, and tourism was in its infancy.

While the larger cities in the Dominican Republic had relatively consistent electricity and might have had a true grocery store, the people outside of the cities often lived without electricity or with inconsistent electricity. People did their shopping daily or every other day at fruit and vegetable stalls, at the butcher and at a kind of general store called a "colmado." Colmados ranged in size from a small section of a front room or porch to the size of a large garage and could stock just basic items or virtually everything – similar to a general store, with the larger colmados frequently owning their own generators. Because people might not have refrigeration, a typical purchase might be 2-3 eggs, a cup of milk, some rice, some bread, and the shopper would bring a metal cup that the vender would fill with cooking oil which was sold by the ounce. Living and working in that environment for 25 months provided a very clear understanding between wants and needs. This experience further reinforced the lessons I'd learned during my childhood and my early 20's living on my own. I also witnessed daily how people could be content and happy without all the excess "stuff" that so many of us have in our lives.

When I came back to the States after completing my service in the Peace Corps, I'll never forget the first time I went into an American grocery store. I rounded the corner of an aisle and was standing in another aisle entirely filled with canned fruits, vegetables, and meats. I stood there enjoying the air conditioning in the vast American grocery store and marveling at all the options available for buying canned peaches: whole, halved or sliced; in heavy syrup, light syrup, or juice, and all the combinations those choices generated. I recalled how at the colmado, a shopper might approach and ask, "Hay leche?" to ask if they had milk before requesting the exact amount she needed. Then she'd buy milk and anything else she needed. Not whole, skim, 2%, low fat, almond or soy milk. Just milk. Those images have stayed with me all these years and help me keep things in perspective, especially when contemplating the difference between wants and needs.

When you're working on your budget, it is critical to understand the difference between wants and needs. I shared the above experiences and perceptions from my time in the Peace Corp to highlight that it's not uncommon to spend money on things we want but don't really need, or to overspend when something more basic might serve just fine. If your budget is tight, finding ways to reduce spending and save money is crucial. Those cost reductions can build your savings and support you and your child(ren) when the unexpected occurs.

Even if you're not living paycheck-to-paycheck, it's a good idea to consider reducing discretionary spending to build up a financial cushion. As a parent, having extra money for the unexpected is critical. If you get paid with direct deposit, an easy way to save is to have a set amount from each paycheck deposited directly into a savings account, with the balance of your paycheck put into your checking account. I did that, and honestly, I'd forget about the amount that went into my savings account and did all my planning and budgeting around the amount of my paycheck that was in my checking account. Hopefully, you can do the same. The goal is to have your savings build automatically. Ideally you leave that money for a rainy day or for an opportunity. Likewise, if you receive a bonus, a tax refund or unexpected money, unless you have debt that that you can pay off or reduce, try to save all or most of that extra cash.

As a parent, I was always conscious of not wasting money on more "stuff." I appreciate everything that we have and hate waste. I always tried to make sensible purchases that supported my children's well-being and fed their creativity, while also always striving to build savings. Sticking to my budget and building large savings balances eliminated so much stress from our lives. It provided me with the ability to deal with unexpected expenses and splurge on experiences for my family. It also enabled me to give my children a substantial leg up in life by funding their college education, so they were able to start their independent lives debt free.

I've included a section in the Appendix about saving for and paying for college. Check it out. The short story is that mentally, I initially linked saving for college to our daycare expenses. With three kids, at one point I was paying approximately $18 thousand a year in day care expenses. Our budget supported that and still let me direct deposit about $50 per paycheck to my savings account ($2,400 per year). When my day care costs declined as the kids went to school and thus spent fewer hours in daycare, I increased the amount of money I saved by the amount of the reduction. For example when my daycare costs declined to $13 thousand per year, I increased my annual savings by $5 thousand (from $100 a month to over $500 per month). That discipline forced me to keep a close eye on my budget and my spending while seriously amping up my savings with the goal of covering their college expense. By the time we were completely done with daycare, I was saving over $25 thousand a year and had well over $100 thousand in savings. It helped that my salary was increasing over that period, and as noted, I tried to keep our expenses from growing just because I earned more money, but the real accelerant was diligently socking away all the extra dollars as my daycare costs declined.

Between mortgage and daycare costs, there wasn't a lot of extra money in my budget when the kids were young, but we made it work, and I saved small amounts automatically every month. As noted above, my savings were my way of creating a safety net for myself and my family. In a single parent, one income household, savings were imperative. While they were minors and through their college years, I also carried term life insurance of at least $1 million (the cost was around $50/month or $600 per year). I also always took advantage of life insurance through my employer (usually equal to a multiple of my annual salary).

Life is uncertain. Whether you're parenting on your own or with a partner, you have to think about what would happen to your child(ren) if you or your partner died suddenly. I'd suggest that even if one of you is the primary or sole breadwinner, that you consider the costs of how life would change for your family if the lower wage earner or stay at home parent died. All the work and support they provide would have to be paid for, potentially over many years. Put a dollar figure on that and to the extent possible, find a way to make that amount of term life insurance for those contributions fit into your budget as well.

Savings gives you the ability to manage the unexpected without negatively impacting your daily lives. Savings can provide peace of mind and more control over both your present and future. Savings gave me the ability to leave jobs and pursue better opportunities. By always understanding our evolving budget, I was able to aggressively save and make choices about how and where to spend my money wisely. You can do the same. It just takes awareness, effort, and discipline.

Below is a simplistic version of a budget that will help you to identify your current earnings and spending. **A comprehensive budget is provided in the Appendix.** As outlined in the detailed template in the Appendix, once you create your baseline or current budget, you'll want to add in the additional expenses that you anticipate that you'll incur related to your child(ren).

As noted above, I used credit cards to pay for most of my expenses and always fully paid off the balance every month. That gave me the ability to use my credit card statement to review the prior month's spending. Using a credit card may also provide rewards. I generally let my cash back rewards build throughout the year to offset my increased spending around the holidays.

Earnings		You	Partner	Total
+	Monthly net take home pay			
+	Other sources of income			
+	Bonuses or tax refunds (divided by 12)			
	Total monthly income			
Expenses				
-	Housing (mortgage/rent)			
-	Homeowner's or rental insurance (monthly cost)			
-	Debt payments other than mortgage:			
	Car payments			
	Student loan payments			
	Other installment loans			
	Other debt			
-	Utilities (gas, electricity, phone, garbage, cable, etc.)			
-	Groceries and food			
-	Vehicle use: gasoline, tolls, parking, auto insurance			
-	Entertainment (shows, restaurants, etc.)			
-	Subscriptions/services (gym, lawn,			

	plowing, maid, etc.)			
-	Monthly portion of expenses paid other than monthly			
-	Other			
-	Other			
-	Miscellaneous			
	Total current monthly expenses			
-	**Amount deposited monthly into savings account**			
	Net monthly excess / (shortfall)			

Again, the above is just a simple overview. I'd recommend using the detailed sample in the Appendix. I'd also suggest that you add a separate line for each material expense you have to help you focus on expenses individually. Add as many lines as needed for your situation. Truly, you can't have too much detail. The better you understand your spending, the more control you can have over changing the way you spend. Information empowers you to make informed choices on how to spend or not spend and to differentiate between your needs vs. your wants. Remember as a parent, you have another little human being who is fully reliant on you (and your partner). Part of keeping your child(ren) safe includes striving for financial stability and building savings.

Parenting is hard. At times you will question your decision. You'll experience tough times and have unexpected expenses. But in deciding to become a parent you've committed to something, to someone, outside of yourself. Keep that in mind and decisions about discretionary spending, about money, can be much easier.

As noted, each time I decided to try to conceive another child, I updated my budget with my current income information and factored in the increase in expenses related to another child. As shown both in the template above and in the detailed budget in the Appendix, I also always include a line item for "Miscellaneous." The reason for including this extra unspecified line item was an attempt to capture the things I might have forgotten, infrequent purchases and to build a bit of additional cushion for unexpected items such as new brakes for the car, an unexpected medical expense, replacing or repairing a broken washing machine, etc. You can put in a fixed dollar amount or a percentage of your total monthly expenses. While ideally you are building a rainy day savings account, it's a good idea to also have another allocation for miscellaneous in your budget that can hopefully cover those unexpected costs or the slightly higher grocery bills without having to dip into your savings account at all.

As you contemplate being a parent, another thing to consider is whether you'll need to make any changes to your living space, your vehicle, the hours you work and/or your job itself. If so, you need to estimate those costs and any impacts on your income. Obviously, babies and kids require lots of extra equipment and items to keep them safe and help you to manage. You'll need to buy a crib and/or a basinet, a car seat, a stroller, and dozens of other things. I did not include the cost of those items in the budget templates. My reasoning was that these are not repetitive purchases, rather they're one time or infrequent purchases. In my mind, they were covered under my "miscellaneous." However, you may wish to add a line item to your budget for baby equipment. For example car seats can cost several $100, and your child will graduate from a rear facing seat, to a front facing car seat, and finally a booster seat. You need to figure out how you'll cover those costs and how to account for them in your budget. It's your budget. Modify it as necessary to make it work for you.

If your monthly budget is skinny, you may want to find a way to address these equipment purchases well in advance. Using secondhand baby equipment from friends, family or other sources is a great way to save money, just be sure to check manufacturer websites to make sure that items weren't subject to recalls or have any other concerns. Another thing to consider is whether you want to have duplicate car seats, playpens or other items for your daycare provider or family members. While this added costs, over time, I did buy duplicate items. I wanted to ensure that my babies were safe in equipment that I'd vetted and purchased. While you might consider sharing the equipment with your daycare provider and transporting it daily, I suggest that it be a last resort. I always strove to make the logistics of daily life as simple as possible. I even got away from a daily diaper bag and just left extra diapers, formula, wipes, and clothes with my daycare providers. My providers gave me any soiled clothes when I picked up my kids, which I replaced the next day. The providers also let me know when they were running low on formula, wipes, or diapers. With a daily transition, if you forget anything, you've got to go back home and get it. Not the best way to start your day. That was a level of stress and complexity that I just sought to avoid. As a working parent, I encourage you to embrace things that make life easier for you and your family.

To spread out the cost of all the baby gear, my strategy was that once I knew I was pregnant, I began buying those items. This spread out the cost over 7-8 months and the costs were captured under my line item of miscellaneous. Spreading out the purchases was also fun and kept me feeling like I was continually engaged in getting ready for the new life growing inside me. Obviously, for subsequent children, you can use many of the same items for all your kids such as the crib, changing table, stroller, etc. Baby showers are another source to potentially address these needs. No one ever threw me a baby shower, but I did benefit from friends and work colleagues who either gave or loaned me many baby and toddler items. My daycare providers where also amazing. They gave Avery so many beautiful outfits that their daughters had outgrown. As a result, Avery was by far the best dressed, most stylish member of our family. Once she'd outgrown the clothes, I made sure to give them to friends or donate them to charity so others could also enjoy these lovely outfits.

A big expense for me before having my first son, Nate, was trading in my car for an SUV. I already owned my big German shepherd dog, and I didn't want Ripley in the back seat with my baby. Several months after I became pregnant, I traded in my Nissan Stanza and bought a used Ford Explorer that had just come off a lease. The Explorer was perfect and worked fine when Jack was born several years later, but when I was pregnant with my daughter, Avery, I measured the backseat and realized that I wouldn't be able to fit two car seats and a booster seat into the backseat of the Explorer. Not wanting to risk having 5 year old Nate ride in the front seat (even with the air bag disabled), I traded in my Ford Explorer for a used minivan.

This was a very challenging move for me. I personally detest minivans. I hate the way the doors slide open. I hate the appearance of minivans. I hate the stereotype of a mom in a minivan. In short, a minivan was completely inconsistent with my own self-image. My ego is more of a "Mustang Sally" kind of gal. But a minivan was the most practical, economical vehicle for my growing family, so I sucked it up and traded in my Explorer for a used minivan. My only concession was to buy one with a V-6 engine rather than a V-4. We all make sacrifices as parents. For me, driving a minivan was one of many. As a single parent, when the choice was between ego or money, money and practicality won every time.

As noted above, while the budget templates I've provided focus on monthly income and expenses, be sure to think about other considerations that could have a major impact on your finances. As detailed above, twice I had to trade in my vehicle to accommodate kids and dogs. In addition to vehicles, ask yourself if your home or apartment will accommodate room for your child(ren). Will you need to move? I added a second story addition to my house after Jack was born, expanding our modest 2 bedroom, 1 bath home located in a wonderful neighborhood into a 4 bedroom, 3 bathroom house. To fund it, I reduced my 401K contributions down to the minimum amount to still get the full employer match and refinanced my mortgage from a small mortgage with roughly 6 years remaining into a big mortgage stretched over 30 years. But it worked. When I got pregnant with Avery, I just needed to move the kids around as we had plenty of room for all.

In short, a budget is a critical tool. Understanding your own (and your partner's) personal finances makes you smarter and more powerful. A simple budget can start you on the path towards identifying ways to build savings, better understand your spending and make better choices with how you allocate your hard earned money. I am very intimate with my spending and encourage you to become the same. As a parent, it's critical to not only know your budget, but the difference between wants and needs. Before I'd built up significant savings, we occasionally skipped spending on "wants" as there just wasn't enough extra cash.

As a parent you need to protect your children from harm. Harm also includes financial harm. Building savings is the first step. You need to think about and protect your child(ren) in the event you lose your job, become injured, or even die. Please think about savings and insurance as essentials. Perhaps it was my blue collar upbringing, working my way through college and/or my Peace Corps experience which further reinforced my understanding of the difference between wants and needs, but I've always been able to prioritize savings. As long as my needs are met, I'm good. More clothing, eating out more often or obtaining more stuff doesn't make me happy. Nothing made me happier than knowing I had the wherewithal to take care of my children and keep us safe. Having extra money to fund adventures with my children and pay for their college education filled me with pride and happiness.

Money represents both security and opportunity. Having savings enables you to address the unexpected expense or job loss. While I felt stress at those times, being able to fully pay our bills, pay the mortgage and buy groceries while I searched for another job, went a long way towards keeping me from freaking out. It also enabled me to keep my family safe and on track without material disruption to our lives. Savings also provide opportunities for pleasure or investment. While always retaining a comfortable cushion of excess funds, savings enabled us to take vacations, enjoy weekend adventures and make occasional splurges. As the kids got older, the large savings balances I'd been able to amass enabled me to write the big checks to fully pay for their college education.

My final comment regarding financial matters is to encourage you to write a will. There are many online options available, and certainly engaging with an attorney or other financial professional is an option. As a single parent, not long after Nate was born, I wrote a will. Like my budget, I've also updated my will over time. Whether you're parenting on your own or jointly, the most important considerations in your will include 1) deciding who will raise your kids if you (and your partner) die and 2) how best to communicate your goals and desires for your children while providing flexibility to ensure you're not trying to dictate from the grave. Whether you're on this journey alone, or embracing parenting with a partner, write a will, talk to your potential guardian(s), and ensure you have appropriate levels of life insurance for both you and your partner to support your child(ren) minimally through age 18. At the end of the day, our role as parents is to protect, nurture, teach and launch these new beings on a path towards independence and success even in the event that we're not there to witness it.

Reading is a gift that never stops giving. Read to your children often.

Life's too short to hold a grudge.

As a parent you're at the bottom of the food chain.

Make sure your kids are pursuing their dreams, not your dreams.

If it were easy, everyone would do it.

SELECTING YOUR VALUES

Once you're sure that you can financially afford a child(ren), dig deep, and determine your most important values and guiding principles. What do you stand for? What are your most important beliefs? What do you wish could've been different about your childhood? What were some of the things that made it great? Take the time to think about and answer these questions. Your answers will help form the foundation of your parenting strategy.

To illustrate how critical it is to define and agree on your core values, imagine how difficult it would be to play a game if everyone didn't agree on the rules, or the rules could change because someone was in a bad mood, or if mom had one set of rules, but dad had another, or the rules applied differently to each player or the rules could change if someone threw a fit . . . you can see how quickly a game without rules could spiral into chaos. Life's a game. Teach your kids to play it well and have fun doing it.

Understanding your core values and your principles is foundational to successful parenting. They will help you establish the rules and guardrails for everyday living. I like to think about core values and guiding principles as your personal mission statement. Since we're focused on kids, let's look at a company that captivates many kids and parents alike - The Walt Disney Company ("Disney"). According to the company's website, Disney's mission statement is *"to entertain, inform and inspire people around the globe through the power of unparalleled storytelling, reflecting the iconic brands, creative minds and innovative technologies that make ours the world's premier entertainment company.'*[1]

In addition to its mission statement, Disney has Standards of Conduct that expand and clarify how everyone associated with the company can understand and implement Disney's mission statement and values in their day-to-day activities. For Disney, these include[2]:

Integrity

Trust

Teamwork

Honesty

Play by the Rules

Respect

Stop for a moment and read those again.

Those are great values for a company, for a family, for life.

Think about how Disney's values might apply to parenting. Now think about what each of those means and which of those values, and what other values are important to you as you think about your role as a parent.

I've listed my core values and guiding principles below. They will be discussed in detail in the ensuing chapters. Your values may be similar, overlap a little, or be radically different. Regardless, the process and discipline of knowing your core values, your guiding principles, is critical in maintaining consistency between you and your partner. Your values can serve as a road map keeping you on track across different situations and throughout the years in your role as a parent.

Sally's Core Values and Guiding Principles:

- Consistency and Expectations

- Honesty and Transparency

- Empathy

- Consequences and Responsibility

- Delayed gratification, plus understanding money and credit

- Strategic thinking

- Family Adventures and Traditions

This book is structured to explore each of these core values and show how I applied them to my parenting. To help illustrate, I've shared examples and stories from our lives in the belief that they may be beneficial to provide a fuller meaning and understanding.

I want you to understand how and why I selected my values as well as how I applied them to parenting. My hope is that understanding the process I used will be beneficial to you as you think through ways to reflect your own values in your parenting.

Throughout the book, I've also included what I've called "Strategy" boxes that provide tactical solutions. I tried many things that didn't work or didn't work well but have only included strategies that were highly effective. Feel free to try them or adapt them to your values and principles. I expect you'll also discover other strategies and solutions on your own that work well for your family. Be sure to share them with your family and friends. Afterall, it takes a village to raise a child. Share and celebrate your successes and pay them forward for others.

Rainbows are magical at any age.

Embrace experiences.

Listen to your kids' stories.

Jumping in mud puddles is FUN! Encourage your kids to enjoy simple pleasures.

Friends will come and go, family is forever.

CONSISTENCY AND EXPECTATIONS

The reason "training dogs" was included in the title of this book was to illustrate, simplify and underscore the importance of consistency in parenting. Raising good dogs and raising good kids have lots of parallels. Dogs, babies, and toddlers have limited understanding of words, so you need to use consistent actions and consistent words to teach them. Everything you say and do needs to be repeated, patiently and consistently multiple times. I trained my dogs and raised my kids with love and attention, by discouraging inappropriate behavior and by acknowledging positive actions and behaviors. Consistent schedules, consistent behavior, consistent responses as well as addressing stressors for the child or dog helped support happy, contented well behaved family members.

I don't believe in hitting or caging dogs or kids for that matter. With consistency, repetition and love, a typical dog can learn 25-40 words and good behavior. Dogs can be housebroken, learn not to bite, be taught to stay off the furniture, to come when they're called, to not jump on people, to stop barking, to sit, stay, walk at a heel, shake, and not beg from the table. They learn through consistency, loving attention, repetition, and patience. I did not use treats to train my dogs, rather the reward for good behavior was extra attention - petting, rubbing, playing together and lots of saying "good dog."

My body language and tone of voice reinforced my message. I gave my dogs treats after long walks or other activities such as after a bath or trimming their nails.

When my dogs chewed up something they shouldn't have, barked excessively, got on the furniture, etc., I addressed the behavior immediately and gave them a sharp "No," "Enough," or "Off." I used the same word every time for commands related to desired actions and the same specific word to address undesirable behavior. If they were on the furniture, I pushed them off and said "Off." When I wanted them to stop barking, I carefully held their muzzle and said "Enough," while looking them in the eyes. If they acted contrite or submissive after the process, I ignored them to let my disappointment sink in. After a few minutes, I'd behave normally with the dog and move on. I repeated as many times as necessary for them to learn.

I remember one of Gary Larson's *Far Side* cartoons that showed a dog sitting looking up at a man who was talking to it. The caption was: "Blah, blah, blah, Ginger, blah blah, blah." If you're inconsistent with a dog or talk to them in sentences, they'll only hear "blah, blah, blah." Your words will just be noise. If you're inconsistent with your kids, you'll teach them that your words are meaningless. "Blah, blah, blah."

Between the ages of 1-3 the typical child may know and understand only fifty to a couple hundred words.[4] In addition to everything else they're learning like how to roll over, sit up, crawl, and walk, babies and toddlers are learning to understand language. I surrounded my kids with words. I read to them, talked to them, and kept up a stream of chatter when we were out on errands or strolling through the neighborhood. While all that was great and I presume it helped build their vocabulary and understanding of syntax and grammar, most of it was likely just noise to them.

When you're trying to teach your toddler, keep it simple. Think of them like a puppy when you're trying to modify their behavior. Use actions and ideally the same one or two words to communicate about their actions. For example, if they're hitting with a toy, calmly and firmly hold their hand, take away the toy and say something like, "No hitting." Then redirect your toddler to something else that they can play with instead. Engage with them for a few minutes (or longer) to make sure they've shifted to a new, good activity and behavior. Reward them with a smile, a caress, and/or continued attention. You can never provide too many positive interactions for your baby or toddler. The added benefit is that if they are surrounded by positive interactions, the negative interactions – such as "No hitting" – will be more impactful due to the contrast.

Most books about babies discuss how important it is to engage with infants and toddlers. Engagement and interaction are critical for development and bonding. It's also crucial from a teaching perspective that you make the time to engage with your child regularly and consistently so that you share lots of positive and neutral interactions. You never want to create an environment where your toddler or child needs to use bad behavior as a means of getting your attention. It is so rewarding for both you and your child to spend time actively interacting. Make the time to play with them, to discover and celebrate the unique wonder of this little human being in your care. Watch their expressions and reactions and try to figure out what's going on in that little brain. Get down on the floor and look at your home from their perspective (you may also discover some safety hazards you missed). Watch their expressions as they discover something new. Share in their wonder and joy. Laugh and giggle with them. The moments are fleeting. Be sure you experience them because those memories will last a lifetime and strengthen the bond between you and your child.

But let's be honest, parenting is not a series of Hallmark ™ moments, and many parents are juggling work, household chores, and personal well-being. That's why it's so important to consciously think about parenting. It shouldn't be an afterthought when you're tired after dealing with work and household tasks. Parenting needs to have equal importance. You and your family will benefit by having a game plan that incorporates time for you and your child(ren) to interact together while supporting your values and parenting goals. Just as you have responsibilities and objectives at work, and regular chores and activities to maintain the household, so too, I recommend that you have a vision and plan about your parenting. That way when you're feeling exhausted after a busy day, you just decide which things to use from your playbook. It will help reinforce positive routines, reduce stress, and generate better outcomes for everyone.

When I decided to become a single parent, I was determined to succeed. I started my journey with a clear understanding of my parenting goals. I'd learned the value of consistency in successfully obedience training German shepherds twice in my life. I selected consistency as a parenting value because I knew it would help my kids learn, it would make life more predictable, and I believed it would reduce conflicts.

What does it mean to be consistent? The dictionary defines consistency as: "1. The condition of cohering of holding together or retaining form; 2. degree of density, firmness, viscosity, etc.; **3. steadfast adherence to the same principles, course, form, etc.; 4. agreement among the parts of a complex thing.**" [3] To paraphrase, as a parent, I wanted to be predictable, clearly communicate expectations and show that behavior – good and bad – would have consistent consequences. In addition, I made sure that my parenting principles and values fit together in a logical, cohesive manner that supported and reinforced each other.

Stating the obvious, being consistent meant that if it was ok for Nate, then it needed to be ok for Jack and Avery too. While there might be considerations for age, or if someone had lost privileges as part of a punishment, I treated each of them consistently, equitably and held them to the same expectations and rules.

Being consistent also meant that expectations applied to my kids <u>regardless of where they were or what others were doing</u>. Whether they were at school, a store, a friend's house or at the daycare provider's house, expectations about how they were to behave and treat others still applied. **Expectations weren't rules of our house, they were rules of conduct and behavior wherever they were**. If others spoke rudely or acted inappropriately in their house, that did NOT give my kids license to behave in that way. I also made it clear that while my kids weren't responsible for the behavior of others away from home, they were always responsible for their own conduct.

I wish I could claim that I had the foresight to recognize that this expectation would be super valuable as the kids became teens, but I wasn't thinking that far ahead. Although I didn't think about it in advance, I quickly recognized that by the time they were teens, my kids had internalized a strong sense of what was ok and what wasn't. This understanding helped them navigate many situations as they gained more independence. I'm sure my kids did things they shouldn't have over the years, but I'm equally certain that there were many times that their firm internal understanding of what kind of behavior was acceptable and what was unacceptable kept them safe and helped them make better choices.

The foundation of my parenting plan was to clearly communicate expectations and to be consistent. Just like training a dog, I preferred to encourage good behavior, promptly address bad behavior by clearly communicating that it was unacceptable and redirecting to find ways we could interact and have fun together.

Initial expectations centered on playing nicely and cleaning up. If one of the kids hit, bit, or otherwise acted badly, they got a prompt "No hitting," and might be placed in time out of a minute or so. Putting them in time out meant they had to sit quietly on a chair or the couch – away from the other child(ren) and their toys. The time out was typically in the same room where they were playing so that the child who'd behaved badly could watch as his siblings got to continue to play without him. If two of my kids were fighting over a toy, I'd tell them that they needed to work out a way to share or take turns. If that failed, and they couldn't work out a way to share and play nicely, the toy got put in timeout. Toys on time out were visible to the kids, but they were not allowed to use them. Toys put on time out were essentially in the penalty box for periods ranging from an hour to several days depending on the frequency or severity of arguments over it.

Since they were little, I've always welcomed ideas and comments from my kids and respected their individuality and perspectives. But I've also always made it clear that the ultimate decisions about family expectations and rules remained mine. To be clear, this is not about power, this is establishing that as the parent, you're the one who's in control. You set expectations and make the rules. While you love them and value their ideas and feedback, there will be times when your kids may not be happy with your decisions. That's part of parenting. Parenting is not a popularity contest. You need to do what you believe is right, what you believe is best for your family and the child(ren) and set expectations accordingly.

> **Strategy:** *Time outs provide time and space for the emotions that led to bad behavior to calm. Time outs provide time to think of better ways to behave.*

Time outs were not punishment, rather they were an opportunity to be removed from the heat of the moment to calm down and reset. Bad behavior often stems from strong emotions or frustration being acted out. The goal of a time out was not to isolate or shame my child(ren), rather it was an opportunity to create a little space, to give them a chance to calm down and demonstrate that bad behavior was not acceptable. When they seemed to have calmed down, I'd ask, "Are you ready to play nicely now?" If they said yes, the time out was over, and they could go back to playing.

If a child was in complete meltdown, throwing a tantrum, they were sent or taken to their bedroom and told to stay in bed until they calmed down. When they were very little, I'd check on them frequently from the bedroom door to see if they were ready to come back. I'd sit on the edge of the bed and comment that it looked like they were feeling better, and I asked if they felt ready to play nicely. Once they were older, I'd leave it to them to decide when they were ready rejoin the group.

While one of my children was in time out, they could read a book, play with a toy, etc. while sitting or lying on their bed or sitting on the couch. They understood that it was up to them to decide when they felt ready to rejoin the group and act appropriately. It was also ok if during the time out, they became so engrossed in a new activity and wanted to keep playing on their own. When that happened, I'd typically give them a kiss on the head, ask if they felt ok and said something like, "If you're feeling better and want to come play with us, that would be great. If not, have fun here. I love you."

The goal of a time out was <u>not</u> to make the child feel that I was controlling them or forcing them to be in time out for a set period, rather I was reenforcing that bad behavior wouldn't be tolerated. I was giving them the space and quiet to regain their self-control and decide when they wanted to rejoin the group.

The best teachers, coaches, managers, and leaders in all walks of life listen, engage with, and seek to understand the needs, abilities, and concerns of their charges. However, the responsibility for decision making remains theirs and theirs alone. Parents are all these roles rolled into one. Never forget that you (and your partner) make the decisions, you (and your partner) set the expectations and rules that you, your partner, and your children will all follow.

In our house, setting expectations wasn't so much about having rules, rather I behaved as if certain things were just expected. Just as I taught my dogs not to pee in the house or bite, expectations were both about things we didn't do and things we did do. When it was time for their bath or a meal, we all cleaned up the toys and put them away. Dirty clothes went into the laundry basket. We ate meals together and no one left the table until everyone was done. We treated each other kindly, we didn't hit, we took turns talking rather than interrupting, we used good manners, we all pitched in to get things done. In short, we operated like a family or team that cared for and respected each other. Naturally, I had to give many prompts and reminders, but they were given in a matter of fact manner and neutral tone; I was explaining and reminding not reprimanding or dictating.

To manage our household, especially as a single parent, I expected everyone to contribute. We were a family, a team. We all helped to the best of our ability. I didn't assign my kids specific chores, but over time, they took on more of their own self-care such as brushing their own teeth, getting dressed, making their beds, putting away their clean clothes, clearing their dirty dishes from the table, etc. Their ability to do these things by themselves was seen as growing up, not chores. While I generally fed the dogs breakfast just because I was always up first, the kids often took turns feeding them at dinnertime. Feeding the dogs was something they perceived as nice to do for the dogs who they loved. Feeding the dogs was never perceived as work or a chore.

> **Strategy:** *Use the "Two Bite" rule for new food items. Do NOT require children to eat everything on their plate.*

I always tried to make healthy, nutritious, delicious dinners. Meals also had to be quick, easy, and ideally ready in 20-30 minutes at most. I used the grill year round to cook chicken, pork chops, steaks, and burgers, and the stove top and oven for ham, fish, eggs or spaghetti and meatballs. Two pots to cook frozen vegetables, a side of fruit plus pasta, rice or bread and a glass of milk and we were good to go.

I'd periodically make a new dish and sometimes one or more of the kids would look at the new offering with an expression of utter disgust. That's when we used the "Two Bite" rule. As its name implies, everyone had to try at least two bites of something new before deciding if they liked it or didn't. The thought was that the first bite might be impacted by expectations, with the second bite providing a more honest assessment. After two bites, each of us could decide if we liked it or didn't.

If anyone didn't like something after the second bite, they didn't have to eat it. However, I didn't give them anything else to eat (I refused to be a short order cook). On occasion, if they were hungry enough, the kids might eat something that they'd declared that they didn't like. At the end of the meal, I'd always ask whether we should add the new dish to our rotation or leave it off. We had to have unanimous consent to add a new item. Dinner times were special times in our house, and I didn't want to add unnecessary consternation by serving food that I knew someone didn't like.

I will also highlight that I did NOT require my children to eat everything on their plates. I always tried to serve the right portions to fit their appetites, but if I gave them too much, they just had to eat some of each item – meat, veggies, grain, and fruit – NOT clean their plates. I wanted my children to learn to regulate their eating to match their appetites. I didn't want my kids to eat food just because it was in front of them.

I both modeled and stated expectations and used reminders and time outs when necessary to address inappropriate behavior. Yardwork and gardening are things I enjoy. While I didn't expect the kids to do yardwork, I bought real (vs. plastic) kid sized shovels, rakes, and snow shovels so the kids could help if they wanted to. They sometimes helped dig holes for my new plants and for several years we planted vegetable gardens together. They also dug holes around the yard looking for dinosaur bones, and trampled my flowers, but that's part of being a kid. During the winter, I shoveled the driveway, and the kids would sometimes clear the sidewalks. While their help was often provided in spurts interrupted by snowball fights, making angels, or building snow people, my primary goal was for us to be together and enjoy the outdoors. I was available to teach my children how to use the various outdoor tools and share knowledge if they were interested. As they got older, we'd frequently shovel the walks and driveways of our elderly neighbors, and the kids were expected to help to the best of their ability as we as a family did something to help others.

Regarding schoolwork, I was regularly and consistently very vocal that school was my children's job. I also always tried to talk about my job in a positive way. When speaking to my children, I'd note that my job was something that I liked and was good at. I'd share that I did good things for people, solved problems, and earned money so we could live in our house and buy the things we needed. Household tasks like cutting the lawn, sweeping the floors, or doing laundry, were things that were important, that had to be done, and something to be proud of doing well. My consistent message was that work, and jobs were things that were important, created value, and should be done well. Whether going to the office, making a meal, keeping the house clean or picking up the dog poop, all jobs were important. Likewise, school was important, created value, should be done well and was something my children should take pride in and hopefully enjoy.

Just like me, my children were expected to do their job every day. They were expected to make the most of school – to participate, listen, do their homework, and be prepared for quizzes and exams. If they had homework or needed to study for a test, they just did it. I always asked questions about schoolwork, tests, and quizzes and helped as needed to help them be prepared.

School was their responsibility. Even in elementary school, they were in the driver's seat. Just as I went to work each weekday to earn money and do good things, they went to school. Their job at school was to expand their knowledge, respect and listen to their teachers and coaches and do their best in all their work. School was also a chance to see their friends and have fun, but the primary reason they were there was to learn. I read all the books that my kids did so I could ask questions to help them more fully develop their thoughts for book reports. I'd quiz them on vocabulary, spelling words, state capitals, multiplication tables, etc. often while making dinner or completing household chores. We tried to make it fun and a competition.

Strategy: *Routines reinforce expectations and make life more predictable.*

When my kids were infants, I maintained the same feeding, eating, and sleeping schedule 7 days a week. I also worked closely with my daycare providers to do the same. I believe this helped my children stay calmer when they were infants, and it avoided allowing the baby to sleep too much during the day, potentially leaving them awake at night when I needed to sleep. Regular naptimes and schedules also gave me the ability to have more control over my day as I planned chores and tasks for naptimes and post-bedtime.

As the kids got older, for our weekend errands and adventures, I planned outings around naptimes, so the kids weren't overtired or overstimulated. I also packed snacks and lunches, so my children had good, nutritious food to keep them fueled. Much cheaper for me, and better for them than most kid menu options. We rarely or never ate fast food.

We had daily routines to ensure we all got out the door on time in the morning. Each night before bed, they put their homework and snack in their backpacks. In the morning, they re-checked their backpacks and got their lunches that I'd prepared the night before.

After dinner routines included confirming that all homework had been done and was in their backpack. We rarely watched movies or tv at night, as I valued the few hours a day that I had with my children outside of work, so I tried to find activities that enabled us to interact and play together. Dinner was followed by playtime, bathes, brushing teeth, reading and quiet time before lights out.

The final wind down to lights out reinforced their circadian rhythms and generally resulted in the kids quickly falling asleep. As a side note, twice each year when our country adjusts clocks for Daylight Savings, by following the nighttime routine and adjusting it to the new time, I was able to "trick" my kids' bodies into more rapidly adjusting to the new time.

While my kids were all good students, Nate struggled with 8th grade geometry. The whole concept of geometric proofs was like a foreign language to him. Thankfully, Nate had an amazing math teacher who met with him every day before school to work together. Nate finished the class with a B and that was the grade I've been most proud of in Nate's entire school career because of all the extra effort he put in and his commitment to push through until he understood. I was truly grateful for his amazing teacher. She was one of those wonderful teachers who seem to have infinite patience, an ability to find new ways to explain concepts and an unwavering commitment to her students.

Given our approach and expectations about school, the kids and I never really had arguments about doing homework or studying. They knew they had to get it done. Like brushing their teeth every day, they just did their homework. I didn't care if they completed their homework at the daycare provider's house, before or after playtime, it just needed to be done before bedtime. I would ask if anyone had homework that wasn't yet done when we got home each night. If it was getting close to bedtime, I might suggest that they finish it, but generally, they did a great job of being responsible to complete it early in the day. Bigger school projects occasionally required more active intervention on my part but that was primarily to teach my kids about time management and how to break the project into parts. I'd then monitor their progress and support them as necessary to ensure they were staying on track to complete the project on time.

Clear expectations and consistency helped life flow more smoothly in our house. Expectations were consistently communicated and enforced, and I was always willing and able to talk about why something was expected. By explaining the "why" of my expectations and decisions, and being fair and consistent, vs. unpredictable or capricious, life was calmer. The kids didn't necessarily always agree with me, but they understood what was expected, and I think they felt respected by being listened to and heard. That said, they tested me a lot, especially when they were young or overtired. But I knew how important it was to model consistency and to treat each of them fairly and equitably. Once I had more than one child, I was outmanned, so I needed to make sure everyone cooperated, everyone contributed, and all of us did what was expected.

Strategy: *Use the "Two Minute Warning" to facilitate transitions.*

Transitions between activities can be challenging, especially for young kids. If they're playing and having fun, they want to keep on playing and having fun.

Just as professional football uses the two minute warning before halftime and at the end of the fourth quarter, I used it as a means of communicating that we were about to transition from one activity to another. Whether it was exactly two minutes or not didn't matter but I tried to be generally close to two minutes so that I was consistent, and the kids were able to internalize roughly how long two minutes were. Examples include:

If the kids were playing in the backyard or we were at a park, I'd holler, "Two more minutes," before calling them to come in or leave.

If dinner was ready to be served, I'd say, "Two minutes till dinner."

Each morning I'd call out, "We're leaving in two minutes. Check your backpacks and put your shoes on."

When we were swimming in our pool, I'd let them know when it was time to finish up with the two minute warning.

Once they were in bed and reading or talking, I communicated, "Two minutes until lights out." After two minutes, I'd go into their bedrooms, kiss them goodnight and turn off the lights.

Sometimes the kids might ask for more time after I'd called "two minutes," and if there wasn't some compelling reason to say no, I almost always agreed. Then we'd decide on the amount of additional time everyone thought was good and use that as the time to end the current activity.

Just as all of us have used calendar reminders that give 15, 10 and 5 minute reminders for appointments, I found that giving my children the Two Minute Warning was a great way to ease transitions, enable them to wind up what they were currently doing and minimize pushback.

Another advantage that worked in my favor as a parent was that the technology of the internet and smart phones were in their infancy when my kids were little. I'd grown up believing that only doctors or other really important people had pagers, so getting a mobile phone was not a priority even for me. As a result, my kids didn't get their own phones until high school.

I also don't believe in substituting technology for human interactions or creative play. While we did have a few Sesame Street ™ and Reading Rabbit ™ games on the computer that focused on learning the alphabet and learning to read, I didn't buy any "educational" toys. I read to my kids daily and filled the house with toys and games that fostered creativity. When the kids brought home basic reading books, we'd sit together while they read their books to me. These books are sometimes so basic that I realized that the kids were sometimes memorizing the books and not really reading. Instead, they were using the pictures and the repeated sentence structures to "read." That's when I'd occasionally make it fun and have them read the books backwards. Like watching a film backwards and seeing something broken miraculously pop back together, occasionally, reading a story backwards resulted in comments that sent us into fits of giggles and laughter. While we always appreciated a good laugh, the objective of this was to ensure that my kids were truly reading and understanding, not just coasting through by using cues from pictures and sentence patterns.

The expectation was that my children were able to read. By reading the books both backwards and forwards, they demonstrated that they could truly read. I was holding them accountable, and they were proud and having fun doing so. It is worth noting that when Jack told his 1st grade teacher that we were reading his books backwards, she got angry and told him to stop. Well, we didn't stop. Jack just never mentioned it to his teacher again. I told Jack to follow the directions of his teacher in class and not discuss the things we might do in our house to support or confirm his abilities.

By delaying giving my kids phones of their own, they enjoyed a longer runway to mature and learn self-control before being overwhelmed by the additive features, apps, games, and the potential harm that can arise from too much time online or by focusing on social media. I was consistently able to model good behavior regarding phone usage as I had only a flip or "burner" phone until about 2013. For me, a phone was a phone – not a computer or device to access the internet. Likewise, I could talk faster than I could text and unless there was some reason we couldn't speak, it seemed silly to me to type vs. talk when I had a phone in my hand.

My sole exposure on social media was LinkedIn, used only for job searches vs. posting. Given all the negative feedback from my family regarding my decision to have children as a single parent, I saw social media as nothing but the chance for others to share opinions that didn't matter to me, to judge me, criticize me or otherwise give me negative feedback. Why would I voluntarily expose myself or my kids up to that? I saw nothing but downside in putting my opinions or our lives on display on social media.

My thoughts about social media can be summed up briefly by suggesting that we all try to present ourselves in the best light - in both real life and online. What we present, while not necessarily being a lie, is likely not 100% truthful all the time. Women and girls are especially apt to believe the worst about ourselves. Tragic, but true. Can social media be dangerous or toxic to our kids? Absolutely. Why expose them to that at a young age? Part of protecting our kids involves keeping technology out of their lives until they can use it positively and maturely as well as limiting it so that they can be safe and unmolested in their homes.

When my kids reached high school, they got phones. As my kids got older, especially when my daughter Avery was a high schooler, I typically addressed bad behavior or not meeting expectations by loss of phone privileges or grounding. Being grounded meant not being able to go out after school and athletic practice. If she'd lost phone privileges, I'd take Avery's phone away and similar to the toy time outs when the kids were little, put it somewhere visible and accessible but off limits to her. It was important to me that Avery knew that I wasn't looking at anything on her phone - I was not violating her privacy – rather I was depriving her of the privilege of using her phone to connect with her friends or otherwise use social media. Time without her phone was generally limited to overnight or one day, but it also reinforced that having a phone was a privilege and privileges can be taken away as a result of unacceptable behavior.

Teaching our kids good behavior is a foundational responsibility of parents. A personal pet peeve is when kids are obnoxious in restaurants. At times, child(ren)'s poor behavior can negatively impact the experience of everyone nearby in the restaurant which is grossly unfair. Eating out was always something special in our family. I made sure that my kids were prepared and knew how to behave. If your kids can't or won't behave, then leave. Get take-out or make meals at home. Eating out is a skill that kids need to learn, but not at the expense of everyone else in the restaurant. Help your child(ren) succeed using the steps outlined in the Strategy Box below.

> **Strategy:** *Discuss new situations beforehand. Communicate expectations for the experience or event and help empower your child to succeed.*

Before taking your child to a restaurant, on a train or plane, to a movie, to a funeral, to a wedding, or other new experience, talk to him or her about what they will experience and how you expect them to behave.

Explain what the situation will be like. If possible, compare it to something familiar. If they're very young, perhaps you might role play and act it out.

Give them a sense of how long the activity will take and compare it to a time period they understand, such as the length of a favorite show, the time it takes to walk to school and back or the time it takes to drive to grandma's house.

Practice using their "quiet voice" and make it fun. Praise them when they do well.

If appropriate, pack a small backpack of books and toys that will entertain your child and not be disruptive to others.

Practice sitting quietly and reading or coloring for 20-30 minutes at a time.

To the extent possible, plan new activities for times of day when your child will be at their best, or conversely, when you expect they will fall asleep in their car seat or on your lap.

If your child is just not ready or will be disruptive to others at an event or activity, there's always the option to get a sitter or not go. That's not failure, it's waiting until your child has the capacity and ability to succeed.

When my kids were little, we'd periodically go to IHOP for Sunday breakfast or to Old Country Buffet ("OCB") for dinner. Not only were these special occasions that all of us were excited about, but they were also opportunities to reinforce expectations of how to behave in restaurants. Our family especially loved OCB as there was no sitting at the table waiting for food, there were oodles of choices, and the kids felt very grown up being able to put food on their plates from the buffet - with my help when they were very young and in pairs as they got older. Before we left the house to go to a restaurant, we'd re-review the expectations about behavior and I'd remind them that if they didn't behave, we'd leave. Going out to eat was an infrequent privilege that they enjoyed, so they were each highly motivated to be good.

I don't recall ever having to leave a restaurant for bad behavior, though I did need to give reminders while we were out to use a quiet voice or walk not run to the buffet. On occasion, fellow diners would stop by our table on their way out and complement me on how well-behaved my kids were. While I was always appreciative, realistically, I think these diners cringed when they saw me come in with my 3 kids and anticipated the worst. Instead, they saw my kids acting like civilized and polite little people. I always thanked the well-wishers for their kind words and told my kids how proud I was of them.

Strategy: *Empower your kids to make choices - within guidelines.*

When my kids were old enough to get dressed by themselves, I would listen to the weather report on the radio each morning and then provide guidance about what they needed to wear. My parameters were "short and short," "long and long" or "one short, one long." This guidance pertained to length of sleeves and length of pants. For Avery, if she wanted to wear a dress, on a "long, long" day, the dress needed to be long sleeve, and she'd need to wear tights. "One short, one long" could be shorts and long sleeves or long pants and a short sleeve shirt. It was totally up to each of my kids to decide for themselves.

So long as their clothes were clean (and I did laundry every night), I didn't care what they wore. I didn't care if their clothes matched or clashed. Choosing their outfits gave them a chance to express their individuality. If one picked the same shirt several days in the same week, I might suggest that people were going to think that we didn't have enough money to buy more clothes, but I didn't make them change. I only made them change if their choices didn't fit the "short" or "long" parameters for the day.

Breakfast was also a time for choices. We all ate the same thing for dinner, but I let the kids pick what they wanted for breakfast from a <u>limited</u> menu of choices – cereal, oatmeal, toast (butter, peanut butter, cinnamon, or jam), yogurt, frozen waffle, bagel, or breakfast bar. Everyone had fruit that I choose and orange juice. All the menu choices were easy, quick options for me to prepare and ensured that each of us started the day with nutritious food in our bodies and felt good about having what we wanted.

Foundational to my ability to be consistent was how I used the word "No." As I thought about raising kids, an important decision I made was that my children would understand that "No" meant "No." Again, this wasn't about power, rather, I would use the word "No" sparingly, and where possible, offer alternatives if I wasn't supportive of the initial request. I was committed to never teaching my children that a "No" could be changed to "Yes" by tantrums, whining or begging. I promised myself that I would never teach my child that it took 15 "No's" to get a "Yes." Once the kids learned this, whining or begging was virtually eliminated. They understood that there was no point in arguing. If my answer was "No," they moved on to something else.

Learning that "No" meant "No" however was a process. Before they learned, the kids challenged me with all sorts of acting out. I stayed calm and did whatever was necessary to safely demonstrate that I wasn't changing my mind. This meant that on occasion, I had to:

- Carry Nate kicking and screaming out of a video rental store.

- Tell Jack that if he asked me again, he was going to lose his play time after dinner.

- Ignore Avery wailing on the floor at my feet while I washed dishes.

- At various times, calmly watch my children vent and act out. If this occurred in public, we left. If it was at home, and they didn't stop after a reasonable time, I'd use my normal voice to tell them to lay down in bed until they were calmed down or I'd carry them there if needed.

Consistently holding to the "No" means "No" policy virtually eliminated whining and begging (at least until they became teenagers when everything was negotiable in their minds). It also gave greater weight to all my rules and expectations. In short, my kids knew that I was serious, and that I meant what I said. They understood that complaining, repeatedly asking, or begging just resulted in bad consequences for them. Again, I emphasis, that I likewise always strove to be fair, to try to find an alternative that I could say "yes" to and was always willing to explain why I'd said "no" to something. We had open dialogue about whatever they wanted and tried to figure out something that could work. For example if Jack wanted to have Alex sleep over, but we had to take Avery to an early morning doctor's appointment, we might settle on having Alex come over for dinner and a movie but go home before bedtime or have a sleepover the following weekend. If we couldn't come up with an alternative that could work, they always understood why I said "no," and knew that "no" meant "no."

Despite my "No means No policy," I also taught the kids how to appropriately challenge authority, even when that authority was me. While I was rigidly consistent about basic expectations, I never wanted to break my kids' spirit and always encouraged them to think for themselves. I taught them how to ask questions to gain an understanding of objections or roadblocks to an outcome they wanted. Just as they learned in school how to write a persuasive paper, I encouraged them to make a case and persuade me if they wanted me to change my mind. We talked about how it was good to be passionate about something, but logic, information and factual reasons were the way to change minds, not stomping their foot and shouting. As detailed in Tales from the Homefront below, Nate and Jack convinced me of the value of a Wii and Xbox when they were in middle school, and I modeled how to hold others accountable to follow the rules when the school district tried to unjustly punish Jack and his friends.

I chose consistency and clearly communicated expectations as fundamental values in my parenting plan because they provided a framework for me and the kids. We all understood the parameters under which we were operating. It was like agreeing to follow the rules of a game or the rules of the road. It made life much more pleasant and predictable for all of us. We were all accountable to each other, we treated each other fairly and with respect, and when we each did our part, life flowed smoothly. Being consistent and fair created stability and predictability for the kids and supported me in my role as a parent. Expectations reduced conflict as they presumptively, proactively gave guidance on how the kids should behave. It meant that I didn't have to fight every battle.

Strategy: *Set expectations and establish milestones that demonstrate to your child that they are maturing and earning more responsibility. As they become more responsible, allow them more freedom and more choices.*

Between your child getting to wear underpants and earning his or her driver's license, establish milestones for your kids that acknowledge and underscore their progression towards maturity and independence. These might include:

moving from a crib to a big kid bed

picking out clothes and getting dressed by themselves

taking a shower instead of a bath

getting a desk where they can do their schoolwork

riding a bicycle around the block alone

walking to the park with a sibling or friend, but without a parent

Having sleepovers

Staying out to a curfew

When a child was not meeting the household expectations, not contributing, being rude or sassy, picking on a sibling, etc. they'd lose freedoms and privileges. I cannot even count the number of times I asked one of my middle schoolers or teens, "Are you six? If you want to be treated like a grown up, act like one. Act like a child and I'll treat you like a child."

I made sure that my kids understood that meeting expectations was required. It was also an opportunity to earn more freedom and a way of demonstrating responsibility and maturity. Not meeting expectations resulted in loss of freedoms and privileges. It was a very clear choice. I consistently held my children accountable to meet expectations.

Tales from the Homefront:

At the end of each chapter, I will include some examples from our lives that I hope help better illustrate the concepts in each chapter. My goal is to clarify the concepts and help you to understand the process of converting principles to action plans. Below are a few of our experiences related to the values in this chapter.

Training new dogs: My German shepherd dog and friend, Ripley died in August 2006 at the age of 13. Ripley was the best dog I've ever known and had the privilege to call my friend. I believe that raising kids with pets, especially dogs, is important, so I talked with a neighbor who worked at animal shelter, Helping Paws, to let me know when a puppy to adopt became available. As luck would have it, in October 2006, a litter of puppies arrived at the shelter. The kids and I went with Cindy to Helping Paws one evening to meet the puppies. Unable to decide on one puppy, we selected the most outgoing male and female puppies to adopt. Because my kids loved the music and TV show of the Wiggles, they decided to name the male Anthony and the female Murray. Anthony and Murray were wonderful additions to our family, and I involved my children to help train our new family members.

In teaching the kids to train the puppies, I taught them about the importance of consistency. I made sure that we all used the same words to give commands to the puppies and showed Nate, Jack, and Avery how they could show the puppies what the words meant. In less time than it took me to train Ripley, we soon had housebroken and well behaved dogs. Anthony and Murray learned all the basic commands, didn't bite, didn't jump on people, stayed off the furniture, stayed on the first floor (the main level of our home is all hardwood floors, while the upstairs is mostly carpeted) and learned to stop barking on command. While it frequently seemed that I had five kids or five puppies in the house, we maintained a general sense of order and calm.

It was super important to engage my kids in training the puppies. Not only did it make it easier to train the puppies as all of us used the same words and actions, but teaching my kids how to effectively train the dogs was a great lesson for my children. Other than board games and puzzles, this was the first time I'd actively taught my children a strategy. Sharing, explaining, and reinforcing the actions and behavior of my kids to train our puppies, showed my children how I was teaching them too. The kids saw the effectiveness of all our efforts on our puppies and that knowledge - consciously or unconsciously - supported my parenting efforts. Because the kids understood, they were even more consistent in their actions with our puppies. My children learned a new skill and also developed stronger, more loving bonds with our new family members.

Meeting expectations even when it hurts: Nate and Jack joined Raiders' football when they were 12 and 10, respectively. Both boys were athletic, but this was their first time being immersed in an all-male world. Jack ended up on a team where he was dubbed, "Automatic Jack," for his ability to consistently fight for a first down. Jack's team had a winning season. Nate unfortunately landed on a team that went winless until the final game of the season. Nate was also burdened with a bully for a teammate. Tall for his age, Nate was the target of Chandler, a big boy who seemed to have a compelling need to show that he was tougher and better than everyone else on the team, starting with my son. Sadly, the dad coaches encouraged this aggressive behavior and regularly paired Nate and Chandler for tackling or hitting drills.

Nate's season was painful for me to watch, but much more so for him to experience. One night several weeks into the season, it was pouring down rain and Nate had a scheduled practice that night. Football practice was rain or shine. Nate, my skinny, tall, gangly, pre-pubescent, 12-year-old son sat on his bed in only a tee shirt and underpants crying and saying that he hated football and didn't want to go to practice. He begged me to call his couch and tell him he didn't want to play. While my heart broke, I looked Nate in the eye and said, "You made a commitment to your team. If you want to quit, you need to call your coach and tell him. Otherwise get dressed and be downstairs in 10 minutes." Then I walked out of the bedroom.

Nate went to practice that night. I drove all of us. Avery and Jack hung out in the minivan and played while I stood under a golf umbrella in solidarity with my oldest son as the boys drilled in the rain. It hurt, but I held Nate to his commitment and required him to honor the expectations of his team and his coaches. While his first year was a washout and a brutal challenge, Nate learned a lot, developed into a strong lineman, and earned the position of center over Chandler. Nate's second year of football blessed him with amazing coaches and a season that took the team to the Super Bowl.

Putting myself on time out: Being a single, working parent, I always had some level of tiredness. I'll never forget one night when Jack was about 6-7 months old and Nate 3. Nate was a finicky eater at that stage and had complained throughout dinner, he'd played too rough with Jack afterwards making Jack cry and had generally been pushing my buttons all evening. I was both exhausted and exasperated by the time I finally got Nate cleaned up and into bed. I was just starting to fold the laundry around 9:45 p.m. when Jack woke up crying.

Jack was a gassy baby. Before I'd learned the strategy from my pediatrician of dosing Jack with Mylicon ™ drops daily to avoid gas, I'd address Jack's gas when it occurred. When Jack had gas, he'd cry loudly until he could pass it. I'd pace with Jack on my shoulder patting his back, bounce him on my knee, lay him on my lap and rub his back, flip him over and rub his belly, pump his legs like he was running, etc. to help him pass his gas and relieve his discomfort. That night, worn down by Nate, I lost it. After about 15-20 minutes of trying to comfort Jack without any signs of success, I held Jack in front of my face and yelled, "Stop it! Just stop it!" Suddenly fear coursed through my body. I saw myself from outside myself and I realized how parents could inadvertently shake their babies to the point of injuring or killing them.

Jack was fine, though still crying from the gas bloating his belly. I put him in his infant swing, turned it on then sat down and sobbed uncontrollably. It was too late in the evening to phone a friend or call my dad to come over. Afraid to hold Jack, I sat watching my son cry, adding my tears to his. Finally Jack passed his gas and fell asleep in his swing. That time out for me coupled with the release from crying gave me the ability to reset. Once I was in control of myself, I gently lifted Jack from his swing, kissed his head and took him to his room and laid him in his crib. I sent a silent prayer of thanks to god, finished folding the laundry and went to bed.

Challenging authority: When my kids were born, the internet was in the early stages of development, smart phones hadn't been invented, movies were still on VHS and the Xbox and Wii were relatively new. As I worked full time, on weekdays, I only had about an hour in the morning and 2-4 hours at night to spend with my kids while they were awake.

I filled our house with creative toys like blocks, wooden trains, Lincoln Logs ™, cars, trucks, dinosaurs, puzzles, Playmobil ™, Legos ™, etc. Toys were stored in clear bins with lids that the kids could easily carry from room to room or in open bins that fit on shelves. This made for easy clean-up and generally kept most of the parts together. The tv was rarely on, instead they played, and I frequently joined them. We built towers, drove cars or trucks through them or into them to knock them down. Avery and Nate especially loved to construct elaborate train set ups and traffic jams that wound under tables and around the furniture. We had enough different toys so that my kids didn't get bored. Anything on the floor was expected to be cleaned up and put away before bedtime.

Other than handheld devices, video games and video systems were just being invented around the time my kids were born. My daycare providers had video game systems, but we didn't. Not having grown up with these types of games, and having only played arcade games in bars, I perceived video games as isolating and non-creative. They seemed like a waste of time, and there's no shortage of theories about the impact of violent video games on kids and how addicting screens and video games can be for both kids and adults alike. In addition, my work colleagues regularly shared stories about how they argued with their children over screen time. I saw no good reason to bring video systems and games into our house.

During middle school, Nate and Jack started a campaign during our drive times to tell me all the good things they could think of about video games. They explained how they worked together to solve challenges so they could advance to higher levels. They suggested Wii Sports ™ gave them the chance to learn other sports like tennis and bowling. They noted how Wii Sports ™ kept them active even when they couldn't go outside due to bad weather. They suggested that just like we enjoyed board games, video games were a fun way to play together. They talked about options to play on-line with their friends and talked about how they were being excluded from this option. Overall, I was impressed with their ability to find reasons that had value for me and regularly talk about them in a way that wasn't whiny but persuasive. One day, I told them that they'd convinced me and that I was willing to get a Wii and Xbox. I also set the expectations that if the systems become a problem with getting schoolwork done or a source of arguments, they'd be gone. The kids agreed.

On balance, it was a good decision. While I periodically had to remind one of my children that they'd been playing long enough, we never had arguments over screen time and the kids either bought their own games, borrowed games from the public library or got them as gifts for birthdays and Christmas (usually from me). I've never really played Xbox, but still enjoy family time playing Mario Cart ™, Wii Sports ™ or Just Dance ™ when we have family game days during the holidays. Because I never use the systems except when playing with my children, I'm a weak player, which only adds to my children's pleasure when they consistently crush me whenever we play together as a family.

Challenging authority when it's unjust:

I've never been shy about fighting City Hall or speaking out against something I felt was wrong. I've challenged taxing authorities, had Op-eds published in newspapers, written letters to Senators and Representatives, campaigned over referendums, written complaint letters to companies about product issues and raised concerns with teachers and principals as needed. Each time, I shared and discussed the situation with my kids and used the incidents as real life examples of how to correctly challenge authority.

One incident especially resonated with Jack and his friends. As outlined in the redacted letter below, I fought back against our middle school and District superintendent when they demanded I pay over $1,456 as Jack's portion of a repair bill for broken playground equipment. I was livid at the time of the incident and was ready to raise holy hell when the situation occurred but deferred to Jack's sensitivity as a middle schooler of not wanting to rock the boat. Before drafting the letter, I did my homework, researching relevant issues in the school handbook and laws regarding detention of minors. My goal was not to rescue my son from consequences of something he'd done wrong, rather it was to show Jack, Nate, and Avery that Jack and his friends hadn't done anything wrong and were being treated unfairly. I, for one, was not going to stand for it. I wanted to show my kids how to successfully fight back, challenge injustice and prevail.

After writing my letter, I provided four copies of it to Jack to give to each of his friends who'd been involved in the incident with instructions to share the letter with their parents. I sent the original of my letter both electronically and via snail mail.

I succeeded in my efforts and the result earned me the complementary moniker of "Bad Ass" from Jack's friends. The response to my letter was a communication from the District sent to each of the families indicating the incident had been further reviewed and the invoice deemed "null and void." I was delighted with both outcomes. Mostly however, I was pleased for another opportunity to teach my kids how to fight back against injustice and intimidation from authority.

December 13, 2014

Ref: Invoice for reimbursement for $1,456.39

Dear Mr. Superintendent:

I am writing to inform you that I will not pay any portion of the above referenced invoice (copy attached), and I will strenuously urge the parents of the other four boys involved in this matter to refuse to pay. My refusal is based on the school's violation of both the District policy as outlined in the Student Handbook and violation of my son's rights under IL law.

The incident that gave rise to the invoice occurred on 10/2/14 at xxx Elementary School. My eighth-grade son and four friends, all of whom attend XXX Middle School, were waiting after school to watch the XXX girls' volleyball game. To pass the time, they walked over to the xxx Elementary School playground which is adjacent to the middle school, and decided to have a competition to determine who could hang the longest from the monkey bars. It should be noted that playground equipment has no markings or signage indicating that use is restricted by age or weight. Nor is the equipment limited in usage by a fence or other barrier. The five boys hung from the monkey bars, and almost immediately, one of the brackets holding the monkey bars snapped. The boys dropped to the ground and caught themselves without falling over. Thankfully, no one was injured. An elementary school girl who happened to be playing on the playground at the time, told the boys that her father was a police officer and that he was at XXX to watch the volleyball game. The boys stayed at the site and the girl ran inside to get her dad. The off-duty officer came out, spoke to the boys and they all went over to xxx Elementary School to report what had occurred. The off-duty police officer contacted the city police department, and two uniformed, on-duty officers came to the scene. The incident occurred at approximately 4:00 p.m.

*The boys gave their names and parent contact information very shortly after they were detained by the xxx Elementary staff and the off-duty police officer. **Despite this, no one from the school or the police contacted me.** Instead, my son was held for approximately two hours at the school and questioned by police. It* *was not until after the police had left that I received a call from my son, Jack; the time was approximately 6:00 p.m. Subsequently, at approximately 7:00 p.m., I was contacted at home by one of the officers from the city police dept. to notify me of the incident. The officer discussed the incident and during our conversation indicated that no charges would be filed against my son or the other boys as it was clearly an accident. He noted that the boys weren't doing anything wrong or deviant, and suggested that their combined weight, rather than inappropriate behavior, appeared to be the cause of the breakage. In response to my specific question, the officer informed me that no action would be taken by the school or District against my son or the other boys. It was only because my son would not be charged legally or subject to disciplinary action by the school or District that I did not raise a complaint with the District at the time of the incident. I was outraged over the detention of my son without notice to me and felt that the school and District were fortunate that the equipment failed due to the combined weight of five athletic boys hanging passively from the bars rather than during use by elementary school children who might have been injured. The school and the District were fortunate to have avoided injury and a lawsuit from the failure of the faulty playground equipment.*

*According to the District School Handbook Section 2, Care of School Property, "Students and their parents are responsible for replacing or paying for lost or damaged equipment, school-owned books, buildings or any other school property." The submitted invoice bills for the property replacement at a cost of $820.00. The invoice also bills for "labor" for 3 staff members for 2.5 hours each for regular time ($219.38) plus the labor of 2 staff members for 5.25 hours each of overtime ($417.01). It is unclear why 18-man hours of labor were required to replace the monkey bars. Regardless, the Handbook does not state that students or parents are responsible for District employee labor costs. **The labor charges are not authorized by the Handbook and therefore the District is not authorized to submit for reimbursement.***

According to the District school handbook section 11, Discipline Guidelines, Student Disciplinary Procedures, parent contact is required for behavior that merits a discussion with the student. When I arrived at xxx Elementary School at approx. 6:15 p.m., I encountered locked doors. I banged on two separate locked doors for several minutes before a staff member responded. She indicated that she knew nothing about my son or his whereabouts. I then called back to the cell from which my son had contacted me and learned that my son and the other boys plus their fathers had exited the building and were outside on the playground. The sole "communication" I had from the school or District related to this issue was receipt of the invoice today by certified mail demanding payment of the invoice.

*According to Section II of Policies and Procedures of the Illinois Juvenile Justice System, Police Custody and Arrest (bolding is mine), "Once taken into police custody and placed under arrest, a youth must be informed of his or her Miranda rights prior to interrogation. **Any time a youth is taken into police custody and is not free to leave, they have been arrested.** However, being arrested does not always mean they will be formally charged. Officers may release juveniles from police custody without further action, either on the street or from a police station to their parent or guardian. **Any officer who takes a youth into custody must legally make a reasonable attempt to notify a parent or legal guardian [705 ILCS 405/2-6]."** No attempt was made to contact me by the school or the city police department during the detention of my son. According to my then 13-year-old son, he was not read his Miranda rights. It was only after the two hours of detention by school personnel and police interrogation that my son was permitted to contact me and inform me of the day's events.*

Mr. Superintendent, the handling of this incident, failed to comply with the District policies and procedures as defined in the Student Handbook and failed to comply with IL law. As noted above, I was furious at the handling of this incident, but at my son's request, I did not pursue further action at the time due to the understanding that the boys would not be charged legally or subjected to disciplinary action by the school. If the school or District intends to proceed in its attempts to pass on any of these costs, please be advised that I am fully prepared to raise a complaint against the school and the District for mistreatment of my son, violation of District policies and procedures as well as the violation of my son's legal rights.

I appreciate your attention to this matter and your guidance on next steps. Please contact me at earliest convenience so I know how to proceed.

Sincerely,

Sally Munn

Email: xxxx

Phone: xxxxx

cc: Bxxxxx family

Kxxxxx family

Pxxxxx family

Txxxxx family

Parent ferociously. Love unconditionally.

Check your emotions at the door. Leave your bags at the station.

Dogs and kids flourish with consistency and love.

Watching kids learn to walk is both inspirational and frightening.

Never underestimate the power of a hug and the words "I love you."

VALUE 2

HONESTY AND TRANSPARENCY

I chose honesty and transparency as part of my parenting values because I believe that they are foundational to trust. They also fit nicely with Consistency and Expectations. My childhood underscored how vital these principles are in a family. As mentioned, my parents married right out of high school and divorced 13 years later. Their divorce was a bitter and protracted break up, and they used us kids as weapons both during the fighting that lead to their break-up and for years afterwards to hurt and punish each other. Lies were the currency of the day with my mother fabricating horrible stories about my dad, and my dad withholding child support checks to torment my mother. As an adult, I know that they were reacting from their hurt and anger, however, the corrosiveness of their behavior and the lies my mother told about my dad resulted in me severing ties with my dad for roughly 7 years, and later permanently ending all contact with my mother. The impacts of my parents' behavior and actions on my siblings, our extended family and me were far reaching and negatively impacted family relationships for decades.

Given this experience, I vowed that not only would I embrace honesty as one of my key personal traits, but I would also never subject my children to such an environment. I was committed to being as honest and transparent as possible with my children. I believe that honesty is foundational to personal character, trust, and successful relationships. I was both proud and saddened when each of my grown sons told me recently that I am the only person they know who is always completely honest with them.

Despite the importance I place on honesty, I'd suggest that I don't think that people are inherently honest. I believe honesty needs to be taught. I think our survival instinct and our knee jerk response related to being called out for bad behavior – embarrassed, uncomfortable, or caught with our hand in the proverbial cookie jar - is generally to lie to save ourselves from punishment, embarrassment or to avoid hurting others' feelings. During her teen years, my daughter Avery told me many times that she lied because she didn't want someone to feel bad or because she'd rather tell me what she thought I wanted to hear to avoid confrontation. While I completely understand that being fully truthful might not be the best course for societal reasons or kindness, I made it clear that I expected honesty from my children and myself at all times within our family.

Children are born without filters. On occasion, their communication can be brutally honest. Therefore, as I taught them to be honest, I also needed to help them to understand social structure, manners, and the nuances of polite society. Children and especially toddlers while they are learning language may say things that are perceptive, funny, rude, or seemingly mean because they haven't yet learned how to disseminate their thoughts. For example, I once had a new neighbor who had a prosthetic arm. A group of neighborhood moms and I were just welcoming her to the neighborhood when 6-year-old Sarah, the daughter of one of the moms in the group, came over to join us. Sarah looked at the new neighbor and asked, "What happened to your arm?" It was the obvious question that all of us wondered but were too polite to ask. The new neighbor explained why she had an artificial limb and all of us felt more comfortable. Sometimes however, the situation is not so pleasant. Once during our weekend errands, 4-year-old Nate saw another shopper who was very obese. Seemingly at the top of his voice, Nate said, "Look at that man. I've never seen anyone that fat in my whole life!" In a voice loud enough for the man to hear, I scolded my son for saying mean and unkind things about others. Later as we drove home, I suggested that in the future Nate whisper or ask me questions privately later to avoid hurting other people's feelings.

I tried to teach my kids that while honesty was expected, that on occasion, good manners may require us to be not fully honest. I explained it as manners and made it clear that being dishonest to avoid bad consequences was not ok. I strove to both teach my children to be honest and also know how to address touchy situations such as:

- When they received a gift of an item they already owned, rather than saying, "I already have one," to say something like, "This is great. Thank you!"

- When faced with a request for feedback from a friend regarding a new haircut, new cloths, etc., that they did not personally like, to say something such as, "That's really cool." Or "I'm glad you like it."

- When eating at a friend's house and being offered something they didn't like, to say, "Thank you, I'm really not that hungry."

None of the above are a lie, but they gave my kids a path forward to be both truthful (though not fully) and avoid hurting someone's feelings. I viewed this guidance as providing my kids with skills/responses that were tools in their toolbox to use when necessary. I also expected them to be honest with themselves and with every member of our family, including me.

As suggested above, being honest doesn't mean we have to be brutally honest. It's important to teach our kids to be honest and not lie to avoid consequences. But it's equally important to teach our kids to be sensitive to others' feelings (Empathy is the next chapter) and sensitive to the times when it may be appropriate to be less than fully transparent.

Embracing honesty and transparency, I was also open and honest with everyone about how I conceived my children. While my family was not thrilled with me as a single parent, my dad and his wife agreed to be available to take me to the hospital when it was time for Nate to be born. Each time I got pregnant; I shared the news with each of my neighbors and told them that it was via artificial insemination, and on subsequent pregnancies, I let them know that it was using the same anonymous donor's sperm. I didn't want anyone to speculate or make up stories about me or my children. I left it to my neighbors to decide how to explain to their own children while also being very clear that I would be honest and open with my kids and everyone else.

During my maternity leave with Nate, in addition to everything else, I had to find a new job. When I was pregnant with Nate, I discovered that my manager was a misogynistic jerk. Even if he hadn't been, at the time, I was working in Chicago and knew I couldn't find or afford daycare for 13 hours a day. Gratefully, I found a job in in the suburbs and was blessed with an amazing manager.

Before starting my new job, one day I took the train to Chicago with infant

Nate to show him off, officially resign, clean out my desk and say goodbye to my former colleagues. During the visit, I was truly astonished by the number of professional, single women who told me that they wished they'd had my courage to have a child on their own. Many of these women were amazing, talented people who I admired and respected. I believe they could've been wonderful mothers. I was saddened that they hadn't taken the chance to experience the amazing journey that comes from creating and loving a child. Their comments also made me even more committed to my own choice.

I'm extremely grateful that I had a very supportive manager as a single parent, especially once I decided to expand my family. I worked at the company for eight years and earned several promotions. While I'd had Nate before starting at my job, my manager, Michelle was completely supportive of me as a single mother. After becoming pregnant with Jack, I told Michelle how I conceived my children, and she seemed genuinely delighted. Other than my friends from the Peace Corps, Pat and Kathryn, I think Michelle was the most supportive person I had in my orbit at the time.

Michelle was both an amazing woman and a terrific leader who went out of her way to uplift women, including giving training sessions to teach female colleagues how to navigate their careers. Michelle was also always willing to mentor or coach women at all levels at the company. Michelle was a Black woman and had an honest understanding of the challenges faced by women. She seemed to have a personal mission to help, support and empower women to succeed. Truly it was a blessing to have Michelle in my corner as I navigated this new territory of both advancing in my career and building my family. I only left the firm when after several acquisitions, executive leadership consolidated groups and moved our division to Atlanta. That was the first time I was laid off unexpectedly. While I received a fair severance package that enabled be to transition smoothly, it was scary. At the time, I had three kids aged 7, 5 and 2 ½ .

Once my kids were old enough to understand that most people had both a mom and dad, I told them the truth. They were too young to understand sex, so I explained that just as I had regularly donated blood over the years to help people in an emergency, there were men who donated the thing that was needed for a woman's egg to start growing into a baby to help people like me who wanted to have kids but didn't have a husband. As the kids got older, I shared more detailed and relevant information (see Appendix for information on Insemination and communication).

> **Strategy:** *Use High, Low, Medium to talk about and characterize your day.*

Dinner times were family time in our house. Because we spent so much time apart during the day, conversations were an important way for me to learn about their day. We sat together at the kitchen or dining room table and ate and talked. To facilitate conversations, I used the mechanism of High, Low, Medium as a tool to talk about our day. In addition to providing a framework for communication, it also required each of us to not just focus on the good things, but to think about and talk about various aspects of the day.

We went around the table, and each had a turn to talk about our day and share events. While we weren't allowed to interrupt, the stories frequently resulted in discussions and comments about what someone had shared. On some nights, our extended conversations outlasted our food, but it was all good and underscored the importance of being a family.

Once the kids were all in elementary school, we added the additional category of "Cool at School" which was a catchall category to share a funny story and talk about something else that was interesting, funny or otherwise noteworthy that might not fit into the other categories.

Requiring the kids to rate the things they discussed also gave me insight into their emotions, sensitivities, sense of humor, and how they perceived situations. These discussions provided open, honest insight into my children's view of the world and their place in it.

Once my kids were all in their teens, I created identical folders of information for each of them. In the folders I included copies of all the newsletters I'd received from the Sperm Bank over the years, the summary sheet and 15 page medical history about the donor from whom I'd conceived my children and his open ended responses to a dozen or so questions about himself, including why he'd become a sperm donor. Years prior, my dad's oldest sister had prepared a genealogy of our family, tracing us back to the Revolutionary War, so I made copies of all the information and photos that Martha had compiled and included that information as well. Finally, I made copies of photographs of our extended family from my childhood photo album to round out the information in my kids' folders. I gave my children the folders and explained that I wanted to be sure that they knew everything that I knew about the donor and our extended family.

I believe that part of my strength comes from being honest. I wanted to impart that source of strength, that source of power, to my children. Throughout my life there have been people who didn't like me or who disagreed with me. While I think we'd all agree that it's preferable if people like you, I was ok if someone didn't like me and I tried not to let it affect my sense of self-esteem. I also never wanted someone to like me or think better of me based on a lie. I never wanted anyone to think I was something I wasn't. From my perspective, being fake or lying about myself was giving others power to call me out or to discover that I wasn't what I claimed to be. It was ok if someone didn't like me for who I was or for what I believed in. None of us can please everyone. I've always tried to be honest about who I was, who I am, what matters to me, and I was willing to face the consequences of being myself. Again, I've always felt that being true to myself and my beliefs was a source of power. It was my shield from unexpected harm or manipulation. I chose honesty as a value that I hoped my children would embrace so they too could find the strength that being honest can provide.

As a parent of kids who participated in lots of different sports, I had many "bleacher friends" – parents of my kids' teammates. I was an avid supporter and was the mom at the top of the bleachers with cowbells cheering for the team during six years of high school football. I tried (not always successfully) to have all my cheering be positive. While I have been unhappy with the general shift in coaching since my childhood from one focused on building the talents of all the kids to seemingly wanting to win at all costs, I believed that most of the referees and umpires tried to be fair and do their best every game. Whenever my kids groused about unfair refs or officials, I always said that I believed that the missed or bad calls seemed to balance out for both teams, and I felt that the officials had done their best to be fair. In other words, I didn't allow my kids to play victim and claim that the game was somehow unfair or rigged. In addition to being honest, it was also about sportsmanship. I was honest with my kids, and I wanted them to be honest with themselves, honest in their self-assessment of how they'd played – good, bad, or average – and not try to blame a bad outcome on someone else.

Sitting in the bleachers or walking on the sidelines of my kids' sporting events, I've seen too many parents give false praise to their kids. While I formed many rewarding relationships with other parents, I also noted that some parents communicated with their kids in a manner that I thought was counterproductive and dishonest. They conveyed directly or indirectly that their kids were superior athletes, that the coach was wrong for not playing them more, that the refs were unfair in their calls. I believe that this type of communication is harmful. Instead, I'd suggest that parents should take the time to notice how their kids are genuinely special and give legitimate compliments and encouragement about those aspects. Also, unless you're raising the next Michael Jordan or Caitlin Clark, your kid is likely not the "best." Be honest with yourself and your child. If they're playing a team sport, encourage both the importance of supporting the team and trying to do their personal best to contribute to the team's success. False praise is a form of lying. It teaches your kids not to trust you. As indicated above, honesty doesn't have to be brutal; honesty with our kids should always be kind. Acknowledge their efforts and the ways they truly excelled, suggest areas where they might improve, and always be honest.

Whether you also choose honesty and transparency as part of your core values or not, in your role as a parent, please give your kids honest information and feedback as you help them to learn about the world. It will help your child(ren) to trust you and come to you with questions and fears. Small events can be great opportunities to demonstrate honesty. Examples include:

- At the pediatrician's office before getting a vaccine: When my kids asked if the shot was going to hurt, I always said yes. Then I explained that the shot would give their bodies medicine to help keep them from getting germs that might make them very, very sick. I assured them it would only hurt a little and would be alright. I reminded them that I was there to make sure they'd be ok. Of course they cried when the nurse gave them the shots, but they quickly calmed down and were distracted by the cool band aid.

- By the time each of my kids got to the end of their rounds of childhood vaccines they didn't cry, they grimaced and took the shot in stride. It's important to be honest with your kids and empower them to deal with situations or unpleasant tasks. **Lying doesn't change reality; it only undermines your credibility and your kids' ability to trust you.**

- They get a big pimple on their face and are self-conscious: Don't say, "You're so beautiful, no one will even notice." Just tell them that it's part of growing up and that yes, while people might notice, their friends will likely be glad it's not them who has a pimple. Remind them that it will go away in a few days and not pick at it or pop it.

- They make questionable fashion choices: I recall once when my daughter Avery was a teen and snapped at me when in reply to her question about her outfit, I said something like, "I'm glad you like it, but I don't think it's very flattering." Using a chastising tone, Avery told me that as her mom, it was my job to tell her she looked nice. I replied that it was my job to be honest so that she'd know that when I told her she looked good, she'd know I was being sincere.

- <u>After a disappointing sporting event</u>: Don't tell them they played great if they didn't. Ask them what they thought they did good and what they wish they could've done better. Ask them how they think the team did and if they had fun. Remind them that everyone needs to practice and if there was something you can genuinely praise – a good play, a nice throw, how they encouraged others, etc. – then do so. Ask them if they'd like to practice throwing, batting, kicking, (whatever) with you or if they'd rather wait to do it with the team. And somewhere in the conversation, be sure to shift their focus to having fun, being a good teammate, spending time with friends and improving their skills.

  In the event your child had the chance to make the winning shot, the winning play, etc., but missed, remind him or her that while it would've been totally amazing if they had made it, that it wasn't their fault that their team lost the game. The loss was the result of all the other good, bad, and average plays by both teams up to that point. Your child may've missed the chance to win the game, but it wasn't their fault that the team lost.

All of us feel uncertainty at times, occasionally fail to do our best and will experience disappointments in our lives. By modelling honesty and being truthful with your kids, you're helping them to face unpleasant situations and move past them. Facing the truth, sometimes an unpleasant truth, and helping your kids to deal with it, demonstrates your support and confidence in their ability to manage all kinds of situations - including disappointments. It helps your kids to overcome fear and embarrassment. It encourages them to try new things when they see that failing is ok; failing is just a chance to learn how to try another way.

These types of conversations and experiences can be great ways to help your children build resilience. Reinforce your love for them daily regardless of how they look or how they performed in the game or how they did on their last test. Offer your help and support. Also be sure to let your kids see you deal with disappointment and adversity; again, always trying to model the type of behavior you'd want them to emulate while also being careful not to overshare regarding your problems.

Strategy: *Encourage your kids to write about experiences*

Personal computers were relatively new technology when my kids were growing up. We had some educational computer games that they liked to play and starting in elementary school, occasionally they would write stories on the computer. Early stories tended to be detailed play-by-play accounts of sports games or adventures in which they were the stars. While most of these stories lacked a compelling plot, the kids had fun and were learning. They were expressing their creativity, developing keyboard skills and spell check helped improve their spelling skills.

As detailed in Tales from the Homefront, I also used writing when I felt that one of the kids needed to consider a situation more fully. I believed that making them produce a document would convert the "punishment" into a chance to better understand the situation, reflect and learn.

We're all only human and it's tough to be great every day in everything we do. Especially with sports and creative activities, try to encourage your child(ren) that these are things to enjoy. These activities shouldn't be threats to your kids' sense of self-worth. Honest feedback regarding sports helps your kids gain perspective and know that a loss is nothing more than a loss. There will be more games in the future. Some games they'll win, some they'll lose. Sports should be about teamwork, individual contribution, being strong and agile, improving skills. Sports are games, and playing games should be fun and enjoyable even when we don't win.

Nate, Jack, and Avery were all talented athletes. They each played multiple sports at school, and I juggled work as much as possible to attend as many games and meets as I could. My children made many good friends, learned new skills, and had lots of fun. In high school, encouraged by their coaches, each of my children also took it upon themselves to find time for the weight room and rapidly saw the value of drilling and extra workouts to improve their skills and strength.

In our family, sports always remained about fun, teamwork and being good competitors. Especially as they were going through puberty, I also loved that sports helped hone and strengthen their developing bodies. My kids didn't participate in travel leagues or clubs because I couldn't manage the logistics and honestly couldn't afford the price tags. In addition, while I think sports are very important, I didn't believe in making any sport the center of my child's life. I wasn't trying to raise future Olympians, just good, strong, healthy kids who understood teamwork and the value of individual contribution. Throughout the years, my kids and I had many conversations about the politics and favoritism of some coaches; the risks of taking nutraceuticals, supplements or god forbid, steroids. My kids and I have discussed what it takes to be a good leader and the value of pushing ourselves to be better. I strove to teach the great lessons of team sports and avoid the ugly aspects that seem to have filtered into sports at many levels.

Youth sports have changed a lot since I was a kid. When I was growing up, everybody played at least a part of every game. Of course we all wanted to win, but effort, learning and improving skills and embracing sportsmanship were emphasized. I'm not sure when the stakes changed, but in my opinion too much of youth sports have been corrupted. Despite each of my sons and daughter having solid athletic abilities, we decided as a family that the kids would not pursue athletic scholarships for college. Instead, they each played intermural sports in college. They embraced fun, friendship and teamwork and avoided the transactional and political nature of college athletics. While they all know that winning isn't everything, they are each serious competitors and supportive teammates.

Strategy: *Board games are a great way to teach that the purpose of a game is to have fun and enjoy each other's company. Playing games is <u>not</u> just about being the winner.*

This was a hard lesson for my kids to learn. I'd remind everyone that with 4 players in a game, 3 of us would lose and only one would win. Naturally, they each expected to be the winner. I'd point out that in some games, a lot can be based on the luck of the draw or roll of the dice. That said, for games like Sorry ™ or Monopoly ™ that had strategic aspects I'd try to teach them various strategies and explain options. Unsurprisingly, there was frequently frustration and disappointment that led to name calling when one player killed the other and got sent back to home. Tears were also not uncommon. But we played to the end. No one was allowed to throw a tantrum, quit, or knock over the board.

We also generally continued to play after someone had won to see who would come in 2nd and 3rd place. I think having the ability to finish the game took the edge off of the disappointment of losing.

When she was little, Avery's favorite games were Candyland and Chutes & Ladders (we also had Snakes & Ladders). Chutes (or Snakes) & Ladders is 100% luck as each player has one token and all moves are decided by the roll of a dice. Statistically, with two players, each player should win roughly half the time. However, I lost virtually every single game that Avery and I ever played, and we played hundreds of times over the years. Given the statistical absurdity of the results, I jokingly complained during our games each time I got sent down the chute (or snake). I complained it wasn't fair; I asked if Avery was cheating and whined that it was impossible for me to lose so many times. Avery would laugh and cheer at my antics. I believe that watching me lose and making it seem funny helped Avery and my boys understand that playing games really was about having fun together.

Respecting privacy is part of being honest and demonstrating trust. As technology and smart phones have become ubiquitous, parents literally have the ability to track their kids' movements, to follow them on social media platforms and invade their privacy to varying degrees. As mentioned, my kids didn't have phones until they were in high school. As they were older and somewhat more mature, we avoided many of the issues that can arise when younger kids have access to technology. While understanding the genuine safety concerns parents have, I think making thoughtful choices that demonstrate trust in your children while still providing a safety net are important. Just as our kids learn to ride a bicycle without training wheels or without you holding onto the seat and running beside them, so they need to learn to navigate other aspects of their lives without you hovering over them or second guessing their every move. Our kids need to develop confidence in their ability to navigate the world without us holding their hand or looking over their shoulders all the time.

As outlined in several Tales from the Homefront examples, my kids did lie to me on occasion and sometimes they got caught. But catching them in a lie was generally due to circumstances rather than "trust but verify" actions by me. If there was something I was really worried about such as a party when the parents wouldn't be home or a request to stay overnight at a friend's house who I knew had parents who didn't place limits on their kids, I'd just make my permission conditioned on my talking to the parents first or I just said "No." My goal was not to shelter my children from the dangers of the world, but rather to try to ensure that my kids had the maturity and skills needed to deal with potential situations on their own before being thrown into the deep end. At those times, my kids often complained that I didn't trust them or that I was too controlling or overly protective. I'd just had had too many experiences growing up that were beyond my maturity. I'd suffered the consequences, generally alone, and I saw no value or reason to let my children repeat my experiences. The same challenging situation for a 15 year old vs. a 17 year old is night and day in their ability to successfully navigate it. I would much rather deal with an angry disappointed teen, than the consequences of an unwanted traumatic situation experienced by my child.

Never forget, parenting is not a popularity contest. Sometimes you have to be the bad guy and deal with your child(ren)'s disappointment and anger to keep them safe. I'd also recommend always talking about your concerns and reasons if you don't let them participate in some desired activity. Be open and honest and share your concerns. Those conversations can help your children to understand a situation more fully and may even make them feel more grown up and respected, even if they're disappointed and angry with your decision.

My kids and I had a lot of conversations about what was ok and what wasn't ok on social media. But I never read their posts or followed them. I also never searched their rooms or took their phones to read their text messages. While that may make me sound naïve or foolish, the kids and I had many daily touch points, open dialogue and their friends were frequently at our house. Based on their actions, feedback from teachers, daycare providers and others, I felt reasonably confident that my children had internalized many of the expectations about proper behavior and I tried to keep my antenna sharp to detect and address potential problems early. I'd also known growing up that my mother sometimes searched my room. When I was young, I stopped journaling and threw out my diary as a result. Just as I'd never snoop in someone's medicine chest while visiting their homes, I wouldn't betray my kids' privacy by searching their rooms, following them on social media or reading their text messages. To me, it would have been betraying their trust. It would've been dishonest.

When you're raising kids, everything is potentially a learning experience. Always provide your kids with honest, age-appropriate information and where there are opportunities to broaden the narrative, help them connect the dots and recognize patterns and similarities. In my role as parent, I've always felt a responsibility to help my kids to honestly understand people, their motives, and to help them see the world both as it is and as we might wish it could be. I always tried to be open and honest with my kids in all our conversations about good and bad things. I never lost sight of the fact that as a parent, I was always striving to work myself out of a job, to let my kids be fully in the driver's seat. We discussed failures and disappointments as well as successes – theirs and mine. They saw me fail. They saw me get frustrated, and they saw me try again in a different way. By analyzing what went wrong or what went right, we all learned how to do better, find areas for improvement, and improve at what we were already doing well.

My grown kids continue be supporters, critics and advisors for each other. They demonstrate good self-awareness and seem to have an honest understanding of themselves. They consistently try to lift each other up and don't hesitate to call each other out if they believe one of their siblings is making a bad decision or slacking when they believe their sibling can do better. They also reach out to each other for their thoughts on potential opportunities or when faced with challenges. At times they have (and may still) collude together behind my back, but I likewise sometimes reach out to them individually when I have concerns about one of them and want to ensure they are aware of issues and available to support each other. Honesty is a value that they've each embraced to varying degrees and listening to them, I believe that they are honest with themselves about their own strengths and areas for improvement.

I created a beautiful, amazing family. While I have encountered people who disagreed with my choice to be a single parent or for whatever reason didn't like me personally, I always felt that that was their issue not mine. While I might've disagreed with their perspective, I never tried to argue with them or lie about who I was to try to gain their approval. Being honest and open gave me strength. My self-esteem came from within, based on making choices and decisions that were true to me, my values, my family – not based on the opinions of others. I wanted my children to likewise to be proud of themselves and comfortable in their skin. I didn't want others to have power over my kids by catching them in a lie about who they were or what they could do. I tried to teach my children to recognize their own unique value and worth based on their own self-assessment, their achievements, and their contributions - not the approval of others, even me.

As noted, part of my rationale for embracing honesty as a core value was a pendulum swing against the pain and harm caused by my parents' divorce and their corrosive lies and behavior. Honesty is such an intrinsic part of my personality, of who I am, that it had to be one of my core parenting values. I believed it was critical that my children knew me as the person I truly am. I wanted them to know that I am a loving but imperfect person. I wanted them to see that I had high self-esteem even though I made mistakes, didn't always achieve my goals or do my best. I wanted them to have confidence that I would always love and support them no matter what. I felt that it was imperative that Nate, Jack, and Avery each trusted me and knew with 100% certainty that I would always be honest with them, even when my feedback might not be the answer they wanted.

Tales from the Homefront:

Appreciating your children's humor: As mentioned, dinner times were family time. We crowded around our kitchen table, enjoyed a good nutritious meal together and used High, Low, Medium, Cool at School to ensure everyone had a chance to talk. One night the kids were wound up and misbehaving at the table. Trying not to get irritated, I stood up from the table and started putting my dishes into the sink and rinsing the pots and pans. As I walked around the table, I said to my kids in a teasing voice, "I can't wait until you're all parents and you call me up one day and say, 'Mom, the kids are driving me crazy. Can you please come over and watch them?" Walking around the table back to my chair, waggling my hands in the air, I added, "And you know what I'm going to say? 'Nope, I'm going out dancing!" Almost immediately, 8-year old Nate, sassed back, "With who? Your imaginary husband?"

The room exploded with laughter and everyone's mood changed 100% for the better. From that day forward, my kids' "Imaginary Dad" was occasionally called out as a great guy always willing to support their every desire with a comment such as, "My Imaginary Dad would buy it for me." Or "my Imaginary Dad would let me do it." My standard response was, "Well, your Imaginary Dad can buy it with his imaginary money," or "Imaginary Dad's going to have to convince me that's a good idea." Imaginary Dad became our inside joke and was always a source of laughter. I also believed it was a healthy way for my kids to call out that they only had me as a parent; being honest that they didn't have a dad. Again, no topic or subject was off-limits in our house.

Santa Claus: I obviously didn't invent Santa Claus, but I had to decide whether to embrace the cultural aspects of Santa or not include Santa as part of our traditions. Having grown up in a household where money was tight, loving the Christmas shows on tv, the magic of Santa, and being able to ask Santa for presents I knew we couldn't afford; I decided to include Santa in our celebrations of Christmas. So we had gifts from Santa, stockings, and all the trappings. As our house didn't have a chimney or fireplace, I purchased a Santa key – a skeleton key with a Santa head as the top part - that we'd hang on a ribbon on the front door. I told the kids that is was a key that would only work for Santa. The kids loved leaving out cookies and milk on Christmas Eve and during elementary school, as students, they also made reindeer food - dry oatmeal, glitter and who knows what else - that they scattered in the front yard on Christmas Eve.

Our house is over 100-years old, and we have kind of a creepy, unfinished basement with several small rooms which my brother (a cop) dubbed "*The Silence of the Lambs* basement." Taking advantage of this creepiness, I hid Santa's presents in one of the side rooms in the basement. I used different wrapping paper, different labels, wrote only in red ink on the gift tags from Santa and used slightly different handwriting in the way I wrote their names. For presents from me, I just left them in a corner of my bedroom covered by our swimming pool towels. I told the kids if they peeked, or if I even thought that someone had peeked, I'd return all their presents. Because my kids knew I never made idle threats, they took me at my word and did not disturb the gifts. It also likely helped that they weren't home without me, so sneaking into my room to peak would've been a very high risk proposition. Once I wrapped the presents from me, I'd put them under the tree. I used evenings after they were asleep to wrap presents from Santa and would return them to the basement. Then each Christmas Eve after I was sure the kids were all asleep, I'd sneak to the basement, bring up Santa's gifts and the bags of stocking stuffers.

As the kids got older and began questioning me about whether Santa was real or not, my answer was typically, "Some people believe, others don't. Just like some people believe in God and others don't. I believe in God, and I believe in Santa." While not exactly truthful, my belief in Santa was believing in the value of the myth and message of Santa. I wanted my kids to experience that. By middle school, I sensed when their questions wanted the truth, versus an extension of their childhood belief and innocence.

In response to his questioning one year, I told Nate the truth. I asked if he'd enjoyed believing, which he admitted he had. So I asked him to keep the secret and not tell Jack or Avery. Nate was delighted to play along and felt superior and much more mature than his younger, still believing siblings. I also think it gave Nate a richer understanding and appreciation of the fun and magic of Christmas. Nate continued to receive presents from Santa as part of the charade, which likely helped too. A year or so later, Jack was part of our conspiracy with only Avery left still believing.

One Christmas Eve a year or so later, I crept downstairs around 2:00 a.m. and brought the Santa gifts up from the basement. As I put down the stack of gifts, I heard a noise. Turning around, I saw that Avery was sleeping on the couch! I froze then quietly tiptoed back to the basement for more presents and the stocking stuffers. As I quietly began filling stockings, Avery sat up from the couch and yelled, "I knew it! I knew it was you!" I looked at her, cracked a smile and replied, "I'm proud of you Aves. Now go upstairs, get in bed and we'll chat in the morning."

At breakfast, Avery's discovery was a source of laughter, hijinks, and general hilarity. The boys were especially proud of how Avery had sneaked down to sleep on the couch to find out for herself. They also disclosed how they'd played along and rather than seeming dishonest everyone walked away feeling that Santa and their discovery of the truth was a source of great fun. We all also agreed that we'd keep putting out stockings, which by the way, I continue to do to this day.

Getting caught lying: Once the kids reached middle school, I still used loss of privileges as the primary form of punishment, but occasionally, I required them to write about an experience. There are two incidents that I'll highlight.

The first was when Nate was a freshman in high school, the other when Avery was 16, I've shared Nate's story in the Empathy chapter (next section) and relate Avery's below. I'll also circle back to Avery's response in the section on Teens as her comments clearly illustrate the push/pull that characterized those years.

I always encouraged my kids to join clubs and participate in school activities including dances. In both middle school and high school, my kids typically went to dances with a group of their friends. While high school proms meant going as a couple, if my sons went, the took friends who were girls as I didn't let my kids "date" or "go steady" until they were 17. My rationale was that puberty is confusing enough, and I figured by 17 they'd have a better basis of emotional maturity. That was fine for Nate and Jack, but a source of on-going conflict for Avery and me.

During my sons' high school years, our house was filled with boys. We lived three houses away from the high school, so our house was a great place to hang out after school, especially before my son's friends had their driver's licenses. It was not uncommon for 2-4 friends to stop by until their parents picked them up after work, with some occasionally joining us for dinner if their parents were running late. As a result, Avery grew up surrounded by and totally comfortable with boys. She was also protected by her brothers and their friends when she got to tag along for a trip up town with them on the weekends to buy lunch or shop at Dollar Tree. I used to joke that Avery had her own mini Secret Service watching over her.

I welcomed all my kids' friends into our home. We had an above ground swimming pool, and during the summer, it was not uncommon for them to invite friends over to swim. Other times, they went to one of the three beaches in our town. Being confident in herself and very comfortable with boys, Avery saw no reason not to date despite being only 16.

In my kids' generation, when a boy and girl were a couple, the boy would give the girl a sweatshirt and/or tee shirt of his to wear. I'd seen that Avery had a sweatshirt that obviously wasn't hers. I asked her about it, and she admitted Tom had given it to her. I reminded her that she wasn't allowed to date for another year and told her to give it back. (As I learned later, she didn't give it back, instead, she hid it in her room.) I reminded her that while she could go out in groups, which might include Tom, she wasn't allowed to date yet.

One day, Avery invited two girlfriends and Tom over to go swimming.

Even as teens using the pool, I always kept an eye on the kids – so my boys didn't drown each other from too much roughhousing and just in general to make sure everyone was safe. On this particular day, I caught Avery and Tom locked in an intimate embrace in the pool while the two girls hit a beach ball back and forth. I called Avery into the house and spoke to her about the inappropriateness of her actions and again reminded her that she was not allowed to date for another year. Avery was furious and resentful and even more angry when, because of her attitude and refusal to listen, I sent everyone home shortly thereafter.

Roughly a week later, Avery asked me to drop her off at Main Beach to meet her friend, Paige, and several other girlfriends. I dropped her at the beach and drove home. As luck would have it, within a half hour of returning home, I got a text from Paige's mom who I'd become friends with while sitting in the bleachers together. Jorie was out shopping and wanted to tell me about something. On a whim, I asked Jorie if Paige was with her. Jorie said she was.

It was not the first time I'd caught Avery lying, but this time I saw red. I phoned Avery. She didn't answer so I left her a voicemail message telling her she'd lied to me again as I'd just talked to Jorie who was out shopping with Paige. In my message, I said that I would be at Main Beach in ten minutes to pick her up. Furious, I drove the mile or so across town to Main Beach, pulled into the parking lot and waited. No Avery. I phoned again. This time Avery answered. I asked her where the hell she was. Avery was crying, breathing hard and replied, "I don't know."

My world stopped. Every horrible news story flashed through my mind and fear settled over me. I calmly asked, "What do you mean? Aren't you at the beach?" Avery replied, "No, I'm on a road."

Her response only fed my fear as more imagines about tragic things that can happen to young women raced through my mind. I asked, "Where?" Avery replied, "I don't know."

Forcing myself to remain calm, I took a deep breath and replied, "Look around you for any street sign or business." Avery said, "I see Gate 22." I said, "I know where you are. I'm coming to get you. Stay on the phone."

I drove to where I thought Avery would be, maintaining a running commentary with her on the phone. I felt overwhelming relief when I saw her walking toward me on the side of the road. Once Avery was safely in the vehicle, I asked, "So what the hell? Where were you?" Avery confessed that after being dropped off by me, Tom and his older brother had picked her up and driven her to their house. Tom's house was near the west end of the Lake in an area of town that was unfamiliar to Avery. They were just getting comfortable on the basement couch when she got my message. She ran out of Tom's house and tried to find her way back to Main Beach by following the Lake before I got there.

I talked to Avery about the risks of the situation and how angry I was with her defying me and lying. Avery said that they'd only kissed. Though she did later admit that while Tom had wanted to do more, upon getting my phone message, she'd dashed from the house to try to get back to Main Beach before me. As punishment for lying, Avery was grounded from going to the beach or hanging out with friends after school for two weeks. I also required her to write about the corrosive impact of lying on relationships. It took her several days to finish but below is what she wrote:

Lying

Trust is the most important thing in a relationship. Whether it be a romantic or personal relationship, in order for it to work there needs to be trust between each other. Over the past few months I've begun to lie about a few different things. Such as it be about where I am or whether or not I have a sweatshirt either way it's still a lie. I've felt before that these have been justified because I was afraid of the reaction I'd receive if I told the truth. I understand now that what I've done was stupid and ruined our relationship. Trust doesn't come back right away. It takes time and while it stank waiting for about 3 months I felt as though we were getting somewhere, and I think you felt the same. The other day, when I had lied about the sweatshirt I lied because I was afraid, you'd get rid of the sweatshirt if I said I had it. Honestly, while I understand your concerns about Tom and our relationship it puts tons of pressure on us and how we can't really go out and have fun. We can normally just stay here and I'm really grateful you let us do at least that, but it really does make things hard. And I felt that if I had told you I still had that sweatshirt you'd really only think I was disobeying you and just get rid of it. While I can't really remember the times I've lied in the years past but over the past few months I've lied to try to cover up things because I was afraid I couldn't see Tom if you knew. And yes, I understand that's idiotic but it's just those snap decisions. Because every time he asks if we can finally go to his house my heart sinks a little further each time that I tell him I can't. While I've said this is not him personally it's the fact that you think I'm not old enough and can't date, he takes it in a more personal way and thinks you dislike him because of his crazy ex (yes, I know this sounds like some high school drama movie) he's had trust issues and it's hard to get him to believe it's due to our own reasons. I'm not trying to justify my lies or anything, but I am trying to get you to understand how I'm feeling about this situation and see things from my point of view. School is very stressful, and volleyball added another layer of stress and now I feel like as soon as I walk in the door, I get attacked all over again. I've been trying to balance everything, and I feel as though we're seeing two different paths (can't think of a better word) and it's been really hard, especially lately. I think we need to try and understand each other more. Such as trying to see each other's sides of the story and maybe make compromises. For example, I've been doing research on birth control and gone through many different types (a patch, sponge, vaginal ring, the pill, mini pill) and I think I'd be willing to get on the pill if you're willing to work with me in building up to eventually go to Tom's house. I feel as though we're very disconnected right now and that's both our faults. I don't want you to pressure me to say anything, but I also feel as though if I have a problem, I can't talk to you about it and that's not okay. We've both been adding stress to each other, and we need to reconnect. And honesty is a good start. So that's also partially why I've written so much because I thought that if you could try and see how I'm feeling maybe you could be a little more compassionate towards me and try to see things from my perspective. But everything starts with building trust. So I think that's a good place to start. And we build from there.

Parenting isn't a popularity contest.

Kids learn prejudice. Don't teach them that.

Disappointment is part of life. Let your kids experience it.

Embrace the magic of childhood.

It's ok to admit you don't have all the answers.

Life is not black and white. Teach your kids to live in and be comfortable in the grey.

VALUE 3

EMPATHY

E mpathy is the ability to perceive the world from someone else's perspective. Empathy doesn't necessarily mean feeling sorry for someone or agreeing with them. Rather empathy is the ability to understand circumstances or situations from someone else's viewpoint and someone else's values, not your values. You don't have to agree with them, but to be empathic, you need to understand their perspective; metaphorically, to walk or stand in their shoes.

Everyone lives in their own world. Yes, we each have family, partners, friends, neighbors, and work colleagues, but we each perceive the world through our own personal lens. Our experiences and memories are from our own personal perspective. When I was pregnant with my second child, Jack, my oldest, Nate asked me in a worried voice, "After the baby's born, will you still be my mom?" That question stuck with me all these years later as evidence that kids really are in many ways a blank slate and many things that seem obvious to us, kids just don't know until they learn. It's why they need to learn not to touch a hot stove, not to stick things into electric outlets, not to run into the street and how to engage nicely with others.

I chose empathy as one of my core values for several reasons. First, if people and other creatures are hard wired towards self-preservation, it would seem that being selfish or self-centered is somewhat of a natural state. Therefore, I felt that as a parent, teaching empathy and compassion for others would be critical to help my children be likeable people and help them to develop and maintain healthy relationships. The other reason I chose empathy was because during my own childhood, I was conscious of social privilege. I didn't know what to call it when I was a kid, but I was aware that some of my classmates and neighbors had more money, more possessions than my family. I realized that that was just their normal.

I never felt that my school friends looked down on me – I was smart and a good athlete, things that mattered as a kid – but I was conscious that others often had more than my family. While I don't recall ever feeling jealous or inferior, it seemed to me that people were generally oblivious to the privilege into which they were born. Their station in life was just their reality. For them it was normal for their family to fly to Florida every year for vacation. Perhaps trying to teach my kids to understand their own privilege was more about self-awareness, but I also hoped to teach them about privilege, how it impacted them, and also understand how privileges that others enjoyed or lacked might impact their perception of the world and their place in it.

I'm glad that the concept of privilege has gained traction as a topic in our social dialogue. Every child born anywhere in the world is born into a specific situation, a specific socio-economic position. As previously mentioned, when I was 23 years old, I joined the Peace Corps and lived in the Dominican Republic for a little over two years. The first three months of my volunteer experience were spent engaged in language and cultural training on site at a training school with all the other volunteers. During this training period, to assist in language and cultural assimilation, each volunteer lived with a different host family in one of the nearby "campos," or neighborhoods. The Dominican families who participated in the program didn't speak English, which forced us volunteers to really work on our language skills when we were outside of training at the school.

It just so happened that the daughter of my host family, my Dominican "sister" and my older sister in the States were both pregnant at the same time. Both of my sisters gave birth to sons within a few weeks of each other. I couldn't help thinking how different the futures of these boys would be solely by virtue of the situations and circumstances into which they were born. Neither child was more or less deserving than the other, but their lives would have drastically different trajectories based on the privilege and situation into which they were born. As I was raising my kids, I wanted them to recognize this fact as part of the reality of the world in which we live.

While I was growing up, I often felt that others were just clueless about the things that they took for granted. It seemed to me that they just had no awareness that others, such as me, didn't have access to those advantages. In many ways, I felt that others didn't understand me, didn't see me as I truly was. I was accepted, well liked, and had many friends, but I never felt like they truly saw me, knew the real me. I wanted to try to give my children the ability and desire to understand others. I wanted to empower my children to have the perceptiveness to empathize, hopefully without judgment, but with understanding.

Teaching empathy or anything else to toddlers is about keeping it simple and showing them how their actions impact others. I often felt like it was a game of charades with the potential advantage of my child gaining an understanding of basic words. Because toddlers are largely non-verbal, it's about finding creative ways to show them and try to help them understand.

Toddlers' fine motor skills take time to develop. Initially their motor skills are brutish or gross. It's only with practice that their ability to manage their bodies becomes more finessed and gentler. I don't believe a toddler grabs and yanks on a pet to deliberately be mean but tugging on an ear or a tail can cause a dog or cat pain. Likewise, when they are young, hitting or biting is a way to use their senses to learn about the world or a reaction to frustration. But that doesn't make it ok. So how do you teach compassion and empathy?

Going back to training dogs, when I was training Ripley, I tried to focus on his good behavior and provide lots of positive attention, while nipping his bad behavior in the bud. Before babies and toddlers develop language skills, just like puppies, you want to engage with them in positive ways and show them what makes you happy. When a puppy fetches a toy, reward it with petting and rubbing. Likewise, when it pees outside, pet it, and say, "Good dog." If it nips you, gently tap the underside of its muzzle and say, "No bite."

For babies and toddlers, games like peak-a-boo and making faces to try and get the toddler to mirror you (or perhaps you mirror them) is a fun way to help them understand that they can have an impact and generate a desired reaction in others. I believe that recognizing that they have the ability to make others laugh or smile is pleasing and stimulating to babies and toddlers. It's a step on the road towards giving them preliminary exposure to empathy. Likewise when their brother cries because the toddler hit him with a toy truck, if you can quickly say, "No hitting," take the toy away and comfort the other child in front of the toddler, that too can be a chance for the youngster to learn.

When you think about teaching empathy, emotions are a good way to start. While your child is largely non-verbal, you can have fun overacting emotions like happy, sad, scared, sleepy, etc. by making faces and providing the words. This type of activity is another opportunity to see if you can get your child to mimic you. As your children get older and understand the words and emotions, you have the chance to help them talk about how they're feeling and to question them about how others might be feeling.

Stories are a great opportunity to talk about emotions. Not just stories in books, but the events that happen during the day that may be more personal to your child. Talking about what happened at school or the daycare provider's house also provides the chance to learn about things your child experienced and expand your understanding of their world when you're apart. Talking about events and asking how they feel is important. Likewise, asking how they thought someone else felt about an action or situation – happy, silly, mad, sad, scared – gives them the words and the thought process to recognize that others have feelings too and to recognize the behavior and expressions of other's emotions. Remember, your child is hard-wired to perceive and think about the world from their own personal perspective. You need to teach your child(ren) that they are not the center of the universe, that others have feelings too, and that the feelings of others matter.

Getting your kids to talk about their emotions and understand how their actions make you, their sibling, their playmates, the pet, and themselves feel – happy, proud, disappointed, mad, sad, frustrated – are opportunities to reinforce behaviors that generate positive emotions and avoid those that cause "bad" or "negative" feelings. The ability of your child(ren) to step outside of themselves and be empathetic is critical. I believe it's foundational to healthy relationships and flourishing communities. "How did that make you feel?" and "How do you think she/he felt when that happened?" were common questions in our household when my kids were sharing stories at dinner. Those conversations helped my kids be more sensitive to their own and others' feelings. The ability to be empathic also helped them to understand that their actions, their words, their behavior could have consequences for both them and others. At some point, they will realize that their actions and words have the ability to hurt others' feelings or conversely make someone else happy. That's the beginning of real empathy.

Dinner was one of my favorite times. As noted, we all sat together at the kitchen or dining room table and the kids talked about their day as well as any other random topic that came to mind. I loved these conversations as they provided insight into their lives. Once your kids go off to school, there is truly a huge part of their world that you're just not a part of. To be involved and aware, you have to encourage them to share their experiences. Kids are more likely to be eager to share and talk about their experiences and thoughts if you create the regular time, space, and cadence to do so.

Strategy: *Use "High, Low, Medium" to have your kids talk about their day and encourage empathy.*

As mentioned, I used "High, Low, Medium" to give the kids a framework to talk about their day. We later modified it to add the additional category "Cool at School" which was a catchall to both make them dig a little deeper and share ideas or just talk about something that was interesting or funny that they wanted to share.

Highs and Lows were great opportunities to ask questions about how they felt and why, and perhaps how others felt to encourage empathy.

In addition, how your kids characterize their day can give you great insight into what's important to them, and what makes them feel embarrassed or proud. Their stories provide insight into their sense of humor. It's also interesting to hear and appreciate the things they notice about others, their environment and how they interact with and talk about other kids.

I also believe that giving each child the chance to lead the conversation at dinner during their turn strengthened their sense of self-worth and self-confidence. Likewise it strengthened our family bond and helped us to understand and empathize with each other. We all asked questions and shared comments and frequently laughed together about the stories that were shared.

As it pertains to my parenting values, I tried to teach my kids to think about others, how others felt and how those emotions might impact the things that other people did or said. Over the years, we had daycare providers from various socio-economic backgrounds, religions, and educational backgrounds. My kids frequently talked at dinner about something that seemed different or weird that they'd noticed at the daycare provider's house. I believe our discussions gave them new appreciation and understanding that is was ok and interesting for people to have different values, religious beliefs, and ideas, and that while we had our family values, others weren't "wrong" just because they were different.   During their high school years, both Jack and Avery occasionally joined friends to attend church with their families to experience different organized religion. I was completely supportive of their curiosity and interest.

Interestingly, the most important lesson I learned about empathy came from recognizing how my own perceptions were partially sabotaging my parenting efforts. When I chose to have my children via artificial insemination, I denied them a father. I'd always hoped that I'd find a partner later, and perhaps have the added benefit of step siblings, but it didn't work out that way. I viewed my lack of a partner as a "problem" that someday I could hopefully rectify. As mentioned previously, I also expected to rely on my dad as a male role model. He lived two miles away across town, so we saw him often. However, life sometimes throws you a curve ball. Not long after Nate turned 4 and Jack was nearly 2, my dad died at the age of 59.

My dad was a recovered alcoholic who'd been dry for over 15 years, but the damage to his liver had been done. Despite offers from both my brother and I to donate a portion of our livers, my dad refused to consider our offers as he didn't want to create potential risks for us to try to save himself. As a parent I understood his reasoning, but as his daughter I wanted him to survive at any cost. The challenge with my dad's situation was that we all knew that he'd either get a transplant and fully recover or die. It was a very difficult time that played out over 6-7 months. Sadly, my dad died waiting for a liver transplant.

As a parent I'd encourage you to maintain a robust support system and to the best of your ability be prepared for the unexpected scud missiles – death of a loved one, loss of a job, serious illness or injury – that can shatter your normal life. It can feel overwhelming to try to handle your own grief, fear, panic, confusion, etc., while trying to maintain normalcy in your children's lives. While my dad's death wasn't unexpected, I was unprepared for how devastated I felt by his death and the overwhelming grief I experienced.

It's worth noting that at the time, I was in the midst of our major home remodel that added a second story to our house and knocked down some walls to renovate the first floor. My sons and I lived in our house during the construction which wasn't as bad as it sounds since on weekdays, my boys were with the daycare provider, I was at work and the contractors didn't work on weekends. However our house was a construction zone and a bit of a disaster, but we treated it as an adventure and loved seeing the daily changes.

When it was close to the end of my dad's life, I left Nate and Jack in Dee's care, and my extended family and I were with him at the hospital. After he passed, I sat in my car in the hospital parking lot in Chicago for a long time just crying. Then before heading home, I left a message for my general contractor to please contact the trades scheduled for that day and ask them not to come to my house. I arrived home around 7:30 a.m. It appeared that my contractor hadn't gotten my message or for other reasons had failed to keep the trades away. I walked into my house as the flooring guys were patching the hardwood floors where walls had been removed. I looked like and was a complete wreck. One of the guys looked at me and said, "What the hell happened to you? Did your dog die?" I looked at him and replied, "No, my dad." Then I walked upstairs.

I spent that day staining trim and doors on the partially completed 2nd floor. The flooring guys came up and apologized for their comments, shared their own personal stories of loss and around 9:00 my general contractor arrived and did the same. Strangely, it was therapeutic for me to work and have the tradesmen there. As I stayed quietly upstairs for most of the day, I think that after a while the workmen forgot about me and fell into their normal routines. My dad was a "blue collar" guy who both worked in and with the trades so hearing their banter, their laughter and their music choices was very comforting to me and made me feel close to my dad as I started to grieve.

I struggled with the grieving process for my dad. I seemed unable to get a grip on my emotions. Due to the fallout from my parents' awful divorce, I had severed ties with my mother in my early 20's, so my dad dying made me feel like an orphan. My stepfamily also used the occasion of my dad's death to take the gloves off and let me know that they fully disapproved of how I'd created my family. Seriously? How could anyone be so cruel? The loss of my dad and the added vindictiveness of my stepfamily plunged me into a tailspin of reevaluating my rationale for having kids on my own. What was I thinking? When I had decided to try to get pregnant with Nate and Jack, I knew that I was denying them a father. Because my sisters had had their kids 10-12 years earlier, I was also denying my children cousins. Now, I'd lost my dad, so on top of everything else my kids now had no grandparents. I hated myself and I didn't know how to "fix" this problem.

I was a walking zombie. I went through the motions of providing the care my sons needed. I went to work every day and did my job, but I couldn't get myself together. I had friends who gave me emotional support and checked in frequently, but I was stuck in grief. I couldn't move forward. I couldn't sleep, I cried every night, I started drinking to excess at night and felt lost. Because my dad and I lived in the same town and he also worked in town, many people knew both of us and knew I was his daughter. As a result, I was periodically approached by random people to express their condolences while I was out walking with my sons or doing errands. Intellectually, I knew that they meant well, but each encounter was like a scud missile landing on me to reactivate my raw grief. Each time it happened I took two giant steps backwards. I felt that I was on a downward spiral. I was scared. I felt powerless. I was failing myself, but more importantly, I was failing my sons.

Then I had an epiphany. I realized two things. First, that I had been focusing on all the things that my family didn't have – didn't have a dad, didn't have cousins, didn't have a grandpa. Second, I recognized that the times that I was at my best were when I was pregnant. While I was pregnant, I treated my body – and thus myself – as a temple. While pregnant, the life growing inside me was worth any sacrifice. I was up to any challenge to help that new life flourish. So from the depths of my despair, still gripped by overwhelming, unrelenting grief, I contemplated the idea of getting pregnant again.

Ok I admit it sounded crazy even to me given my then current state of barely functioning. I'll also note that I was 39 years old at the time and the math of having another child wasn't the best. But I felt that I needed a seismic shift to get me back on track. Just as I'd joined the Peace Corps for both altruistic and deep personal reasons to generate a hard shift in my life trajectory, I knew I needed a major change to save me from my downward spiral.

With my crazy idea in mind, I started charting my menstrual periods, my mucus, and my basal temperature again. I updated my budget. For context, I'll note that my menstrual cycle was fairly predictable, and that conceiving Nate took two months, Jack four. Given my somewhat fragile state and my age, I decided that I was going to try once to get pregnant. I decided that if this was meant to be, I'd conceive. If not, the universe would be sending me a message that I shouldn't have any more children and should look to plan B.

While I had no plan B, just taking the steps to prepare for another pregnancy attempt was helping me recover, helping me to actively live (vs. just exist) in the present and look forward to the future. It focused my mind and put hope and excitement back in my heart. It enabled me to push back against my seemingly unending sadness. I updated my budget and leaned into my parenting plan. I was taking baby steps to get past the rawness of my grief, and I was re-embracing life.

I conceived my daughter on my first attempt. When I peed on the stick and confirmed that I was pregnant, I felt that the universe was solidly in my corner. Seemingly overnight, I regained my perspective, strength, and confidence. I celebrated life again. Being pregnant forced me to recalibrate. Being pregnant forced me to set aside my grief and focus on protecting the life growing inside me and fully re-engage with my boys. I was once again able to actively nurture my amazing sons and start preparing them for a new sibling. My feelings of sadness became less frequent and manageable, and I was able to move forward. Avery was born a couple months before my 40th birthday.

As indicated above, changing my focus from what my family lacked to appreciating and embracing what we had was a huge shift in my perception. It took the death of my dad to make me see that my prior focus had been wrong. I'd always considered myself a pragmatic optimist, but losing my dad forced me to acknowledge that I'd been wasting energy worrying about what I'd denied my kids rather than focusing 100% on all the amazing things that I was able to give them. My paradigm shifted completely to building traditions and playing to our strengths. For the first time, I truly perceived my beautiful family as whole and complete without limits on our ability to flourish and succeed.

As part of teaching empathy, I wanted my children to understand that there are other countries, languages, and cultures in the world. I bought a big world map and had it dry mounted. I hung the map in our sunroom. I also bought, hung, and labeled 8 clocks around the sunroom with the names of major cities from around the world, and set the clocks based on the world time map. I wanted my kids to understand that the world was round, that people lived lives very different from ours, and that when it was daytime here, it was nighttime on the other side of the world. I also saved currency from other countries. I had artwork from the Dominican Republic and Haiti and bought local artwork when they were older, and we traveled overseas.

I had been fortunate to have engaged grandparents and great aunts and uncles growing up who exposed me and my siblings to the many top-notch museums in Chicago. My great aunts and uncles also shared stories and relics of their own world travels. As my own children grew, our adventures included visits to virtually all of Chicago's museums and zoos. As they got older, I took them to high school plays and later to professional productions across all genres. I played lots of different types of music and some evenings our dining room became our "dancing room" and we all danced in goofy ways while I took turns holding and spinning my kids. I wanted my children to have an appreciation of the arts, other cultures, ideas and different ways of expression.

> **Strategy:** *When you anticipate a challenging transition for your kids, discuss it beforehand and during the conversation(s) try to guide the kids to discover the solution you want to implement as their idea.*
>
> *As part of our home remodel, Nate, Jack, and I frequently looked at the blueprints for our new second story addition and pointed out which would be each of their bedrooms. As the house took shape, they took special pleasure in watching as their individual bedrooms and shared bathroom were built. By Avery's due date, the boys had been living in their own rooms for several months.*
>
> *Once I was past my first trimester, I asked the boys what they thought about having another sibling. They were totally excited about the idea. I then posed the question of where the baby would sleep. My sons suggested my room or our upstairs family room. I considered their suggestions and provided reasons why I didn't think those would work in the long term. Finally Jack suggested that he and Nate could share a bedroom. Nate added that as they both had bunk beds it would be easy. I praised their ideas and let them take the lead on deciding which room would be theirs vs. the baby's room. We worked together to decide how best to set up their new shared bedroom. The boys also were helpful in arranging Avery's room and especially glad to help select and test new toys for their baby sister.*
>
> *By making it "their idea" and engaging their input and suggestions, the boys were excited both about sharing a bedroom and about the new baby. There was no resentment and only eagerness about our growing family.*

I also used movies to teach. In addition to movies about local Chicago greats, Michael Jordan, and Walter Payton to celebrate individual athletic greatness and team contribution, I exposed my kids to movies that portrayed racism, its impact and how some were able to push back against it. Movies we watched included: "Remember the Titans," "Glory Road," "The Help," "Straight Outta Compton," and "The Hate U Give." I wanted my children to understand both how far we've come as a society and how far we still must go when it comes to racial equality. As the kids got older, we discussed politics, events in the news, and issues at school. No topic was off limits in our house.

I was recently walking with my son Nate and his dog, Sam, during one of their visits home. Nate shared with me that our house was the one place while he was growing up that he was able to express his thoughts and feelings freely and openly. I was elated. A critical part of empathy is the ability to accept and understand yourself so you can understand others. Knowing that my children felt comfortable being their true selves in our home hopefully provided them with the latitude to accept and understand others.

While I have no shortage of opinions, in our house, we always took turns sharing our thoughts, especially at mealtimes. I functioned as referee when needed to prevent interruptions or discussions that became too passionate. I likewise played devil's advocate by asking questions when I thought someone's perspective was too one-sided. I frequently challenged my kids with questions like, "What if killing a rhinoceros for its horn let a dad feed his family for a year? Would that make it ok? What if his kids might starve without the money that he could earn from selling the horn?" I obviously wasn't trying to support poaching but rather pushing my kids towards empathy. I wanted them to understand that sometimes people might be forced to make difficult or impossible choices. There were no right or wrong answers. I wanted to get my kids to think outside of their comfort zones, outside of their situations, and try to see the world through others' eyes. I wanted them to be empathetic and understand that people make choices in life based on their circumstances, their privilege, their beliefs, and their options.

Again, empathy isn't necessarily about agreeing or condoning, it's about understanding the perspectives and rationale of others. After our most recent family vacation to Morocco and Lisbon, I asked each of my kids which place they liked better. Avery chose Lisbon as she felt safer and more comfortable there. She added that while she'd loved our experiences in Morocco, it was too far outside her comfort zone. Nate, Jack, and I each selected Morocco for the very reasons that Avery didn't.

Strategy: *Read the books that your kids read.*

Reading has always been prioritized in our family. I read to my kids since infancy and sat with each of my children as they learned to read themselves. I often read to them during weekend lunchtimes as they ate their food and also read to them at night until they became old enough to read for themselves.

I cannot say enough good things about public libraries. We visited our library every weekend and brought home armfuls of books each week which we read that week. My kids participated in library reading programs, diligently recording their minutes, and earned prizes. I required that my kids read a minimum of 20 minutes each day.

Once your kids get familiar with the library, their book choices reflect their interests and passions. It's so easy to engage with your kids about subjects that they're interested in. By reading those books yourself, you can gain insight into your child and the authors and ideas that fuel your children's imaginations and dreams. You can also talk about books just like discussing a movie or experience you shared together. Reading provides so many wonderful opportunities to connect and engage with your child(ren). Don't miss it.

I also read all the books my kids were assigned to read in middle and high school – I just checked out a copy from the public library. I flew through the Young Adult books and classics and was then able to help my kids with book reports and other writing assignments. My approach was to have my child discuss the book, their assignment and what they thought they'd write. Then I'd ask questions and because I'd just read the book too, I was able to ask about aspects of the book I thought were important that they hadn't mentioned. We'd have good back and forth conversations that helped them flush out their ideas to complete their assignments and then they'd frequently read the completed assignment to me. It was fun and it made me feel like I was helping them to be better students and readers.

Drive times and dinner times are such great opportunities for sharing thoughts and ideas. Families that park themselves in front of a tv screen at mealtime or don't make the time to eat and talk together miss a golden opportunity. As noted in several of the Strategy boxes, I intentionally created mechanisms for regular conversations and sharing of ideas, especially during dinnertime. I truly believe these conversations helped build my kids' sense of confidence and self-worth; while also reinforcing the notion that no subject was off limits. Our conversations and family back and forth also helped strengthen my kids' comfort with public speaking and gave them practice in developing, expressing, and defending their ideas.

There's a saying that character is doing the right thing when no one's looking. So much of what we teach our kids is black and white; right or wrong. But real life is lived mostly in the grey. Empathy is not always easy or expedient, but I believe that the more you can expose your kids to different ideas, lots of perspectives, people from different backgrounds, and varied experiences, the better the chances that they have of being empathetic and respectful and truly be able to understand another person's point of view or perspective even when they don't agree.

While I encourage you to always try to do what you think is best and is true to your values, part of empathy is understanding how your children feel. Again, sometimes we have to disappoint our kids or not give them what they want, but I recommend that you strive to be sensitive, to be empathic and identify the passions and ideas that excite your child. I've always had a strong personality and as mentioned was always conscious of not wanting to quash my children's spirit. While I tried to create many different opportunities and experiences for my children, my objective was to try to discover what turned them on and got them excited. On occasion, I've seen parents try to relive their youth by pushing their own passions on their kids. My mother enrolled my older sister and me in ballet. I was a tomboy not a prima ballerina. I went to the first lesson and after the instructor tried to make my leg bend behind me so my toe could touch my head, I refused to go again. Ballet was my mother's dream, not mine. I never went back.

While you encourage your kids to try different activities, listen and watch to discover and support the things that truly light them up inside. Look at the books they select from the library. Use your own empathy to try to understand why your kid finds something amazing and then nurture their interests and excitement with your support. Ideally, we help our kids become the best version of themselves; but it should be their vision, their passion, not ours.

As I approached parenting, I tried always to be mindful of the values I wanted to teach and model. I also wanted to be sure that the kids respected my authority but also saw my humanity and fallibility. There were times during our dinner conversations when I used my "low" to share stories about how I hadn't done my best in a work situation and had let someone down or perhaps apologized to one of my children for snapping at them when I was really frustrated about something else that had happened to me during the day. I wanted to give my kids the opportunity to have a glimpse into how it felt to be me, to have some empathy and understanding of what drove my actions.

Strategy: *If you have more than one child, at some point let the kids select gifts for each other. Similarly, let them choose gifts (up to a dollar limit) for a friend's birthday party*

My kids are each roughly 2 ½ years apart in age. When my youngest, Avery, was about 5 years old, I suggested that the kids start buying Christmas gifts for each other. When they were young, I provided the money and made it clear that if they didn't spend all the money, then I'd keep the excess, not them.

Nate, Jack, and Avery had fun getting together in pairs to compare ideas. They'd periodically come to me to ask about costs, which kept me busy trying to help them stretch their dollars. Regarding gift selection, I gave no advice, the kids were their own decision makers.

As the years have passed, my kids agree on general spending limits and pay for gifts themselves with the wages they've earned. It has been my perception that they look forward the most to the gifts they give and receive from each other. There have been years when someone got a clunker, but the bad gifts have become something to tease each other about and I believe the gift giving process helped them to better understand what their siblings value and appreciate as well as helped them to become closer.

Jack also added his own touch by stashing gifts he didn't like inside an ottoman in his room. It took a few years for the family to discover this collection of misfit gifts. When we did, we found that all of us had given Jack gifts that had been banished to "the box." Perhaps Jack was trying to spare our feelings, but several years ago, I made a new rule in our house that if someone didn't like a gift they'd received, they should say so and the gift would be returned — no hard feelings. I hate waste and couldn't stand the reality of the wasted money represented by all the gifts in "the box." Dealing with "the box" was another learning opportunity for us all.

One of the things that makes us human is our ability to be empathetic. I believe that we are hard-wired for self-preservation, so empathy, like honesty, is a skill that needs to be learned. Teaching empathy is not easy. Everything we perceive is from our own personal experience. By making empathy a core parenting value, I focused on talking about and being aware of emotions – our own and other's. I strove to give my kids the tools to understand and talk about their feelings and be sensitive and preceptive about the feelings of others.

We noticed how some families had more money, others less than ours. We recognized that some people were very religious and others came from other countries and had customs that were different than ours. I wanted my kids to be able to see themselves from outside themselves, to see how others might perceive their words and their actions. As detailed in Tales from the Homefront below, I was so proud of Nate for befriending a blind schoolmate and including Giovanni in his birthday celebration one year. Nate's actions helped all of us to appreciate not only the feelings of others, but especially the strength and resiliency of people with disabilities.

Tales from the Homefront:

Appreciating the special abilities of others: Birthdays were a big deal at our house. I decorated the first floor with streamers, "Happy Birthday" signs and balloons that remained for several days before and after the big day. When the kids were in elementary school, we had birthday parties at home with school friends. The number of guests was determined by their age; if they were turning seven, they got to invite seven friends. We lived 1 ½ blocks from the grade school, so after getting permission from the school and the parents, on the day of the party, I took a vacation day from work and collected my kids and the party goers outside of the school and we walked home as a group to our house.

Our parties were comprised of lots of games – pin-the-tale on the dinosaur, Bozo Buckets, dropping clothes pins into a jar, coloring, etc., culminating with a treasure hunt comprised of two teams who had to find and follow 5-6 clues stashed around the house that led to a treasure chest (cookie tin) filled with candy and small toys. The parties ended with cake and ice cream and opening of presents. Winners of each game selected a prize (little gift-wrapped toys purchased from the Dollar Store). All of the kids were able to fill their goody bags with candy and toys from Bozo Buckets and the treasure hunt as well as with the prizes they'd won.

One year, when he was turning 9, Nate asked if his blind friend, Giovanni, could come to his party. I was both nervous and elated that Nate wanted to include Gio. Giovanni's parents only spoke Spanish but using my language skills from my Peace Corps stint, I was able to convey to his mom over the phone that I understood that her son was blind, and I promised to keep him safe. She told me that it was the first time in his life that Giovanni had been invited to a party by a friend.

I was so proud of Nate and his friends. On the walk to our house, the boys took turns holding Gio's arm to guide him the entire way. As with most of our birthday parties, the event was barely controlled chaos, but tons of fun. Gio participated in all the games, sometimes with assistance. The kids even insisted that Gio be blindfolded for pin-the-tail - they weren't taking any chances of giving him a potential advantage! Gio's huge grin seemed to suggest that he loved being treated just like all the other kids.

At all my kids' parties, at roughly the midway point, we play something I call the Memory Game. It's fun and slows down the energy level as it takes about 30 minutes. Prior to the party, I collect 25-35 or more random items from around the house – a spoon, a playing card, a pencil sharpener, a yo-yo, a flashlight, a comb, a ruler, a dice, a toy hammer, a golf tee, a battery, a feather, a super ball, etc. I place the items on a large cookie sheet and cover them with a kitchen towel. I also make sure that I have enough paper and pencils equal to the number of party guests + my kids.

To play the game, I have all the kids sit on the floor in a circle and explain that I'm going to bring in a bunch of things and they need to try to remember as many as they can. Then I put the cookie sheet in the middle of the circle, remove the towel and give everyone approximately 10 minutes to examine all the items. There's generally a lot of chatter. Giovanni joined in with the kids, picking up one item after another as I told Giovanni what each item was as he held and touched it. When the kids agreed they were ready, I collected all the items, took away the tray and gave each child paper and pencil. Everyone moved away from the others to write down all the things that they could remember being on the tray. I told them spelling didn't matter, just do their best.

Giovanni and I found a place away from the others where he could whisper to me the things he remembered. After about 10-12 minutes I asked if everyone was done. I collected the pencils, everyone came back to the circle with their papers, and I brought out the tray. Invariably, there were moans and yells about things they forgot. We'd then go around the circle and determine who remembered the most and was the winner. That year it was Giovanni! He had remembered nearly twice as many items as the next closest kid. Gio immediately got the admiration of all the kids and beamed a giant smile. Looking around the room, it was obvious that all the kids understood Gio in a new way.

"The Awesome Place:" I always tried to nurture my kids' imaginations. We checked out books and materials from the public library every week, hiked on the trails in the state and local parks, built forts in the living room and their bedrooms and spent oodles of time outside catching bugs and digging holes in the yard looking for buried treasure or dinosaur bones. At some point I introduced my kids to the 1974 TV series "Land of the Lost" which essentially tells the adventures of a father and his two kids who accidentally go through a time portal and end up in prehistoric times with dinosaurs. My primary reason for showing it to my kids was to demonstrate how bad special effects were when I was a kid so they could appreciate how revolutionary "Star Wars" was to me when I was a teenager. While they appreciated the improvement in special effects, it was the concept of the show that captivated Nate and Jack. Their fascination blossomed into an imaginary world that they regularly discussed and dubbed "The Awesome Place."

Anything was possible and everything imaginable existed in "The Awesome Place" – dinosaurs, pirates, dragons, space travel . . . The boys would weave stories about this imaginary world during drive time, dinner time and sometimes at night after lights out, I'd hear them talking to each other about it. It was pure joy to hear them and during those times, I felt that I understood and could experience this magical place through my sons' stories and almost see their souls dancing as they created stories about their experiences in the Awesome Place.

Thank you notes: Part of parenting is teaching good manners, and that includes sending thank-you notes. While good manners weren't called out as a separate value in my parenting plan, they were most definitely part of the overall expectations of how we all acted. They are also part of empathy and recognition that others care for you and needed to be thanked for their kindness.

The request to write thank you notes was sometimes met with bellyaching. My standard response was something to the effect of, "Dee worked to earn money. Then she took the time to think of a great gift for you, went to the store and bought it, brought it home and wrapped it. How do you think she'd feel if you couldn't be bothered to spend 5 minutes writing her a thank-you note?"

To help with the process, I also gave my children a formula for writing that acknowledged the gift, mentioned why they liked it and expressed their appreciation typically both for the gift and for coming to their party. Whether my kids were genuinely appreciative or just feared that I'd donate their presents to charity, they always wrote thank you notes and always remembered to say please and thank you when they were out and about or visiting at a friend's house.

Writing an apology: As noted in the prior section, once the kids reached middle school, I used loss of privileges as the primary form of punishment, but occasionally, I required them to write about the experience. I shared Avery's story in the Honesty and Transparency section and relate Nate's below.

One weekend, when Nate was a freshman in high school, he, Jack, and their friends Charlie and Cam were in the dining room playing Monopoly. Avery was watching. As a side note, I'll share that Monopoly was banned from my dad's house because our games became way too vicious. I hadn't played Monopoly since my early 20's but I'd purchased the game and had it as one of many in our game's closet. Remember, the object of Monopoly is to bankrupt your opponents, not just win, but force them to sell all their assets and properties, give you all their money, and literally to drive them out of the game. In hindsight, probably not the best game for kids.

While the kids were playing, I was outside weeding and trimming our front gardens. I'd periodically come inside to drink some juice to stay hydrated. During one of my many trips inside, I walked in on a heated argument. Nate had rolled the dice during his turn, and one dice had fallen off the table onto the floor. The roll was exactly what Nate was hoping for. The other kids all felt that Nate had to roll again arguing that both dice had to be on the table in order to count. As I walked through the dining room, having no context, Jack asked me, "What happens if one of the dice falls on the floor?" Without breaking stride, I shrugged and replied, "Just roll again." Nate looked at me and yelled, "Fucking whore!"

The collective gasp from the other four kids seemed to suck the oxygen from the room. I stopped, glared at Nate and in a deathly calm voice said, "Nathan, go to your room." Then I turned to the rest of the kids and said in my normal voice, "You guys are welcome to continue playing or you can clean-up." I've never seen kids move that fast to clean up and flee the house.

In his room, Nate was fuming. I told him that he shouldn't use such foul language and certainly not directed at me. Nate complained about how I'd been unfair to him. I pointed out that I didn't know whose turn it was or anything about the game, I'd just given what I thought was a fair answer to a question about the rules. I told Nate that he had to stay in his room, think about what had happened and when he was ready, sit down and write me an apology note. I left, closed his bedroom door, and went back outside to continue my yardwork.

About 30-45 minutes later, Nate came out onto the front porch, note in hand. I stopped weeding and asked him to read it to me. His note was a rant about how unfair it was that the roll didn't count. Nate wrote about why he was angry and why he had said what he'd said. I listened and when he was done, I explained to Nate that an apology was not about him, but about me and how what he did and said had impacted me and had made me feel. I sent him back to his room to try again.

I honestly don't recall if it took Nate 2 or 3 attempts to finally generate a satisfactory note, but he did. The final version of his apology was:

Dear Mom,

What I said today while playing Monopoly was unacceptable in more ways than one, and I will not tell you that it was the right thing to say or do at all, under any circumstances. I do understand that I haven't shown a lot of respect to you on more than one occasion, this being a fine example of such an occasion, but I do want to apologize for this time, because it was completely uncalled for.

I should not have said something like that to anyone, much less an adult, and as I said before, I want to apologize for saying it. For the next couple of months I will work on both the amount of respect that I show to you, and my problem with swearing. For the respect part, all I would have to do would be things like paying more attention and not using a voice like I'm bored with what you're saying. However, these habits will not become instantly visible by tomorrow, but I am going to start working on it and hope to see a lot of improvement by the time school starts. As for the problem with swearing, I have tried to break this habit before, and did so for a while, but I will go back to trying to stop myself using all curse words excluding both hell and damn.

Not only will I show more respect to you, and stop swearing, but I will also show more respect to both Jack and Avery. In doing so I mean that I will no longer swear at either of them or you and will be nicer person overall to all three of you.

In conclusion, I will show much more respect to you and my younger siblings, due to the fact that I am very sorry about such a rude and disrespectful outburst. Not only that, but I will also be cutting down on swearing almost entirely. As I said before, these habits will not occur overnight, but by the time that school starts there should be a very visible difference in both the amount of respect that I show towards you, and the amount of swearing that I do.

Nate Munn

After he finished reading, I took off my work gloves and extended my hand for his note. I said, "Nate, I know you said that horrible thing because you were angry and frustrated. I get it. I appreciate what you wrote and know you can do it. Thank you for your apology. I love you."

Being present goes a long way.

Kids are smarter than we realize. Listen to them.

No behavior is gender specific. Don't limit your kids. Help them become their own beautiful selves.

Fireflies defy explanation and make summer evenings magical.

Say "I love you" every day.

VALUE 4

CONSEQUENCES AND RESPONSIBILITY

My next core value and additional foundational part of my parenting plan was holding myself and my kids accountable – accountable to meet expectations, accountable to each other and accountable for our actions. I wanted my children to understand that actions and words had consequences, and we were all responsible for both. The common connotation of words like "consequences" and "accountable" are frequently deemed to be negative, as if you're assigning blame or pointing fingers. That's not how I think about them.

Being responsible and accountable means keeping your promises. Doing what you say you'll do. It means having self-control and taking responsibility for your actions and the results of your actions. Consequences can be good, bad, or neutral as well as intended or unintended; expected or unexpected. But the whole concept of consequences and taking responsibility is meant to be empowering. It's meant to demonstrate trust in your kid's ability to do what's expected, to allow them to make thoughtful choices and to require them to think about what they do and what might happen as a result. It also means recognizing that they are still responsible for the consequences of their behavior even when the outcome was unforeseen or unintended.

Clearly, toddlers and little kids are figuring out the world and can't realistically be held responsible for all their actions. Likewise, accidents do happen. However, just like training puppies, once the dog has learned that chewing on the table leg is not ok, she should be scolded if she continues to chew on the furniture. So too if one sibling continues to hurt the other and you've already shown them many times that hitting or biting or whatever is not acceptable, you should examine what you're doing and find a better way to demonstrate that this behavior is not ok. Your child needs to understand that this kind of bad behavior will not be tolerated. In other words, you need to show your child that hurting a sibling has negative consequences. Again, I don't advocate striking a child, or as some have advised, biting your child to show that being bitten hurts, but you need to find a way to teach the misbehaving child that the behavior is unacceptable and should not be repeated.

It's my experience that dogs and kids respond to both positive and negative displays of emotion and feedback. When addressing undesirable behavior, I showed and expressed my negative emotions of disappointment and anger by the tone of my voice, my body language, and the words I chose. If they're old enough to understand empathy, and are sensitive to your displays of emotion, show and tell your child that their brother is crying because of what they did or said. The goal is to show and communicate with words, body language and tone of voice that what they did was wrong and not ok. They need to understand that if they can't or won't behave appropriately, there will be negative consequences. If the child who behaved badly doesn't seem to understand or seemingly not care. Ask them how they'd feel if they had been hit or bitten or whatever. Again, don't hit or bite the child who caused the harm, lean into empathy, and help them to see and understand that hurting others is not acceptable. They wouldn't like it if others hurt them, and they need to learn that they shouldn't hurt others, but if they do, there will be negative consequences.

Consequences for bad behavior might include loss of privileges, a time out to get control of the negative emotions that drove the bad behavior and/or engagement by you to steer them towards better behavior. Engage with your child(ren) frequently. Be on the lookout for escalating situations and to the extent possible, try to preempt bad actions by intervening, diffusing rising frustration and steering your child(ren) toward other activities and better behavior. In addition, strive to notice and call out or reward good behavior with positive attention and pleasant emotions. You want your children and your dogs to learn that good behavior can result in good consequences and positive attention, and bad behavior always leads to bad outcomes.

Consequences can be rewards. If there's an activity that you want everyone to pitch in and/or finish quicker, perhaps the consequence (reward) of cooperation and additional contribution is that there's extra time allocated to watch a special show together, read an extra book before bedtime, or eat ice cream on the porch. The goal is to show your children that they have the ability to control their actions and can choose to generate positive or negative outcomes. I always clearly verbalized and demonstrated consequences to my children. I wanted them to know that if A then B. By communicating expected outcomes, I was giving my kids the power to make choices, reinforcing the discipline of delayed gratification (if it was a reward for us after we completed an activity) and the ability directly see how their actions generated good or not so good outcomes. I wanted them to know and understand that they could and should control their words and behaviors. I wanted them to see that they had the power to drive desirable outcomes.

Earlier in the book, I talked a lot about expectations. Certain things weren't negotiable, they were just expected. Recall that through communication and actions, my kids understood that homework was their responsibility, school was their "job," and they were expected to do their job well. When the kids did well on tests, in addition to praising them, I tried to highlight that their strong results weren't just because they were smart, rather the good grade was a result of them completing their homework, participating in class, and asking questions when they didn't understand.

I regularly connected the dots verbally for my children. I wanted them to clearly understand that when they took responsibility for learning, put in the time to do the homework, good things happened. When I helped them practice things like spelling, vocabulary lists, state capitals, or multiplication tables, I always tried to make it fun – cheering and celebrating when they got them right and moaning and groaning comically if they made a mistake; always encouraging them to try again. I wanted practice and learning to be things they felt good about even when it wasn't easy. I also wanted them to know that I was always there to help them as needed.

My goal regarding school was to emphasize and have my kids see that the result of their hard work and preparation was both knowledge and good grades. While we always acknowledged good results, the lesson I wanted my kids to internalize was that their success was a result of their preparation and the effort that they put forth. A good test result was therefore almost a foregone conclusion, a consequence of learning the coursework and being prepared. The added benefit was that in addition to helping them see the consequences of their hard work, I was emphasizing the importance of good study habits and a strong work ethic.

Strategy: *Help your children learn how to negotiate and resolve problems on their own.*

With three young kids, disagreements and arguments between siblings were not uncommon. I generally tried to give them the space and time to work out their disagreements. If they reached out to me to resolve a minor dispute and emotions were under control, I'd typically reply, "I'm not a cop or referee. You guys need to work it out yourselves."

Naturally, this didn't always work and sometimes they became physical or one of them was reduced to screaming at the top of their lungs. Then I obviously had to step in. Through questioning and giving each of them a chance to tell me what happened, it was typically easy to get to the root of the problem. It was usually squabbling over a toy, not playing fair, or one of them just behaving selfishly or acting like a jerk.

If they'd been arguing over a toy, I found it effective to put the toy on time out from everyone. Regardless of the root cause, once the emotions had calmed down a bit, we'd talk again about what had happened and I'd ask how they thought that they could do better next time. I tried to guide them to think of solutions that could've avoided the fight by being fairer to each other in the first place. So even when I was the one who stepped in and had to defuse or resolve the situation, I wanted them to think about it and have a strategy to generate a better outcome the next time.

Kids need to learn how to resolve disputes and negotiate solutions. The more practice they have, the better. Listen to them and help guide them to consider potential solutions. You want to fill their little toolboxes with skills to use next time or in the future. Different situations and different people may require different solutions. The more experiences your children have at working through these issues, the better they'll be at building healthy friendships, avoiding conflict and resolving disagreements when they do arise.

Unfortunately, it seems that too much of our education in the US for K – 12 has become a regurgitation of class lessons, with instruction geared towards doing well on standardized tests. I recognize that student achievement is tied to funding and evaluating schools, teachers, and curriculums, but I think in some respects it shortchanges our children. Ideally, kids should see the value of the skills they're mastering, not just as a means to do well on a test. They should be encouraged to learn, discover new ideas and information, to have their curiosity encouraged and nurtured. My kids did have some amazing teachers who far exceeded my expectations, and others who just did a good job. I encourage you as a parent to support your children's teachers and help keep political views and non-secular thoughts, comments, or opinions out of the classrooms and school board meetings. Our children need a safe, healthy, non-biased environment in which to learn. It's best for everyone when our teachers can spend their energy and efforts focused on our kids, rather than having to address bad behavior from parents or having too much effort expended on standardized test results just to keep their jobs and funding.

Another trend that evolved when my kids were in school that concerned me was teachers giving kids multiple tries to retake exams if a student did poorly. When I was in school, teachers occasionally gave re-tests, but only if most of the class had done poorly. But when I was a kid, the highest grade that could be obtained on a retest was 90% if someone got all the answers right on the retest. In my kids' generation, teachers were offering retests for full credit. What's that about? Seems to directly eliminate negative consequences as a motivator to study harder next time. It was the anthesis of what I was trying to teach my kids. I also noted that some teachers were only testing things that had been discussed in class, not all aspects of the assigned textbook. As a result, my kids had a rude awakening when they went off to college. I'm sure many others did as well.

Freshman year of college for every kid is a period of many adjustments as they learn how to take responsibility for all their daily needs while living away from home. They also need to step up to meet the enhanced rigor of college courses. Freshmen need to figure out time management, establish good habits and adjust to an environment that offers so many new opportunities within guardrails that tend to be very, very wide. Some kids implode and fail, but thankfully, most find their way even if it's not perfect.

Before they headed off to college, I wanted to ensure that my kids had internalized the lessons I'd been teaching over all the years. I knew that they'd need to rely on their own self-discipline and self-control to avoid going off the rails. I provided lots of advice, and we had many conversations about their schedules, time management, and allocating time for basic needs like meals, laundry and sleeping. Each of my kids talked about how big the adjustment college was for them, but they all ultimately found their footing and did well.

When it was time for Avery to attend orientation and move into her dorm in the OH university she'd selected, both Nate and I helped her (at the time, Nate was living and working less than an hour away from the university that Avery's attending). We all met at the university. We liked Avery's roommate and when Nate and I left, Avery was feeling very positive and excited to be there. I drove the six hours home and was sitting with Jack and his girlfriend in our living room sharing how appreciative I was that Nate had come down and how happy and pleased I was with Avery's choices when my phone rang. It was Avery. She was in tears and begged me to come get her and bring her home! Apparently, Avery and her roommate had been walking through town when a car full of guys yelled catcalls at the girls as they drove by. The hecklers also leaned out the car windows to film the girls' reactions on their phones.

This experience was completely foreign to Avery, especially as she grew up with her mini Secret Service of her older brothers and their friends always keeping her safe. She felt threatened, afraid, and just wanted to come home. Thankfully both her roommate and I were street smart and helped talk Avery off the ledge. I explained that it was logistically impossible for me to get Avery that day (though I had no intention of doing so even had it been possible) and that I had to work the following day. After calming Avery enough that she'd stopped crying, I shifted into tough love mode.

I helped Avery to see that it would be foolish to let this one event – regardless of how upsetting – to derail all the plans and good decisions she'd made about picking this university. I encouraged her to stay through orientation week and see how she felt at the end of the week. From a financial perspective, I also made it clear that if Avery attended the first day of classes, she'd need to stay through the full semester as I'd have no chance of getting a refund. I also told Avery that if she did decide to come home, she'd need to get a full time job. I reminded her that her big brother, Nate, was nearby and hopefully he might be able to also help her put this event in perspective and visit with her on weekends as needed.

While Avery was blindsided by this occurrence, she chose to stay. After the first several weeks she was thoroughly delighted with the university, her classes and all the friends she was making. She was gaining confidence in her new environment and learning how to manage her new responsibilities. Tough love combined with support from her roommate, Nate, me, and her growing circle of friends, gave Avery the support she needed to enable her to settle down and realize that she'd made good choices and was in the right place for her to achieve her goals and have fun.

While college had other challenges that Avery needed to work through – with support from me and her brothers - she's flourished. In fact, Avery landed a local summer internship during her sophomore year and hasn't been home since Christmas of last year. Rather than come home for Spring Break, Avery, her roommate and another girlfriend drove to FLA; Avery's first road trip with friends. After completing her sophomore year Avery moved into an apartment provided by the company where she interned the weekend after the school term ended. While I relish spending time with all of my children, I do the happy dance every time they create or embrace opportunities to enrich their lives or careers - even when it reduces the time that we get to be together. As a family, we text, we talk, we share pictures, we email, we have periodic family FaceTime calls. The kids visit each other, and we strive to minimally see each other over the holidays or any other time we might be in the area. We stay close even when we're apart.

There is a saying: "If you love something, set it free. If it comes back, it's yours forever; if it doesn't, it never was." While the original author and exact wording of the quote is undetermined, I love the idea as it applies to my children and everyone else who I care about in my life. As parents, we should always be striving to work ourselves out of a job. We should be empowering our children with skills, knowledge, strategies, and confidence to navigate this amazing, yet sometimes crazy and confusing world. Ideally, our kids become independent, self-sustaining, capable individuals. Holding them accountable for the consequences of their actions or inactions, ensuring that they're responsible for their behavior and their decisions goes a long way towards helping them succeed in this goal.

Going to college was a sea change for my sons too. Although they didn't have an immediate incident like Avery experienced, each of them had to find their equilibrium as they were faced with a wave of choices, opportunities, and decisions about how to successfully navigate the college experience. They witnessed students who floundered, students who spent too much time partying and others who tried but seemed unable to navigate on their own. Gratefully, all my children had each internalized many of the values and lessons from their childhood. Those values, lessons, and experiences coupled with the knowledge and self-confidence they'd gained growing up helped keep them on track and enabled them to find their way.

When it came to the difference between high school and college courses, all three of my kids really had to step up despite each of them having taken several AP classes in high school. At one point or another, they each complained to me about an "unfair" test that asked questions about material not covered in class. I offered no sympathy and instead directed them to the syllabus and course reading materials. I basically busted their chops and reminded them that they were responsible for their education. They had to do work both during and outside of class time. They needed to read the materials listed for the course even if those materials weren't discussed in class. I reminded them that if they didn't understand a concept, they needed to go to office hours, work with the TAs and/or get tutoring assistance. I drew a bold line under the expectation that they were in the driver's seat and solely responsible for their grades, which should be reflective of their learning. I also upped the ante by reminding them that if they expected me to continue paying for their college education, they needed to earn A's and B's. I refused to let my children play the victim. I've never stopped holding my children accountable.

My rationale for using tough love was to remind my kids that they were responsible for their own success. I left no doubt that their effort, extra effort, or insufficient effort would drive their outcomes. Only they had the ability to choose how to allocate their time to ensure they spent sufficient time on learning and schoolwork. That said, I was also available to help them navigate the university to obtain additional resources, cheerlead, and offer advice from the sidelines and consistently remind them of how confident I was in their ability to succeed. Freshman year of college was a bit of throwing them into the deep end of the pool knowing that they knew how to swim; while also standing nearby just in case they required some assistance. Especially in the first year of college as well as during the semesters when that were particularly challenging due to a heavy course load, I supported them via text communication, emails, and phone calls. I used my knowledge of navigating institutions, learnings from my years working in management and playing to the different strengths of each of my kids to talk through issues and help them develop strategies and potential solutions. As Jack and Avery entered their college careers, I also encouraged them to engage with Nate and each other to share best practices and discover how their siblings had solved problems as their siblings' experience might also be helpful – especially as it was much more recent and likely more relevant than my college experiences which were virtually all from night school.

At all ages, school athletics was another area where consequences were obvious to my children. Due to economics and logistics, other than Nate and Jack playing youth football during middle school for a couple years, and Avery playing softball for three years, we rarely participated in athletic clubs or clinics. Instead, my kids tried out for and made the middle school and high school athletic teams. The schools managed travel logistics, which was invaluable for me as a single, working parent. I didn't have the extra money to afford clubs, plus most clubs involved some level of travel, and as a single, working parent that was just not possible. As a result, my kids found other ways to hone and improve their athletic abilities.

When he was around 11-12 years old, Jack asked if he could start lifting weights. I said no. I explained that his body was still growing and while I was fine with him doing calisthenics and exercises, no weights for the next couple years. Jack tried to persuade me to change my mind to no avail. Jack knew that "no" meant "no," so he started doing sit-ups and push-ups instead. As Jack started to see the results of his efforts, he exercised more and more. After several months, Jack was doing around 800 push-ups per day, countless sit-ups and developing a strong chest, defined abs, and big arms. Jack's friends didn't believe that he wasn't lifting weights and taking supplements. However, Jack was proving to himself daily that his actions, extra efforts, and commitment could generate wonderful results. I was delighted with his discipline and how his actions reinforced the values I was teaching. It may sound crazy, but at times I actually had to tell Jack to stop exercising.

Once both Nate and Jack reached high school, I purchased a set of weights and a lifting bench. The boys lifted together regularly in the basement, spotting for each other. During high school, each of the kids participated in 2-3 sports each year as well as clubs and Student Council. All the high school coaches encouraged their athletes to use the school weight room. Having already learned the value of putting in extra effort, when they were in high school, all three of my kids got out of bed early each school day to go to the high school weight room to train before class. We lived just down the street from the high school, so Nate, Jack and Avery were able to complete weight training and dash home for a quick shower before classes. They each worked hard daily, and both my sons achieved the 1,000 pound club – the ability to lift a total of 1,000 pounds combining the weights that they could bench press, squat, and dead lift. While Avery wasn't striving for the 1,000 pound club, she quickly saw the benefit of strength training and box jumps. Avery was soon repping weights in amounts greater than many of her male classmates and by her sophomore year, Avery's vertical jump was one of the highest on her volleyball team, a great asset when spiking or blocking at the net, and a direct consequence of countless box jumps performed in the weight room. I also encouraged my children to do wind sprints, biking and longer running to improve and maintain good cardio. They each developed great individual routines that balanced schoolwork, sports, and personal time.

Sports, workouts and good sportsmanship supported many of the values I was striving to teach my children and were tangible evidence of consequences driving outcomes. I was proud of their scholastic and athletic abilities and strove to attend as many games and meets as possible not only to demonstrate my support, but because I really enjoyed watching them participate. While I occasionally felt bad about not being able to afford clubs and clinics – especially when high school coaches often made decisions about starting rosters based on participation in clubs - I'm old fashioned enough to believe that playing multiple sports and using different body muscles was healthier and better for my kids than specializing in one activity. In addition, the cost of travel leagues, clinics and clubs had become so costly that paying for them would've reduced or eliminated my ability to save enough to pay for college. Many of my bleacher friends were parents who paid for these activities with the expectation that the clubs and skills acquired would increase their child's chances of getting a college athletic scholarship. I understood their strategy but chose a different path. While Nate, Jack, and Avery each had genuine athletic talent, I never believed that I was raising future Olympians and specializing in sports and all the time and money that entailed, just wasn't an option for our family if I wanted to ensure I was able to pay for their college educations without being reliant on athletic scholarships.

We did explore potential college scholarship opportunities in football for Jack, but after a severe concussion senior year of high school that essentially sidelined him for the season, we did a complete 180 degree pivot. Each of my kids had occasionally sustained sports injuries, but Jack's severe concussion rocked me to my core. I watched my talented, wonderful son lie in bed in a darkened room, miss school and slowly recover from a brain injury. Jack and I also watched and discussed the movie, "Concussion," starring Will Smith. Thankfully, Jack fully recovered, and he played intermural flag football in college. However, I saw the potential devasting consequences that could happen, had experienced it in my own son and never viewed contact sports the same way again. We perceived the potential negative consequences for college football as just way too high. I opted to pay more for college rather than expose my child to potentially devasting harm.

As I've said many times, a central goal of parenting is working yourself out of a job. I'm not suggesting that you'd ever stop loving your kids or stop being available to help them if needed, but I constantly strove to find ways and experiences to teach my kids how to become fully functioning, fully capable and fully independent beings. If I was hanging blinds, doing home repair, unclogging a drain, or painting a room, if any of them were at home, I dragged them over to explain. I showed them how to use power tools and hand tools. While I was teaching them specific skills, I was also trying to instill the confidence and willingness to attempt things on their own rather than just contact someone else to address problems or issues. When they each went off to college, I literally gave them a toolbox full of basic hand tools and hardware. While I knew we'd need several of the tools to assemble some of the items we'd purchased for their dorm rooms, I wanted my kids to have ready access to these tools when needed in the future.

As previously noted, none of my kids had phones until they reached high school. This was a constant point of friction, but to the argument that all their friends had phones, my standard answer was, "Great, then you can borrow a phone to call me if you need to." Nate bought himself a phone in high school and I finally broke down and got basic phones for each of Jack and Avery when they were in high school too. However their phone plans had severely limited data plans, so they had to self-monitor social media usage or run out of data during the month. We all quickly appreciated the advantage of being able to check in via text or a quick call. Having a phone did enable them to have a bit more freedom, but it likewise created more problems and worries when they failed to check in or didn't respond to my calls or texts. The other upside to the kids having phones was my ability to take the phones away as punishment. Having their phones on time out and thus unable to communicate with their friends quickly demonstrated to my kids that ignoring my calls or failing to text me when expected was not a good choice.

Curfews were another topic for frequent discussion. From my own teenage years, I'd learned that it's very rare for good things to happen in the wee hours of the night or early hours of the morning. Choices and decisions I'd made after midnight were frequently not the best. Not to say I didn't have fun and some very memorable and crazy experiences, but again, if I'm being totally honest, things that happened in the wee hours were far and away not my best choices. Fair or unfair, I generally held my sons to curfews of 10:00 on school nights and midnight at the latest on weekends. While I strove to treat my children equally, I believed that our society and social norms required me to be more protective of my daughter, Avery. While Avery enjoyed the benefits of protection from her brothers and their friends on daytime outings (her mini "Secret Service"), when Avery wanted to go out with friends, rightly or wrongly, I gave her tighter parameters.

Be sure to check out the chapter on Teens. I'll honestly admit in hindsight that I could've done better for my kids during their teen years. However, I can only say that there were too many times during my own teenage years when I found myself in situations and facing experiences that were well beyond my maturity and ability to handle. My parents were distracted with their own issues post-divorce, and I felt lost and alone for the majority of my teenage years. While my kids often accused me of being too controlling while they were growing up, I gave them more freedom and latitude as their age and maturity dictated. When they were teens, I also regularly verbalized that the more they were able to demonstrate their responsibility, the more flexibility I could give them. Despite that, curfews and parties were constant topics for discussion.

As my parents were divorced but still battling each other, I didn't feel much parental support as a teen. I was regularly grounded for disobeying rules but was made to sit in my room with no conversation or feedback from my mother. As a result, I learned nothing other than resentment. I most assuredly wanted a different experience for my kids. As a parent, I struggled to both give my teens enough room to grow and yet keep them safe within acceptable boundaries. While I encourage you to be equitable with your children, you may find that it makes sense to have different guidelines for each of your kids depending on their personalities, their maturity, their gender, and the environment in which you live. It wasn't easy to find the right balance and if I erred, I did so on the side of caution, figuring I'd rather deal with an angry teen than the fallout of any of my children mishandling a bad situation or experiencing a traumatic outcome.

Regardless of the curfews set for my sons and daughter, it was understood that they needed to text me when they got to their destination and needed to be home on time. Occasionally, I embarrassed my kids when they failed to text me or answer my repeated phone calls. When they didn't respond, I had no problem showing up at a festival or event to ensure they were ok. My boys quickly learned and adjusted their behavior to avoid the embarrassment of me showing up. Avery was slower to learn this lesson, or perhaps it was her way of pushing back against me. As a result, Avery and I frequently butted heads over communication and accountability.

Strategy: *Ensure kids understand that driving and having a phone are privileges not rights. If they act irresponsibly or inappropriately, privileges can be taken away.*

When Nate had his driver's license and Jack was in Driver's Ed, I bought a used Camry as a second vehicle for the kids to share. I paid for insurance and maintenance; the kids paid for gas. They also understood that it was my vehicle, and they were responsible for keeping it clean and were not allowed to leave personal items or sports equipment in the backseat or trunk.

They were also prohibited from eating in the car. They were inexperienced drivers, and I felt that they didn't need the distraction of eating while driving. If I went to use the Camry and found crumbs on the driver's seat, I made the guilty child vacuum and Armorall the car. Then he or she was grounded from driving for a week.

For summer jobs, the kids had to coordinate with each other for work schedules as well as for the times they wanted to use of the car for pleasure. On balance I rarely had to get involved except to periodically remind one of them if they hadn't spent money on gas in a while.

Avery and I had confrontations in front of her friends when she conveniently silenced her phone and thus missed my attempts to reach her when she hadn't checked in or was late. I made it clear to Avery that the negative consequences she experienced were the result of her poor choices, not me trying to be a jerk. I consistently and repeatedly communicated to all of my children that the price of freedom and greater latitude was demonstrating responsibility, not defying my parameters. When I asked Avery and her brothers to check in, I meant it. Trust was a two way street, and I was willing to trust them so long as they acted responsibly. I wanted them to have more freedom. I wanted to work myself out of a job. During the teen years, the price of more freedom was my children's willingness to check in, be honest about where they would be and to be home before curfew.

Recall, my first parenting value was consistency and expectations. Holding your kids accountable for the consequences of their actions is a form of being consistent. In addition, I strongly encourage you to say what you mean and mean what you say. Don't <u>ever</u> threaten negative consequences that you're unwilling or unable to enforce. While there were times I wanted to yell,

"You're grounded for life!" or something equally stupid, I didn't.

There was one time that I shocked all three of my kids at dinner. Avery went through a very brief stage during 3rd grade when she would suck on her hair. It was gross and disgusting to witness. One night during dinner, Avery repeatedly kept sucking on a small section of hair. After I'd told her to stop several times, I told her if she did it again, I'd cut it off. Well, she did it again, so I pulled out the scissors from the kitchen junk drawer and cut that section of her hair off at her jawline. All three of the kids just gasped in disbelief. As I dumped the lock of Avery's hair into the kitchen trashcan, I looked at Avery and said, "If you do it again, I'm going to cut all your hair short, so none of it will reach your mouth." I never saw Avery suck on her hair again.

Holding your children accountable for their actions and consequences is critical. While your child may be angry or sad over the loss of some privilege for an hour, a day, or a week as punishment, never forget that you are teaching your children to respect your values, have personal self-control, and behave appropriately with others. You are teaching them the importance of being responsible and meeting their commitments. You are holding your children accountable. You're helping them to build good character. You are teaching them life lessons in a safe and positive manner. They may resent you at the time, but they will thank you later. Their future employers and significant others will also be grateful to you for teaching your children those lessons. You are helping your children to become the best version of themselves.

Strategy: *Teach kids how to be ready on time by adding up time and counting backwards.*

I always expected my kids to be ready when it was time to leave the house – whether for school, errands, or a weekend adventure.

To help the kids understand planning, we'd discuss how long it would take to complete all the tasks we needed to complete before leaving – getting dressed, making their beds, eating breakfast, brushing teeth, etc. Then we'd estimate how long they thought they'd need to complete each activity and add up all the minutes. We'd also typically add in an extra 5-10 minutes just because.

The kids and I would then do the math. If they felt they needed 40 minutes and we had a 5 minute cushion, we'd all agree that they needed to get up at 6:45 if we planned to leave at 7:30. This process and agreement reduced grousing when I woke them up and helped keep everyone on schedule as we all worked together to get out the door on time. As detailed in a prior Strategy box, I also used the Two Minute Warning each day as we got close to our departure time.

This tactic also taught my children a helpful strategy that they used for school projects – breaking down each step in the process, estimating time they'd to complete it and thus keeping them on track to complete it on time. I also showed them how I used the same strategy for making meals so that everything was finished and ready to be served at the same time.

Most kids have a backpack that they take to school. As previously mentioned, part of our evening routine was for the kids to put their homework plus tomorrow's snack in their backpack each night. Every morning, I always gave a reminder to grab their lunch from the fridge and asked them to recheck their backpacks one more time.

Occasionally as we were driving to the daycare provider's house, one of the kids would cry out, "I forgot my book report," or something similar. I would tell them that I was sorry, but they'd just have to tell their teacher that while they had completed the homework, they had left it at home. I also offered to email their teacher when I got to work to confirm that my child had done their work, it just hadn't made it into their backpack.

Only once do I remember turning around and returning home to get the forgotten items. That was when both Jack and Avery were in tears because they'd both forgotten something. But after we'd returned home and were heading again towards the daycare provider's house, I told them that because of their forgetfulness, I would have to explain to my manager, Michelle, why I was late for work. I wanted them to see that by saving them from negative consequences, their actions had potentially created negative consequences for me. Yes, I wanted my kids to feel some guilty. I wanted this experience to help make them more likely to be responsible going forward.

It's natural to want to shelter, protect or bail your kids out of unpleasant consequences, however I believe that letting them learn lessons at an early age when the stakes are low is best. Holding your children accountable for the consequences of their actions (or forgetfulness) motivates them to internalize and be responsible for their own success going forward. The real impact of 1st or 3rd grader failing to turn in one homework assignment on time is negligible. However, by making them bear the consequences of that mistake, you can strengthen their desire and ability to meet their obligations and be responsible for getting things done on time in the future. Especially when they were young, I gave my kids lots of reminders and our routines created a cadence that helped keep them on track. But at the end of the day, the way they felt when they had to face negative outcomes because they'd messed up, was often the thing that truly drove the lesson home.

Again, learning these lessons and mastering responsibility when they're young is low cost and one more step on the road to success for your children. One more step towards working yourself out of a job.

There was a lot of tough love in our house, but with the toughness, there was always love. Even when I was angry or disappointed by their behavior, I don't think my kids ever doubted that I loved them. I told them, "I love you," every morning when they got up and again every night when I kissed them goodnight. When they left for high school each morning I said, "I love you. Have a great day." Through our daily interactions, they could see that they were valued and appreciated. They also knew that I considered them responsible for their behavior and the consequences of their actions. When I was angry or disappointed, they knew exactly why. As they demonstrated their responsibility and maturity, they were given more freedoms and more privileges. On balance, I believe this approach was empowering for my children. They were always in the driver's seat to generate outcomes – good or bad.

Consistency, honesty, empathy, holding them accountable and tough love helped shape my children into the strong, reliable, confident, resilient people that they've each become.

Tales from the Homefront:

Stealing: In addition to bringing lunch to school, when the kids were in elementary school, they needed to bring 25 cents each day to buy a carton of milk. To make life easier, I kept a small container on the kitchen windowsill full of quarters so the kids or I could put one in their lunch bag each night. When it got low, I'd buy another $10 roll of quarters from the bank and add it to the container. One weekend while I was making lunch, I noted that the container of quarters seemed rather low despite my having just refilled it the prior day. I dumped it out and counted the quarters. I found that approximately $4-5 was missing.

I called Nate, Jack and Avery into the kitchen and told them what I'd discovered. I asked if they had any ideas about where the missing quarters had gone. They looked at each other and at me and then Nate suggested, "Someone must have stolen them." I said, "I think you're right, Nate. Since it's only been us in the house, it seems that one of us must've taken some of them. Is there anything any of you want to tell me?"

The kids looked at each other again and at me. They each shook their heads, and we just stood there silently for a minute or so. I asked again, "So no one can tell me what happened?" I waited another minute looking in turn at each of them as we all felt the pressure of the silence. Finally, I said, "Well, since no one is willing to confess, I guess I will just have to punish you all and stop giving you allowance until someone confesses." There were shouts of "What?!" "That's not fair," and then suddenly Jack burst into tears and said, "I didn't do it, but I'll pay the money. I don't want everyone to get punished."

To this day, I don't know if Jack was taking one for the team, as the middle child often does, or if he was both admitting and denying his guilt. Jack had been caught previously trying to steal Star Wars ™ figures from a daycare provider and when confronted jointly by me and the sitter claimed the figures must've fallen into his backpack; rather improbable since the figures were kept in the basement rec room and his backpack was by the front door. Whatever the truth regarding the milk money, there was never a problem with stealing again in our family.

Having a car on campus: During Nate's junior year of college in Iowa, he earned a co-op opportunity through the University, but the job was located in Nebraska. I bought a used Kia Sportage making it clear to Nate that the vehicle was mine, but letting him know that he could use it so he could move from IA to NB and use the vehicle during the semester while he lived and worked in NB. The additional upside was that I no longer had to make 5 round trips to Ames, IA each school year to bring Nate home for breaks. Unsurprisingly, post-graduation and 3 years later, Nate continued to have the Kia. Once he turned 25, I transferred title of the vehicle to Nate. Nate paid all the taxes and fees to transfer title and registration to his name. As the owner of the vehicle, Nate now pays for all maintenance, fees, registration, and insurance.

Once both Jack and Avery were in college, I suggested that Jack take the Camry and keep it on campus so he could drive himself back and forth during breaks. I clearly didn't need two vehicles sitting in my driveway at home with just me. In addition, with Avery and Jack both away at college – one basically south, the other west - giving Jack a method of transportation home simplified the logistics for everyone getting home for breaks and holidays.

Within 6 months of Jack having the car on campus, I received a notice of a speeding violation in the mail. Of course I was angry. I called Jack who explained how he'd been driving a classmate and fraternity brother home. This classmate lived in some distant town and Jack got caught in a speed trap. Jack got an earful both for the ticket and for using the car in that manner. I reminded him that while I was fine if he used the car for errands around town, it was my car, and his acting like "big man on campus" to take his frat buddy home was outside of the approved parameters. I also explained how his moving violation would increase my car insurance premiums for the next 2-3 years. Jack paid the speeding fine and promised to do better.

After Jack graduated from college, he got a job and moved to Chicago, where having a vehicle was both unnecessary and very expensive to own and insure. Again, mostly to facilitate visits home, I let Avery take the Camry to college in Ohio during her sophomore year. At the start of the summer before Avery took the car, I had four new tires installed. In less than two months of her having the car on campus, Avery drove through a huge pothole and got a flat tire, a non-repairable flat tire.

It was a good learning experience for Avery. We had several phone calls as she worked through getting a new tire. I assisted Avery with the process to ensure we got an appropriate tire to match the exiting new tires, and of course, I made Avery pay for it. I continue to hold my kids accountable.

Selecting punishments.

When the kids were in grades K-12, a tactic I found highly effective to both drive empathy and face the consequences of their actions was to let the aggrieved kid recommend a punishment when he or she had been mistreated by a sibling.

As noted, our punishments tended to be loss of privileges and as they got older and understood money, payment if they broke something belonging to someone else through carelessness or meanness. I followed their recommendations about 90% of the time.

What I found interesting was that my children typically suggested more lenient punishments than I might've given, and the child who was deciding the recommended punishment often made comments about how he or she had done something that had contributed to the bad situation. Perhaps they were feeling empathy for their sibling, or perhaps they were hedging against the time when the shoe would be on the other foot and their brother or sister got to name a punishment, but I think it was a good learning experience for all of us.

My goal in punishment has always been to demonstrate that bad behavior brought negative consequences and if possible, mitigate any damage or harm done. I wasn't trying to make someone feel bad or sad, rather, I was merely holding them accountable to understand that what they'd done was not ok and ideally understand how they could do better next time.

I firmly believe that learning these lessons in childhood has made my children more reliable friends, better employees, and more tolerant, thoughtful, empathic people.

Successful parents are both selfish and selfless.

Lies are toxic. Be honest and kind.

Be gentle in your criticism. Egos are fragile.

Teach independence, but don't rush childhood.

Try never to say, "I told you so." They already know.

VALUE 5

DELAYED GRATIFICATION, PLUS UNDERSTANDING MONEY AND CREDIT

I choose delayed gratification as one of my core parenting values as I wanted my children to master self-control and impulse control. I also tried to educate my kids to recognize the pervasive marketing that seeks to compel them to actions that are not necessarily in their own best interests.

I love this country and all its possibilities; however I wanted to equip my children with the ability to disregard external stimuli and follow their own genuine desires. I wanted my kids to understand that it is impossible to "keep up with the Jones," and recognize that there is no value or pleasure in even trying to do so.

Fundamentally, delayed gratification is about self-control. Self-control may be demonstrated by a 1st grader trying to sit quietly in his chair until recess, a high schooler not posting a reply to a provocative text or someone not clicking the "place order" button for something she doesn't really need. Money is a great way to teach about delayed gratification. In America, the deck is stacked against all of us striving to avoid the pitfalls of immediate gratification. Social media platforms and their algorithms try to stimulate our base desires in ways that are beyond our conscious understanding. The ability to master delayed gratification is about being true to your genuine needs vs your perceived wants as manipulated by marketing and media.

The internet, Amazon, Uber Eats, Facebook "likes," Apple Wallets. . . all feed both our desire and ability for instant gratification. Companies have made it so easy to pay that it is virtually frictionless. You barely have time to think before your money's been spent. With all this "convenience," you can easily lose track of spending.

We are all bombarded with options and enticements. Pop-up ads. Saved payment options. Free trials that convert into subscriptions if not cancelled. Everything is just a click away and packages are delivered to our doorsteps. Our marketplaces are designed to pander to our every whim, the moment they occur. Marketers encourage us to buy, buy, buy.

"Buy now, pay later"

"3 years, zero cost financing same as cash"

"Express delivery"

"Pick up in 2 hours"

"Low monthly payments"

How can we as parents teach our kids to ignore those enticements and swim upstream against the torrent and satisfaction of easy gratification? Why should we try?

I believe that a steady stream of immediate gratification is bad for your soul, bad for your character, and can be ruinous to your financial well-being. For those reasons, delayed gratification was one of my core parenting values.

The COVID pandemic and the related shutdowns demonstrated that we do not need to have retailers open 24/7. Unless you are experiencing a medical emergency, waiting is ok. In fact, waiting is good. Waiting provides you with the opportunity to consider your decisions more thoroughly.

Among other benefits, the ability to delay gratification is a critical aspect of:

- Impulse control

- Self-control

- Financial health and savings

- Waiting in line for your turn

- Successful navigation of social situations

- "Zippering" in traffic

Strategy: *Use allowance as a tool to learn about managing money, rather than payment for chores.*

Basic expectations in our family were that everyone contributed and as the kids got older, they took on more of their own self-care. While there were household and personal tasks that needed to be completed, no one had "chores" assigned in our house.

Taking care of our house and our dogs had no economic value. Homework was part of my children's "job" to succeed at school, keeping their rooms clean and putting away their clothes, toys, etc. were their responsibility. Everyone was expected to contribute and to do more as they got older.

Allowance was not a payment for services, rather it was money received that enabled my children to make discretionary purchases and gain experience with managing their own money.

I did NOT require that the kids allocate a portion of their allowance to charity. Instead, I talked about the organizations we as a family supported and why. As the head of the household, I funded our family's charitable contributions.

As a single, working parent, I paid thousands of dollars in daycare to cover working hours. I was hard pressed to justify paying additional costs for sitters to watch my kids at other times too. Our social activities therefore revolved around kid friendly activities and activities that included other friends with kids. When they were too young to stay home alone, it also meant that my children had to come along while I completed our weekend errands. While each week varied, weekend errands typically included visiting the grocery store, Walmart, or Target, perhaps the bank, the post office, the dry cleaners, etc. We all got up early (see comments in the section on Consistency and Expectations regarding maintenance of a consistent schedule) and we were generally finished by mid to late morning. This left the kids ample time for play, friends, homework, and downtime and also permitted us to have half or full day adventures on most weekends.

Taking the kids with me on errands also exposed them to many aspects of running a home, managing purchases from a shopping/grocery list, using coupons, taking advantage of sales, and sticking to a budget. I explained how I made my list to support the meals I'd make that week and why I'd purchase extras of the items that were on sale that we regularly consumed. (If you have room for a chest freezer in the basement or garage, it can be a wonderful investment to take advantage of sales to reduce grocery bills. Meat, vegetables, bread, butter, all of those items can be frozen.)

Strategy: *Wait a week before making non-essential, discretionary purchases*

I gave my kids lots of latitude in their spending choices but made them wait a week before actually buying. Impulse buying was not permitted in our family. For me or my children.

Each week, I read the grocery flyers and shopped off a list. If the kids wanted to buy something, they had to tell me before we left the house. If they remembered they wanted to buy something only once they saw it again in the store, too bad, so sad. They had to wait another week. My rationale was that if they couldn't remember a desired purchase outside of the store, clearly it wasn't that important to them.

I used the same strategy for myself. I've thrown out countless catalogs with purchases that I was considering ordering. Nine times out of ten, I decided not to buy after thinking about it for a week or two. Likewise, I've left many items in on-line shopping carts that I never bought.

Discretionary items are just that – discretionary, optional, not necessary, things we may want but don't actually need. Teaching your children to think and rethink about how they spend their money is priceless.

As a financial person, it's easy for me to talk about money. But teaching kids the basics of money is not complicated. The grocery store provides a wealth of teaching opportunities. As the kids were forced to come along with me, I tried to make our errands more interesting and fun. Some of the money lessons to consider in a grocery store include:

- Comparing the cost of buying a melon vs. buying a container of cut melon pieces.

- The cost of buying prepared meals vs. making meals at home.

- Purchasing produce that's in season vs. out of season.

- Buying bulk vs. individual servings.

- Using store brands (when comparable quality) vs. name brands.

- Recognizing that the cheapest items in a section are generally on the bottom shelf, with more expensive items at eye level and on end caps.

- Adding up the cost of items to make a great dinner to feed all four of us at home vs. the cost of us eating at our favorite restaurant.

- Considering prebagged items sold by weight vs. unbagged items sold be weight. By law, the prebagged items must weigh at least the amount advertised so they generally provide extra. I'd have one of the kids weigh the 3 lb. bag of apples before putting it into the shopping cart to see how much extra we were getting for free.

- Evaluating packaged items on a cost per serving or per weight unit to accurately compare different items or to decide which size to buy. The shelf labels often provide this information, but make sure it's relevant. For example, laundry detergent labels show the price per ounce, but depending on concentration the number of ounces per load varies. For laundry detergent, I showed my children how to compare the cost per load to determine the best value.

In addition to money, the produce section of an average grocery store also provides opportunities to talk about lots of other interesting topics such as:

- Recognizing that part of the price of an item includes the cost and challenges of transporting it from where the product was grown and harvested to our store. So perhaps the pineapple travelled on a truck, a boat and another truck to get to our store. I wanted my children to recognize that some of the cost included transportation expense.

- Making a game of estimating how much grapefruit, a bunch of bananas, a watermelon or other item weighed and then weighing it.

- Showing kids how to select the best quality produce by smell, look, color, firmness, etc.

- Guessing if items grew on trees, on shrubs, on vines, on the ground, underground, etc.

The list goes on and on. Kids are curious and there are learning opportunities everywhere. Keeping that mindset also added fun and discovery to our mundane chores that might otherwise have seemed like drudgery. There are opportunities for fun, discovery, and adventure everywhere. It just takes a smidgeon of creativity and attention. Do it for your kids. If they're having fun, they're more apt to learn and remember the knowledge that you're trying to share.

As indicated, my kids all received an allowance. Initially, I gave them $1 each week, plus a quarter that had to go into their piggybank for saving. As they got older, I changed their weekly allowance to correspond to the dollar amount equal to their age and continued to also give them 25 cents per week for savings. Allowance was not tied to specific chores. As already noted, my kids were expected to contribute as members of the family and be responsible for more of their own care as they got older, (making beds, putting away clean clothes, etc.) so I never considered "paying" my children for these contributions by linking them to allowance.

There were occasional times when Nate, Jack or Avery wanted to save money for something and earn extra money. At those times we'd figure out some job that they could do that I was willing to pay for. Examples included picking up the dog poop at the end of the week, weeding one of my many gardens, vacuuming the minivan, etc. We always agreed on the price for the job and mentally, I always compared it to their weekly allowance and tried to arrive at a value that would be meaningful for them and fair to both of us. I also always inspected the job prior to paying to reinforce a good work ethic, and on occasion had them address minor issues before I paid them. More tough love with a purpose.

Subject to the "wait a week" rule, my kids were able to spend their money on whatever they wanted. I paid for their clothes, school supplies, all our needs and all our food. Perhaps because we ate such healthy meals and only occasionally had sweets and goodies, the kids typically weren't interested in buying candy or junk food. If they had focused on those types of items, I would have come up with parameters to limit those purchases that made sense.

As outlined in the Strategy box above, to avoid whining or impulse purchases during our errands, before we left the house for our Saturday morning errands, I always asked if there was anything that any of my children were thinking of buying. Generally, none of them could think of anything they really wanted to buy. Once we were out and about, if they saw something they wanted to buy, they had to wait a week to make the purchase and tell me about it the following Saturday before we left the house.

When we went to Walmart, Target, or another big box department store, I generally allocated time for us to linger in the toy section, or when they got older, the electronics section. This gave my kids a chance to understand the cost of things they desired. I highlighted for my kids how merchandise linked to a movie or TV show compared to the price of similar items that weren't tied to a movie or show. We judged the quality and cost of major brands like Lego to cheaper knock-off brands. We also compared the cost of toys they wanted to the total spent on our weekly grocery bill, the cost of all of us eating at our favorite restaurant or to their weekly allowance to give them additional context. All of these conversations helped build my kids' understanding of money and what things cost. While time hanging out in the toy department lengthened the time spent each week on our errands, it was something the kids looked forward to and seemed a fair reward for them having to come along with me. I also took mental notes of the items that my children were consistently drawn to as potential ideas for birthday and Christmas presents.

Requiring my kids to wait one week before making a purchase and having context and a backdrop around the value of money saved us thousands of dollars and eliminated the negative drama that goes with public arguments.

As the kids got older and were able to walk up town with their friends or as a group, they spent some of their allowance at the Dollar Store, or bought lunch from the Pizza Stop or Wendy's. I wasn't present, so the "wait a week" ban wasn't in effect, however my kids had already learned its value. I'd sometimes comment on my children's spending. Regarding buying lunch, I suggested that rather than spending $5 each for a slice of pizza and a pop that they could contribute $4 each for a whole pizza, get more total pizza, and have juice, milk, or water at home. I'd also save coupons for Wendy's so they could evaluate if pooling their money and dividing up a meal deal was a better alternative. I was presenting options for their consideration and left it up to them to decide how to spend their money. Each of my kids learned the hard way that toys priced at $1 were frequently cheaply made and broke easily. They also learned that eating at home was free, healthier, and also left more of their own money for other purchases.

Strategy: **Teach opportunity cost**

The concept of opportunity cost is essentially that if you spend money today, you won't have it available to spend later.

#1: While your child(ren) are under 10 years old, give them a gift of money and let them wrestle with their spending decisions.

When Nate was 7, in addition to birthday presents, I gave him $50. He decided to go to Toys R Us. We spent hours in the store. If he had several toys in the cart and wanted to add something that took the total cost over $50, Nate had to take something out of the cart first. The experience helped him figure out his priorities, use his math skills and see that spending money on one thing meant he couldn't spend it on something else.

At several times in their lives, I repeated this exercise with both Jack and Avery. I expect that shoppers who heard me say something like, "That's $5 more than you have," may've thought I should just kick in the extra five bucks for the kid, but I was teaching a life lesson. I didn't care if a random shopper thought I was cheapskate.

#2: Provide both positive and negative feedback about past money decisions to reinforce opportunity cost. When Jack changed his mind and decided not to spend $3 on a box of marbles (after waiting a week to think about it) and several weeks later bought a toy for $12, I praised him for not buying the marbles as that decision had enabled him to have enough to buy the current toy. Likewise, when he spent $2 on a resin hippo that he almost immediately didn't care about it, and then didn't have enough money to go to the Pizza Stop for lunch with his siblings and their friend, Cam. I reminded Jack of the $2 he'd squandered on the hippo. Tough love, reinforcing an important lesson.

My children and I talked about opportunity cost. I'd always call it out when one of my children found something that they wanted to buy but had to wait 1-2 weeks to save enough allowance because they'd spent most of their money at Pizza Stop or Dollar Tree the prior week. Just like grow-ups, kids often learn more from their mistakes than their successes. Learning these lessons at an early age can lay a good foundation for your children to understand these concepts when the dollars involved are very, very small.

Back to the 25 cents I gave each week for savings. I opened up minor savings accounts for each of the kids at the bank when they were in elementary school. Banks typically provide these accounts for free, i.e., no fees, small or no minimum balances. When their piggybanks were full, we'd dump out the quarters, count them and deposit them in the bank. For birthdays and Christmas, in addition to buying gifts, I'd typically give each of them a check for $100 that I deposited into their savings accounts. By the time they were 18, they each had several thousand dollars in savings. While the interest earned on these accounts was virtually zero, the kids learned that small contributions of 25 cents a week and gifts of money could grow into big amounts over time.

When each of my children had finished their senior year of high school and got their first summer job, we went together to the bank to open a checking account (moving some money from their minor savings account to fund the new account). While I also showed each of my kids how to fill out a check, my children quickly adapted to on-line banking and e-checks. Once they had a paycheck being deposited directly into their checking account, we'd go back to the bank so they could apply for a credit card.

I specifically chose a credit card vs. debit card as I wanted my children to start building a credit history and establish good habits around using credit. I was NOT a co-signer on their credit cards, nor did I consider having them as a signer on mine. As a result, their initial credit limits were modest at around $500 - $1,500 to start. I clearly communicated to each of my children that while I loved them with all my heart, there was absolutely no chance of me co-signing or guaranteeing any of their financial obligations ever. If they overspent, it was their money and their credit history at risk, not mine. Again, I was forcing my children to be responsible and accountable. I was putting them in the driver's seat and drawing a bold line under how critical it was for them to learn to use credit wisely. This was their first major step into financial adulthood. The risk was low due to their limited credit lines, but the upside was huge for their future financial well-being.

Each month, they'd open their credit card statements, and we'd review them together. We'd look at how much money they spent on various categories like food and entertainment. This process showed them how a lot of little purchases throughout the month could add up to big dollars and helped them be more mindful of their purchases. I also consistently reinforced the importance of paying their credit card balance in full each month, not just the minimum payment. When early in the process Nate missed paying on time one month and was assessed a $25 late fee plus interest for failing to make even the minimum payment, all the kids got an earful about how Nate had just thrown that money down the toilet. I was livid as I take pride in never paying bank fees. The upside was that to the best of my knowledge, Nate has never paid another late fee and neither has Jack nor Avery. A very valuable lesson learned by all three of my children for the bargain price of $25 plus interest. As a result of this early education and exposure, each of the kids is diligent about managing their credit, finding ways to build their credit score, and paying balances in full. Avery's practice is to pay off her open balance via on-line banking each Sunday. Routines make life easier and support good habits. Encourage your kids to find routines that work for them.

Having had roughly $13 thousand of college debt when I graduated with my bachelor's degree and knowing how oppressive that felt during the roughly three years it took me to pay it off, I was determined to get my kids through college debt free. Subject to their earning A's & B's, I agreed to pay for college up to a set dollar limit. My payments included all tuition, fees, room and board less any scholarships they earned. My dollar limit meant that some universities were just not options as my offer was contingent upon none of us incurring any debt. I also offered to increase the amount I was willing to pay each year by $10 thousand for each year that any of my children lived at home and went to community college. My rationale was that the cost of room and board alone was approximately $12-14 thousand per year and community college would mean we'd completely eliminate that cost. In addition, community college would cost much less for tuition, books, and labs. I estimated that each year of community college would save me $15-20 thousand, so I was willing to pay up to an incremental $10 thousand of those savings. Win-win.

However, rather than community college, all three of my children selected four year universities, lived in dorms the first 2 years and in campus apartments or off-campus housing for the last two years. Nate and Avery attended universities that were within my price limits net of scholarships, and Jack had to contribute a couple thousand dollars each year from summer earnings or campus jobs. All three found excellent schools that had strong programs for their majors.

Building on the knowledge from childhood that school was their "job," each of my children also participated in professional networking organizations affiliated with their areas of study which enhanced their effectiveness at job fairs and improved their chances of earning internships and co-ops. I was especially delighted when Nate joined the Society of Women Engineers ("SWE"). In fact, Nate earned his first internship through a SWE sponsored job fair as he was the sole male student at the event and in addition to being talented and personable, Nate was very memorable.

To further expand their money management skills, prior to the start of each semester, I deposited my college contribution into my kids' bank accounts to cover the known costs and estimated costs for books. Each month, I also gave them $100 in allowance (relatively consistent with $1 per their age per week) which I also deposited into their checking account. If any of them needed more than that, they had to use money from their bank account from summer earnings or work. During the first year I'd coordinate closely with my new college student to make sure they knew how and when to pay their bills via the university system.

To help build their credit history, I also encouraged my children to use their credit cards when buying books and other items, then pay off the balance with the money I'd given them. In this way, they were demonstrating to the credit card issuing banks that they were able to use credit wisely and they always paid off their balances in full each month. These good practices reinforced their good credit habits and generated both larger credit card limits and higher credit scores.

Teaching about delayed gratification is really just establishing habits that work for you and your family to resist impulse buying decisions. The other key aspect is to maintain your spending in line with your cash or monthly earnings. Managing allowance and then credit cards can help your kids learn to be mindful of their spending choices and understand that choices made today can impact potential choices in the future. As noted, giving my kids an allowance, and having a firm, "wait a week" policy around purchases had massive benefits. It created the beginning of a solid financial foundation for understanding money and made our time together much more pleasant as it virtually eliminated arguments about buying things while we were in the stores. Jack recently shared how this lesson continues to underpin his day-to-day monetary decisions.

Once my kids were in high school and earning money from summer jobs, we'd talk about the cost of things (going to a movie, buying a video game, eating out, going to prom, etc.) in terms of the hours they had to work to pay for it. I wanted my children to understand not only opportunity cost – "if I buy this, I can't buy that" – but to also have some appreciation around how much of their own effort and time was required to earn the money to pay for the things they valued. If it took 4-5 hours of work to afford the current hot Xbox game, perhaps borrowing it from the library was preferable to owning it.

We'd also sometimes compare my salary converted into an hourly wage to the amounts my children earned. The objective of this exercise was to reinforce the value of a college education and master's degree in potentially enabling them to earn much higher wages.

Nate's first job was working for a friend's parent's landscaping company. Jack's first job was loading cars and bringing in shopping carts at a local home improvement store. Avery worked at Kohls, Target and later segued into waitressing. Each of those jobs had my children on their feet working hard and truly earning every dollar of their paychecks. While their new wealth resulted in some splurging on personal items, they each quickly learned to consider purchases against their paycheck and the hours those costs represented. In addition, once they got past freshman year of college, they also used earnings from their summer jobs to build up their bank balances to ensure they had enough to cover discretionary spending during the school year that was above their $100 per month allowance.

As the kids progressed in their college careers, they worked hard and competed for paid summer internships. In addition to the resources provided through the universities and affiliated organizations to create resumes and hone interviewing skills, I also reviewed and provided feedback on their resumes and gave advice regarding effective communicative at the job fairs, during their interviews and in email communications related to the opportunities.

Nate's college internships gave him valuable paid experience in several different industries in his field. Those experiences helped him build an impressive resume that resulted in several job offers after graduation. At present, Nate's building a strong track record in his career and has earned several promotions. Jack's highly competitive summer internship led to a job offer from the firm after graduation and he is developing a reputation as a strong performer and communicator. Avery has just completed her first summer internship and, like her brothers, she's gained valuable experience, earned an income of roughly twice a typical summer job and is likewise building out her resume in her chosen career field while she is still attending college.

Strategy: *Use your household costs and budget to teach your child(ren) about money and financial matters.*

Some schools have finally begun teaching financial literacy. As your kids gain independence, they'll need to know how to use bank accounts, pay bills, build a budget, understand a lease or mortgage, use health insurance, pay income taxes, save for retirement, and make countless decisions about money. The more you can prepare them the better.

I showed each of my kids how to write a check and understand both their bank and credit card statements. When my kids wanted to move into apartments for junior and senior year of college, they had to send me a copy of the lease. I sent back a highlighted version of the document and either explained why they could not sign that lease or if the lease was ok, stressed the sections that they needed to make sure they followed exactly to the letter to avoid fees and / or additional costs or liability.

The first time each of my children completed a tax return, we did it together using paper forms and walked through both state and federal filings to ensure they understood the process.

The more you talk about money, the easier it becomes. In our family, we all now discuss money matters as calmly and unemotionally as we discuss the weather.

Learning to delay gratification was a hugely valuable skill in many aspects of my children's lives, including managing their money. I equipped my children with a mechanism to reduce impulse purchases, allowed them to manage their money (including letting them make mistakes), taught them the importance of using and paying off credit cards each month, and gave them an understanding of opportunity cost. By the time my kids left for college, they had a solid foundation of how to manage money as well as good habits to help avoid the temptation of unnecessary spending. Again, I highlight that these early experiences were achieved when mistakes were measured in very small dollars. My kids still occasionally waste money and don't always make what I think are the best choices, but on balance they demonstrate a solid understanding of the value of money and how to manage credit. None carry credit card balances; all have savings; and as working professionals, both Nate and Jack are taking advantage of 401Ks, building cash reserves in their bank accounts, and are investing a portion of their post-tax earnings. In addition, all three of them have saved money to fund travel with friends that gave them new experiences as well as opportunities to make choices about how to get the best value out of their money while traveling.

Talking about money is healthy and should be age appropriate. When my kids were young and asked how much money I earned, I merely said, "I make enough money to pay for all the things we need." As they got older, I gradually moved to full transparency in virtually all financial matters including my salary, bonuses and tax returns. It's critical to understand money, contracts, leases, mortgages, car loans, health insurance, auto insurance, renter's insurance, credit cards, etc., so I used myself and our household spending as teaching opportunities. I wanted my kids to know everything about money, including opportunity cost, how to write a check, how to use credit cards wisely, and how to save for retirement and to invest wisely. We also talked about the importance of avoiding fees, the potential benefits of early repayment of debt to lower interest costs and taking advantage of employer 401K matches and programs such as employer tuition reimbursement.

The ability to be able to delay gratification is an essential life skill. Because money is so entwined with enabling us to meet our needs and desires, many of the lessons regarding delayed gratification incorporated learning about money, credit, and savings. As discussed in the sections about Budgeting; while teaching my children about money, I also underscored the importance of differentiating between "wants" and "needs." I'll say it again; as parents, I believe we fundamentally need to work ourselves out of a job. We need to fill our kids with knowledge, skills, experiences, and abilities to make good decisions, be responsible and accountable and navigate the world and their place in it. Money touches virtually every aspect of our lives and equipping your children to understand and control their impulses and their spending is priceless.

Tales from the Homefront:

Win-win investing. At the time of the housing crisis in 2008/2009, I had a very small remaining mortgage balance on our home as I always contributed extra amounts to pay down my mortgage. One of our long-term daycare providers had recently been through a divorce and foreclosure and was renting a modest townhouse while still caring for my kids during the summer when they weren't in school. I pitched the idea to my daycare provider of finding a house that I could buy – using a cash out refinance on my home – and having her and her kids as my tenants. I believed that this could be a huge benefit to her and her family as well as a good investment strategy for me. My objectives included investment diversification, buying real estate when prices were very low as well as income generation from the rent she'd pay. I planned to keep the rental in great shape to benefit from real estate appreciation down the road as the industry recovered. I also thought that if this worked, I might consider buying another property in the future so I could have three properties as part of estate planning for my three children.

It took us nearly a year to find the right property as during that time, one of my daycare provider's children decided college wasn't for her and moved back home. In addition, my day care provider's mom lived in an apartment in town, and she and her family decided that having a three generation household would provide both financial and family benefits.

As part of the search process my kids and I toured countless homes with my broker. When we found ones we liked, we had the daycare provider and her family visit too. The impact of the housing crisis shocked my children. They were stunned that outward appearances of wealth did not necessarily indicate financial solvency. Seeing that people in wealthy neighborhoods and middle income neighborhoods were facing foreclosure was eye opening to my kids. I think this knowledge was also beneficial to them as they navigated the world of social media where perceptions and reality are often very different.

We ultimately found a home that worked for everyone, and I purchased it. I used on-line software to craft a lease that I modified to fit my needs and set the rent at a rate that covered the costs of the larger mortgage on my home, property taxes on both the rental and our house and gave me a little extra income above those costs to cover maintenance. It was an arrangement that was mutually beneficial as I had a tenant I knew and could trust, my daycare provider and her mom saved money by living together and were able to rent a beautiful, spacious home at a below market rate from a landlord who knew and cared about them.

I was completely open about all aspects of the transaction and my kids learned many financial, legal, and real estate lessons over the years.

Finding a way to bend a rule but remain true to your values. One day when Nate and Jack were 8 and 6, we were out shopping at an overstock store when the boys found a Star Wars Lego set of Cloud City (10123) for $85. The boys were over the moon excited. They literally sat on the floor of the store clutching the box and looking at the pictures on it. They were both huge Star Wars fans and both loved Legos. They knew that even combined; they didn't have enough money saved from allowance to buy it. I also recognized that the price was a bargain, that the boys loved and regularly played with their other Star Wars Lego sets. I also knew that if we didn't buy it that day, someone else would purchase it before the boys could save enough from allowance to buy it.

Avery and I wandered around the store and periodically passed by the boys as we browsed. I used the time to try and figure out how to address the situation. Having learned that whining wouldn't work, my sons just looked at me with pleading eyes and clutched the box tighter each time Avery and I passed by. To my delight, Nate suggested a solution that solved the dilemma. He looked at me while he and Jack were clutching the box as said, "You're a banker, you could make us a loan."

Perfect suggestion. I quickly realized the potential to give my boys a lesson on buying on credit, debt repayment and opportunity cost. However, I wanted to reinforce that this was a unique situation that wouldn't undermine our "wait a week" principle. So pretending to think hard about Nate's suggestion, I replied, "That's an excellent idea, Nate. I could make you a loan. But that would mean you'd both be paying me back with your allowance for several weeks and you wouldn't have any money to buy other things during that entire time." Nate and Jack's faces lit up with happiness, both rapidly agreed and then they dashed for the checkout counter with the Lego set in hand before I could change my mind.

When we got home, before they were able to open the set, we all sat down at the kitchen table. On a piece of paper I wrote out the total amount of the purchase, including tax. Then each of the boys brought in all the money they had in their allowance banks and handed over their cash. I wrote down the date and the amount paid, drew a line, and wrote down the remaining amount still due. We put our debt register on the front of the fridge and repeated the exercise each week until they had fully repaid their (zero interest) loan.

I let the boys assemble and play with the Star Wars Lego set the day we bought it as in real life, if we buy on credit, we typically get the chance to use the item before we pay off the debt. I was actually pleased they were still delighted with the purchase by the time they'd paid back their loan. Given the value of the set now, it was obviously a great purchase. More importantly, the boys were elated, they loved the set and played with it for a long time. While I didn't charge them interest, it was a good introduction to buying on credit and requiring 100% of their allowance until they paid me back helped reinforce the concept of opportunity cost.

Feed your children's imaginations with books, walks in the woods, museums, zoos, aquariums, and all sorts of big & small adventures.

Lead from behind. Allow your children to make choices and live with the consequences.

Nothing disrupts your plans like the sound of your child vomiting.

Give your kids the latitude and support to be who they want to be.

Laugh at yourself. Your kids will.

VALUE 6

STRATEGIC THINKING

When trying to explain strategic thinking, I like to use my college education as an example. For me, earning my bachelor's degree taught me lots of technical skills that filled my toolbox of knowledge. The classes I took while earning my MBA taught me how to use those skills and that knowledge. MBA courses taught me how to implement a vision, how to apply my knowledge, and how to motivate and lead others. In other words, my MBA was about improving my ability to think and act strategically.

As parents, all the guidance, rules, values, experiences, and life lessons that we share with our children are ways that we fill their toolboxes with knowledge and skills. For my core parenting values, I wanted to take it one step further. I didn't want to just give my children tools and skills, I wanted to ensure that they had the confidence, knowledge, and ability to use what they'd learned. I wanted them to be able to think strategically. I wanted them to have a goal and know how to develop a plan. To face a problem, understand the root causes, break it down and find a workable solution. And for those instances when there wasn't an obvious solution, I wanted my children to have the wherewithal and confidence to think creatively and develop a solution that might work, and if it didn't, to learn from that result and try again.

The ability to think strategically involves several key aspects:

- **Understanding what may not be obvious but is relevant.** Whether it's understanding how a magic trick works, recognizing a politician's hidden agenda or appreciating that what people present on social media is not 100% reflective of reality, strategic thinking requires seeing past the obvious and trying to understand all the factors at play. I often think of the scene in the "*Wizard of Oz*" when Toto pulls back the curtain to show that the wizard is just a man moving a lot of levers and pulling chains to create the illusion of a great and powerful wizard. Realizing that he's been discovered, the man says, "Pay no attention to the man behind the curtain." As we moved through our lives, I always tried to help my kids to see the man behind the curtain.

- **Knowing the goal or desired outcome**. Whether it's trying to win a board game, deciding how to spend your time, saving for college, or launching a business, you need to know what you're striving for. What you hope to achieve, change, or accomplish.

- **Determining the steps to reach your goal, and if necessary, reevaluate and change those steps as the situation evolves.** Whether it's reacting to an opponent's move in a game that disrupted your strategy, considering the impacts of new technology on your business or adjusting operations due to a global pandemic, thinking strategically is always dynamic. Just like in parenting, it's important to have a plan and a back-up plan and the vigilance and insight to know when the situation has changed, or your efforts aren't working, and you need to chart a different course.

- **Recognizing patterns or similarities.** We've all heard the phrase, "Don't re-invent the wheel." Help your kids to see how situations or problems are similar to something they've already successfully done before. This approach can help reduce stress and anxiety as well as build their confidence to try new things. Implementing a proven strategy is always an option to consider. Help your children to build on what they already know even when they don't have all the information or a definite solution.

Strategic thinking might involve taking an idea or a plan and making it real, putting it into action. Or it might involve taking knowledge you already have and applying it in new ways. Or it might require breaking down a big project or task into smaller parts, some of which you know how to address and others that you don't. Regardless, teaching our kids to think strategically is about enabling them to figure out potential paths forward and deciding which path they believe is the best given the circumstances. And if they fail or discover they're wrong, they have the ability and willingness to try again and make a different decision.

Jigsaw puzzles are a fun and easy way to teach strategic thinking. The great thing is that as your child gets older, you can buy puzzles with more pieces and more challenging pictures. I've always loved doing all sorts of puzzles, including jigsaw puzzles. I'd also read someplace that jigsaw puzzles helped with brain development, so we had puzzles ranging from 4 pieces when the kids were toddlers to up to 1,000 pieces as they got older. Once, we even completed a 5,000 piece jigsaw puzzle as a family.

Putting together a jigsaw puzzle offers the opportunity to apply many strategies. Jigsaw puzzle strategies might include finding all the edge pieces, sorting pieces by color or shape, and selecting parts of the picture to assemble like mini puzzles within the bigger picture. We worked on our puzzles on the dining room table and spent time together and individually working on them. I especially liked it when we all worked together because we each called out what we were going to work on and would give pieces to each other that fit each person's strategy. So for example, if Avery was assembling the border, whoever found an edge piece, gave it to Avery. If Nate was putting together sea turtles, he was given all pieces that had parts of sea turtles on them. If Jack was working on yellow fish, yellow fish pieces went to Jack. I always tried to select the most difficult and boring parts of the puzzles – generally sky, land or water – so that we made good progress, and the kids used their developing skills on the more fun parts of the picture.

In addition to the cooperation and application of different strategies, putting together a jigsaw puzzle gave us a sense of accomplishment. There were no winners or losers, we all worked together for a common goal as a team. We all were delighted when any one of us was able to connect one of the inside parts to an edge or to another partially completed part of the puzzle. Over the years, there was a subtle competition to be the person who put in the last piece. I addressed it by making sure no one was holding back or hiding pieces, then we all put in our final pieces together.

When your children are young, many opportunities to teach them to think strategically revolve around school, sports and playing games. An easy example from school might involve completing a project that requires them to gather and present information. You can coordinate with them to develop a plan around where to get the info, help them to evaluate its relevancy and accuracy, finally help them think through how they will present the information in their own words.

Algebra and math story problems are likewise excellent opportunities to nurture their strategic thinking skills. When my kids were frustrated or stumped while trying to do a math problem, I'd often suggest (if appropriate) that they draw a picture to help understand the question. Then I'd ask, "Well what do you know?" and have them write down those things or add them to their picture. Then I asked how we could use the things they did know to figure out the answer – the thing they didn't know. Sometimes we worked together through a couple of problems. It was always rewarding when suddenly the light bulb would turn on for them. They got it. Not just the answer, but the way to use strategy to help them find the answer.

Teaching your kids to think and develop strategies is captured beautifully in the proverb from Chinese philosopher Lao Tzu, "Give a man a fish, and you feed him for a day. Teach him to fish and you feed him for a lifetime." Especially as they became teenagers, my kids often said that I over explained things, but I wanted them to understand the rationale and thought process behind my answers. I wanted them to think strategically. If they understood how to solve a problem they could use that knowledge in similar situations. If they knew the purpose of an ingredient in a recipe, they had the ability to consider substitutes. If they understood the risks of oversharing personal information, they were more likely to be more cautious and make better choices while navigating social media sites and personal interactions.

Just as I believe being your honest, true self and holding yourself and your kids accountable is empowering, teaching our kids how to think strategically sets them up for success. They'll have some misses and failures along the way, but the more you enable your children to solve problems, figure out solutions for themselves and encourage and celebrate their attempts and their creativity, the better off they'll be. It is impossible to give your children all the knowledge and experience you've learned in your lifetime. Instead, strive to give them solid values, varied experiences, and the ability to recognize patterns and think strategically to address whatever situations arise.

I inserted Strategy boxes throughout this book to share some of the tactical strategies that worked in our family. Each of those boxes is an example of applying strategic thinking with the goal of teaching a method or behavior to successfully parent your children. Rather than just suggest that you talk to your kids about their day, I highlighted the possibilities and benefits of eating together at dinner and using the "High, "Low, "Medium" as a mechanism to encourage your children not just to reply, "Nothing," when asked what happened at school today. Hopefully, you'll find some of these helpful. I also anticipate that you'll develop your own strategies too.

Tales from the Homefront:

Defeating a library bond referendum. My kids and I were huge fans and users of the public library. However, we became part of a grass roots community group that fought against a proposed bond issuance to build a new library. The concerns that led to our opposition included a belief that it was unnecessary, that the proposal was way too expensive, that the proposed new site on the edge of town was poor vs. its existing walkable location in the center of town, that the information being put forth was deliberately misleading and omitted some key information and that there appeared to be several additional agendas that were likewise not being fully and accurately disclosed to the public. As honesty was one of my core values – both personally and as a parent – I had to object. I wanted the voters in our city to be able to decide based on the truth, not spin and partial information.

Something that can be truly great about gathering together a group of people from a neighborhood is that people's jobs and knowledge can be so varied. While we share geography, our backgrounds and experiences can be hugely different. Our group had an amazing skill set including computer technology, web site creation, financial analysis, marketing, teaching, management, and public speaking. We also had lots of different professional and personal networks to utilize to both gather and share information. Because our recently completed remodeled house had a very large living room as well as an upstairs family room for the kids to play while the adults met, our house became the meeting place for our group of neighbors and friends to strategize and coordinate our efforts to oppose the bond referendum.

During our family dinner conversations, I shared how the grassroots group was using each person's skills to communicate and connect with other citizens and deliver our message. I explained how the group formulated a strategy, divided up tasks based on each person's strengths and how we were using social media, newspapers, radio, yard signs and flyers in our strategy. The kids suggested picketing in front of the library and while I applauded their idea, I suggested that we could likely make a bigger impact by distributing flyers to households throughout the town and I soon had them walking with me through different areas of the city rolling and rubber banding flyers to doorknobs. I also suggested that protesting in front of the library might create a hostile environment and while we disagreed with the Library Board's proposal, we all agreed that we loved the library. Our efforts paid off and the referendum was defeated.

Several years later when the Library Board again sought an even larger bond referendum to build a new library on the existing site, I showed my kids how we could borrow from our prior effective strategy – avoiding "re-inventing the wheel" – and with a much smaller group of neighbors, we once again opposed and defeated the bond referendum.

As a result of the two defeats, the Library Board went back to the drawing board and developed a more modest, much less costly plan that resulted in remodeling and repurposing many areas within the existing building as well as constructing a drive-thru book return. The result is wonderful. The redone children's section is larger, more inviting, and absolutely terrific. I almost wish my kids were still young so they could enjoy it. The adult space is more accessible, has a much better, more versatile layout and the library integrated technology to better manage circulation, freeing up staff to have more time for programs and to support patrons.

Playing games: As mentioned, we played a lot of board games in our house. I wanted the kids to learn to be gracious and enjoy the activity whether they won or lost. It was also a good way to show that games have rules, and we all have to follow the rules. I also would remind them before we started that when 4 people sit down to play a game. There would be one winner and 3 losers. Yes, I deliberately stated it harshly. So instead of making it about winning and losing, I always tried to make it about having fun together and figuring out the best strategy for each game.

Sorry(TM) was by far one of our most and least favorite games that we played. Despite my best efforts and all the times we'd played previously, emotions always ran high playing Sorry especially when someone was "killed" and sent back to Home. Tears and horrible remarks were not uncommon. There were many games where Avery was curled up in a ball on the floor sobbing after being sent back to Home. I would calmly rub her back and draw cards for her during her turn until she was once again able to have a piece moving around the board.

Revenge ruled the day. If Jack killed Nate, Nate killed Jack. They all especially liked killing me. I strove to explain that their choices shouldn't be personal and always tried to show them why killing the red piece or blue piece made more sense than killing the green piece, but I always left them free to make their choices. It took a long time, but they finally got it. In fact, given how competitive we all are, my kids took the lesson further than I anticipated. They've each studied chess books, compete regularly in chess matches when we're together, and consistently trounce me in virtually every game we play!

Based on my kids' recommendation, Family Game Day is now a tradition in our house whenever we all get together. Everyone gets to select 2-3 games, and we play different games all day. The games are a chance to compete, to catch up on conversations and to just enjoy each other's company.

Flat Stanley travels the world. During 2nd grade, Nate and his classmates were given a project to color and send a Flat Stanley paper doll to people who would then write back to them, return Flat Stanley, and include a photo of Flat Stanley from their location. Flat Stanley is the main character in a book series written by Jeff Brown. The objective of the project is to improve writing skills and teach children about other countries and cultures. Nate and I discussed his assignment and decided to take advantage of my network of former Peace Corps friends who lived all over the country. I was also working for GE at the time and had work colleagues who frequently traveled the globe, so we decided to tap into that network too.

As Nate and I talked about the project, Nate decided that making and sending multiple copies of Flat Stanley would avoid the risk of someone either not responding or being slow to send Flat Stanley back to him. So we went to the library and made several color copies of Nate's Flat Stanley. Then with Nate sitting at the computer, we worked together to create a letter to send to my friends and colleagues to explain the project and Nate's request. Nate did all the typing, and I helped with phrasing his ideas in a professional way. I also reached out to each person via phone to ensure they'd be ok with helping out. Then Nate mailed the first batch of letters and Flat Stanleys. Each time a Flat Stanley came back, Nate wrote a thank you note and sent Flat Stanley off to someone else on our list along with his letter.

Nate and I were genuinely astonished with the support from people. Not only did Flat Stanley travel to 6-7 different states in the US, but he also had his picture taken in a skybox at one of the playoff NFL football games for the

AFC Championship game that year. Internationally, as part of Nate's project, Flat Stanley had his photo taken in South Korea, London, Madrid, Tunisia and even in Russia next to a statue of Lenin in St. Petersburg Square. I bought a big piece of posterboard, and Nate drew a general map of the world and marked all the places Flat Stanley had visited. What a great project! Nate's idea to use multiple copies of Flat Stanely and tap into my networks made the project even more successful and rewarding.

Changing our college search strategy.   As noted, I offered to pay for my kids' college education so long as they selected schools within my price parameters, achieved A's & Bs, and took on no debt. However, Jack was a very talented athlete and in high school was receiving quite a bit of interest in his football abilities. During his junior year of high school, I paid to have him attend some skill and football camps to assess how he might stack up against other talented boys who were also looking for football scholarships. Our goal was to determine if Jack might be able to attend a higher tier university – all of which were well outside of my price range - and use football as a means to get there.

As detailed in the Paying for College section in the Appendix, when considering potential colleges and universities, we used an Excel spreadsheet to keep track of and compare relevant information to help in our decision making process. For Jack's search, we ran two tabs in our spreadsheet – one for schools that might be in range with an athletic scholarship, and a second for those where only potential academic scholarships might impact the final cost.

As previously noted, Jack sustained a severe concussion during football practice his senior year that was so serious he never played a single football game that season. While he fully recovered, our college search strategy pivoted, and we looked solely at options without consideration of athletic scholarships. In hindsight, Jack's concussion may've been a blessing in disguise. While I'm certain that Jack had the talent and drive to play football at the collegiate level, he had an amazing college experience jammed full of experiences and activities that would not have been possible if he was also a college athlete. Jack has launched very successfully into his career in large part due to those additional efforts and experiences. Equally or even more importantly, Jack didn't risk further brain or bodily injury during his college years. For that I am eternally grateful.

Successful parents work themselves out of a job.

There's no sweeter sound than the laughter of your child.

Sports can provide so many lessons. Michael Jordan wrote, "There is no 'i' in Team"

There's always room for ice cream.

Time outdoors is time well spent.

"I'm sorry" moves everyone closer to forgiveness.

FAMILY ADVENTURES & TRADITIONS

I believe that a commitment to family, lots of shared experiences and traditions are the building blocks of a family's story, history, and memories. Traditions bring continuity across the years and perhaps even generations. Hopefully, traditions are activities that your family anticipates and enjoys. Some may fall away over the years; some may be passed on over multiple generations and new traditions can be added.

Just as consistent routines provide stability and predictability during a day or week, so traditions provide stability and predictability over the longer term. I think of traditions as part of the framework that supports a family over time and a way to pass on heritage and family history. They can also provide milestones or markers for your children as they grow up and start to establish their own households and families. Traditions are a way to reconnect to memories from when they were young and potentially pay it forward if they continue the traditions as adults leading their own families.

When thinking about establishing traditions for your children, you may wish to consider:

- Family traditions from your own and your partner's childhood

- Your ancestry and culture

- Religion if that is an important part of your lives

- Activities that reinforce your values

- Whether activities will be only for your family or include others

- Whether traditions will be activities for certain stages of life or for the long haul.

Conceiving my children via artificial insemination without a partner, I was especially committed to making my kids' childhoods as "normal" as possible. I'd grown up having sleepovers at my grandparents' house and many weekends with my cousins. As previously indicated, my brother never had children and my sisters had kids in their 20s, making their children 10-15 years older than my kids, so the cousin relationships didn't line up. My dad died when Nate was 4 and Jack nearly 2. Not having seen my mother since my own 20s, I was faced with no cousins and no grandparents for my kids. When I was growing up, extended family had been an integral part of my childhood and our holiday celebrations. Without it, I felt like I was playing Monopoly ™ and starting at Go.

However, following my epiphany after my dad's death, I've tried to always focus on the things that made my family great and special rather than the things we lacked. We all have challenges and a laundry list of things we'd consider changing in our lives if we could, but I'd encourage you to embrace and celebrate the things that you have and if desired address things within your control to change, i.e., always see the glass as half full when parenting, not half empty. No matter how rich or wealthy you may be, you'll never be able to do everything you'd like for your kids. Honestly, nor should you. If you did, they'd turn out to be spoiled, entitled, incompetent people who don't appreciate anything. Do your best and what you think is right. By focusing on your values and what's important, building from your strengths, appreciating what you do have and can create, you have a much greater chance of success. And rest assured that especially when they're young, kids really are easy to please and amuse.

Adventures don't have to be grand or big. You don't have to jet off to Paris or be whirled upside down on a rollercoaster to have an adventure. Things as simple as discovering a bird's nest with eggs in your tree, finding a new author who sparks your child's imagination or spending several hours at a park, the beach or on hike can be a fun and exciting adventure for your child. Even just walking our dogs around the neighborhood, my kids would bring little buckets. They'd collect pinecones, leaves, rocks, dandelions, etc. We made a simple walk into a treasure hunt full of possibilities. When the weather grew cold and the local beaches were closed for swimming, we sometimes visited to look for shells and tried to see who could skip rocks the most times on the lake. Being outside and having the lake mostly or fully to ourselves made it special. Adventures are everywhere and it's not difficult to make the ordinary extraordinary by using a smidgeon of imagination and the right attitude.

While my kids were between the ages of 2-12, I dubbed myself the queen of cheap or free adventures. We used all the services of the library - story times, reading programs, free books, free games, free craft projects, and free movies. We visited local and states parks, went to museums and zoos on free days or if we bought memberships, did so every other year and went 3-5 times during our membership year. Whenever possible, we brought our own food for lunch, so we ate better and saved money. We attended high school plays, visited the local beaches, county fairs, watched local parades and visited festivals and carnivals during the hours that were cheapest for little kids. We all looked forward to weekends and all of these activities wove adventures into the fabric of our lives and were anticipated activities that we all enjoyed. Our adventures made life fun and special and fueled my children's imaginations. When possible, we also went with friends or neighbors who had children comparably aged, making our adventures even better as they were shared.

Over time, I learned that many people could fill the void when family wasn't available. As I've noted throughout the book, I was blessed by a friendship with one of my elderly neighbors, Dee. Dee and her husband Bob had lived in their home for 40+ years and raised four children. We'd become close friends over the years, and I found Dee had a wealth of knowledge. Dee had retired from her professional job but took care of the mayor's daughters before and after school as the mayor had been a childhood friend of her sons. Dee was just one of those wonderful people who seemed to know everyone, was plugged into local current events and was always available to help out people in the neighborhood. She attended all my kids' birthday parties and school events, and each time I was in the hospital to have another child, Dee cared for my boys until I came home with the new baby. Dee became a surrogate grandma to my kids and remained a treasured friend to me throughout her life.

Strategy: *Use your public library and all its resources to supplement your family adventures*

Public libraries are amazing sources of programs and resources to support your parenting goals.

Good or excellent public libraries fill the gap between school curriculums and your parenting goals. Librarians can assist in developing resources for research projects, give access to computers, and teach your children how to use databases that are often behind a paywall if accessed outside of the library's subscription. The amazing thing is that most services and programs are free for library card holders.

My kids were so proud to have a library card. It was their first piece of ID, making them feel recognized, important and grown up. Explore your library and take advantage of all the programs and services they offer.

Remember, your role as a parent is to educate, support and launch your children into the world to become fully functioning, responsible and capable people. Public libraries augment and support everything you're trying to achieve. The library can literally offer your children the world. Best yet, they do it for free! Librarians are crazy talented, motivated people. Embrace all they offer to support and inspire your children.

Part of the reason I opted to undertake a major addition to our home rather than move when we needed more space was that our house was located in a fantastic neighborhood. Our home is within blocks of the grade school, high school, library, and is walkable to retail, restaurants, and the train station. In addition to Dee and Bob, we had many great neighbors. Our neighborhood had families of all ages and as well as several elderly retirees. We had the very good fortune to live in a vibrant community of good people. My choice to get a larger house for my growing family was either to move or remodel. As they both would have cost roughly the same, and I could make our existing house into the perfect house for us, I elected to remodel and add a second story. We lived through the turmoil for roughly six months, but we viewed the time living in the construction as an adventure, marveling at the progress and changes as our baby house was transformed into a big house.

Strategically to get to know my neighbors better, when Nate and Jack were in elementary school and Avery a toddler, I decided to organize a block party.

I believed that the more we all knew each other and each other's kids, the better for us all. I grew up in the 60's and 70's when most moms were stay-at-home. I enjoyed the freedom to roam the neighborhood and once skilled on my bike, the town. I wanted to ensure that my kids and the other kids in the neighborhood could roam freely. I believed that the more the families in the neighborhood developed relationships, the safer and better it would be for everyone – especially our kids.

The first block party was a huge success. Everyone had such a great time that after the first one, block parties became both a neighborhood and family tradition with 18-24 families coming to each event. My kids, our neighbors, everyone looked forward to the events and everyone contributed. We closed the street, dragged trampolines to front yards; set up tables, chairs and firepits into the street; we had music, catered food and shared dishes, rented bouncy slides, etc. We had games for kids, adults, and families. We talked and partied, had water guns and water balloons, ate, and played from late afternoon until around midnight. Lighting was provided by outdoor lights in the trees, front porch lights and firepits. As neighbors, we became closer and more invested in each other through these mostly every other year events.

Our city is over 150 years old, and we live in the original part of town. As a result, our neighborhood had greater diversity than a typical new subdivision, so our block party participants ranged in age from their 80s to babes in arms. I think the muti-generational aspect also made the events more beneficial for all as we socialized with people who we might not have otherwise engaged with in our normal day-to-day lives and activities.

What I was unable to offer my children in the way of extended family, I was able to find and nurture through relationships with others who met those needs. Roughly every other year block parties provided a chance for all of us to re-visit and strengthen our community connections. To support that connectivity, I also put together and distributed a neighborhood sheet listing names of everyone in each family - parents and kids, our addresses, phone numbers, and email addresses. Everyone benefited. I continued the tradition until Nate reached high school, a time when my sons' attitudes and concept of entertainment shifted away from this type of activity.

Just as I believe most people are good and willing to help if asked, it just took a little extra effort and a willingness to create opportunities for us to make and strengthen connections. As mentioned previously, I added an above ground swimming pool to our backyard when Nate was 7, Jack almost 5 and

Avery around 2 years old. To both manage and encourage guests, I bought a flag with a pink flamingo on it and when we displayed the pink flamingo flag on our front porch, it meant open swim at the Munn's. Anyone from the neighborhood was welcome. The only rule I had was that kids had to BYOP – Bring Your Own Parent. I had zero interest in being lifeguard to a pool full of active children. The BYOP rule kept the number of guests manageable and added another layer of connection within our neighborhood to ensure that I kept my adult relationships solid. I also enjoyed it when any of my elderly neighbors came by to sit on the back patio and watch the kids swim. I typically joined them and tried to seat us out of splash range.

Between the block parties and visits around the pool, we all stayed connected to the older folks. Dee, Stella, and Violet especially engaged with my kids. They shared stories which the kids who at first only listened to be polite, but soon looked forward to hearing - appreciating how different their lives were growing up from ours. This relationship also evolved into the kids helping out with yardwork and shoveling the driveways and sidewalks of the elderly folks who we had come to love and appreciate.

To the extent your town has them, I suggest reading your city's newsletter or website, park district catalog and library newsletter to find sponsored activities and events that your family might enjoy. Again, adventures don't have to be huge or grand, just new, different, interesting, or exciting. If your city has annual events that your family enjoys, participation can become part of your family traditions.

For many years, it was my neighborhood responsibility to reserve a place for me, my kids, and several families in the neighborhood for the 4th of July Parade. Some years, one of my sons would push Violet and/or Stella in a wheelchair the 5 blocks to our typical parade location so that the older ladies could also enjoy the event as part of our group. Our town has an awesome parade which was such a big deal that I had to save our place 48 hours beforehand to get a good spot. As the kids grew older, the tradition evolved to include swimming in our pool after the parade with the older folks, often watching from our patio while the kids swam and played in the pool. This tradition evolved again to include Dee's adult children, and their kids. We continued the tradition until Dee died, but by then, my kids had already established social media connects with her grandkids and still stay connected. Family is not limited by a blood connection. Family is about shared experiences, history, and traditions.

My kids were truly raised by a village. They felt connected and safe in our neighborhood. They felt like quasi family at our daycare providers' homes and knew that their friends were always welcome in our house. It took extra effort to build this sense of community, but to this day, 31+ years since I bought this house, this is still an amazing community with neighbors always available to help each other when needed. I joked in 1993 when I moved here that I lived in "Mayberry" where everyone seemed to know each other's business, but I soon came to appreciate and nurture the social fabric and relationships that connect us. Most of the elderly folks have died or moved into assisted living, and some families have moved away, but new younger families have moved in and feel welcomed.

While our daycare providers and neighborhood went a long way towards substituting for extended family, I also consciously looked for ways to nurture our own family ties. As I've indicated most days, meals were eaten together as a family. We sat around the kitchen table without screens or phones. Once a month or so, we might have a special movie night when we ordered pizza or better yet, prepared homemade pizzas and watched a movie during dinner, but otherwise, we sat at the kitchen or dining room table together and talked. Everyone stayed at the table until everyone was done eating and talking.

Homemade pizzas are a fun tradition in our house that my 20+ year old kids still enjoy to this day. I buy cheap pizza dough mix, several packages of pepperoni, shredded mozzarella cheese and pizza sauce. I also cut up pineapple, set out lots of spices – Italian, onion, red peppers, garlic, etc. – and occasionally a cut up mushrooms, peppers, onions, or leftover bratwurst. The fun of homemade pizzas is that everyone gets their own cookie sheet and gets to custom make their own pizza with whatever combination and amount of ingredients they want. We each have to spread our own dough to fill our pan and invariably, Jack always needs help to stretch his dough to fill the pan. Jack's need for assistance always brings forth kind spirited taunting from Nate and Avery. While not the most nutritious choice for dinner, the meal aways has two vegetables as sides plus fruit. The value of homemade pizzas was the sense of fun, the pleasure in making their dinner exactly as each of us wanted and specialness of the meal, which is why it became a tradition that we continue to enjoy.

> **Strategy:** *Make dinnertime family time.*
>
> *I tried to move our dinner time to accommodate after school activities and sports so we could all still eat together. Dinner time became our daily clearing house of information. Our conversations helped cement good experiences and offer thoughts, advice or comfort for the things that weren't so good or address issues that one of us was struggling with.*
>
> *I also occasionally shared age appropriate tales about friends at the office or provided anecdotes from my childhood that were relevant to issues raised by my kids. This gave the kids insight into what I had experienced growing up and things that happened to me while we were apart.*

It's easy to create family traditions centered around birthdays, school milestones and holidays. As mentioned in the Empathy section, we had fun birthday parties in our home. To make it festive, I always decorated the living and dining room with streamers, banners, and balloons. The kids loved to have balloon fights and likewise loved ripping down the streamers a week or so after the big day. Birthdays were all about making the birthday kid feel special as well as enjoying friends, games, and fun. Every guest left the birthday party with a goodie bag filled with items earned while playing games. We always opened presents from the guests near the end of the party while everyone was eating cake. Friends were thanked for their gifts at the time and also received a thank-you note afterwards.

The other birthday tradition we had was that the birthday person got to pick their favorite meal for me to make for dinner or they could choose to have us go to a restaurant of their choosing for their birthday dinner. Almost invariably, the kids selected Old Country Buffet. I appreciated not having to cook and with four birthdays in our family each year, it also ensured that the kids had regular opportunities to reinforce proper behavior while eating out.

After each of my kids was born, I purchased a schoolhouse shaped frame engraved with my child's name. Each year, I bought school pictures. Wallet sized photos were added to the frames that hung in in our upstairs hallway. I also bought and hung personalized growth charts for each child to record height measurements. The growth charts have spots for seven photos. Several times each year, typically around birthdays and holidays, I'd measure each of the kids to mark their heights and note the date. As the charts only went up to 5' 2", all the final markings for each of my children are on the wall above the charts. In addition to being fun mementoes, the schoolhouses and growth charts served as visible evidence that the kids were achieving milestones. If you have more than one child, the charts and photos can also be beneficial for the younger child(ren) to be able to compare themselves against their older siblings when the older kids were their age. It's natural for children to compare themselves to others, especially siblings, and having access to photos and heights of siblings when they were the age of the younger child can make a fairer comparison.

Sometimes you have the opportunity to participate in traditions of others and take them on as your own. Both my sons played high school football and developed friendships with many of their teammates. As the boys got older, Thanksgiving became a time for our family to join the annual Turkey Bowl with football friends' families. Several families had been playing an annual game early on Thanksgiving morning between the sons and dads since their boys were little. As our sons had become friends during high school football, they invited our family to participate in their tradition. The Turkey Bowl is a time to drink coffee, juice or hot cocoa, visit with people we generally only see once a year and especially after the kids went off to college, a time for all the boys to see and reconnect with their former high school teammates. It's also interesting to watch as the dads pass the torch to their sons to keep the football game competitive.

For us, Thanksgiving was also the time to set up the Christmas tree and the Christmas village. I always cook the traditional turkey and all the trimmings for Thanksgiving. To highlight the spirit and meaning of the holiday, early on, I asked my children to think about what they were thankful for and be ready to share those thoughts at dinner time. As the years have passed, this has become a favorite time for me as my children understand the importance of this reflection and share genuinely heartfelt thoughts. I am very impressed with the perception and thoughtful expressions of gratitude from my children, especially when they reflect empathy for others and appreciation of issues well beyond themselves. As part of their comments, they each typically also share how important our family is to them. Our reflections and traditions help strengthen our personal and family bonds.

Christmas was a time for many traditions focused on baking goodies to give to our neighbors and friends, purchasing another building for our Christmas village, and each child selecting a new special Christmas ornament. We lived near a florist and nursey that set up 25-30 Christmas trees, each decorated with a different theme. Each year, we went to nursery, in November or December to purchase a special Christmas ornament. The owners of the nursery also made it an event, offering free hot cocoa, hot cider, coffee, and cookies. Unfortunately, the company went out of business in 2020, and we haven't found a suitable alternative. But for roughly 14-15 years, each of my kids was able to wander around, look at ornaments and finally decide on the perfect ornament for them each year.

Strategy: *Build traditions that support your family values and are enjoyable.*

Holidays, birthdays, and milestones like graduations all offer the chance to create something special that can develop into a family tradition. Traditions should be something the family anticipates and enjoys.

Many of our traditions evolved out of something we did once that we decided to repeat. It doesn't matter if the initial activity was planned by the city, the school, or your own idea. For example, high school coaches requested that their players participate in an outing to bag food for the non-profit Feed My Starving Children. I joined each of my children at these events as contributing in this manner was consistent with my Peace Corps goals and experience.

At our library each year, we also select 1-2 cards from the giving trees around the end of year holidays. The library coordinates with local shelters and organizations to take requests from needy families. Library patrons then decide which items they'd like to purchase to donate to fill the requests. While we didn't know the recipients of our gifts, it feels more personal than just giving money to an organization.

We also make at least one annual trip as a family to Chicago during the holidays. The city is so beautiful and festive. We typically take in a professional play or musical, have a meal, explore a museum and visit the Christkindel Market. While our plans vary each year, it's something we all enjoy and anticipate.

As part of our tradition, personal ornaments can only be put on the tree by the person to whom they belong. Our family tree has ornaments ranging from licensed characters to animals, birds, sea creatures, trucks, spaceships, fighter jets, mythical creatures, and gaudy decorations. All of the ornaments reflect my kids at a stage of their life and thus make our tree special. It's my intent that when any of the kids are ready to form their own families, they'll take their personal ornaments with them as the foundation for their own family Christmas trees. If they have children, perhaps they will find a way to continue our tradition of enabling their children to select a new, special ornament each year.

As mentioned earlier, not long after Nate was born, I decided to start a Christmas Village. We started with about 4-5 buildings and some extra people, trees, and accessories. Then each year, we assembled our Christmas village around Thanksgiving and purchased at least one new building that year. Often, trying to decide on just one new building failed and resulted in buying more than one building and perhaps additional accessories. As a result, after 20+ years, our village fills five card tables, my desk, and an end table – an area over 15' long and 2-4' deep virtually filling our sunroom.

Our Christmas village wasn't something just to admire, instead the kids loved to play with the people, animals and vehicles. We also have an ice rink that has 6 ice skaters that move around as if skating as it plays one of several Christmas carols. The characters have magnets on their feet that enable them to glide around the rink and appear to ice skate. One of the figures skates on one leg, with the other elevated. If we don't get this character in exactly the right place counterbalanced by the correct other characters, at some point he wiggles, shakes, and ultimately falls down. We've named this character "drunken dad" and cheer and laugh when he starts to wabble and ultimately, face plants. Quite a few of our villagers have been glued back together after having been accidentally dropped while the kids played with the village. But that's ok, it just makes our village more personal. Many times over the years, we'd turn off all the lights in the house except for the Christmas tree and the Christmas village. In the semi-darkness we'd talk in soft voices about what it would be like to live in our Christmas village. We'd consider which job we'd like to have and where we'd want to live. Our village is a magical place and part of our family traditions.

The third year of our having our Christmas village created a poignant memory that I recall every year when we set it up. During that year, the company that makes the village introduced a building labeled Jack's Diner. While our village has a Victorian feel, and Jack's Diner was more a 1950's vintage, I decided we had to have it in honor of my son, Jack. Unfortunately, during that holiday season, I'd been very busy with work and didn't have the opportunity to get out to buy it until December 23rd. Our local store was sold out, but an employee called and confirmed that another nearby store had one, so we drove 10-11 miles to that location to buy it.

When we arrived, I put Jack who was just over 1 year's old in the umbrella stroller while 3 ½ year old Nate walked. Nate was roaming around the Christmas section nearby looking at all the amazing sights. I found the Diner and was struggling to maneuver the stroller through the narrow aisles within the Christmas section while carrying the Diner in its box under my other arm. I called to Nate to say that we were leaving. As he jogged back towards us, Nate tripped and fell, hitting his cheekbone on the corner of a display counter on the way down. Nate immediately began screaming, crying, and bleeding. Thankfully, while falling, he'd missed his eye, but his cheek was cut and gushing blood. As I picked up Nate to comfort him and assess his injury, he screamed at me, "This is your fault! This wouldn't have happened if we didn't have to get that stupid diner." Knife through my heart as that very thought had just crossed my mind.

The commotion caused by Nate's accident scared Jack who then also started crying. Fortunately, employees and other shoppers rushed over to help us. I handed Jack to an employee and focused on Nate. Somehow, we managed with paper towels and band-aids to get Nate's bleeding under control. I paid for the Diner and left the store. We'd initially gone out right after dinner, so it was late when we got home. Despite the band aids, the cut on Nate's cheek kept seeping blood and wouldn't stay closed. I was afraid to put him to bed without medical care and realized that he likely needed a few stitches. I called my dad who agreed to let me drop off Jack, who fell asleep in his carrier on the drive over, while I took Nate to the emergency room. It was around 9:00 p.m. when Nate and I headed out from my dad's house.

Nate was completely exhausted, upset by the events of the day and frightened by all the hubbub in the emergency room. The emergency room was rather busy that night, and with a non-critical injury, it took a long time for us to be seen. Finally, it was our turn and after the initial contact to collect insurance info and assess the injury, we were moved into a curtained off area. The doctor determined that Nate did need stitches. The doctor instructed me to hold gauze that contained a local, topical anesthetic on Nate's check while he attended to other people in the ER. I sat on the edge of his bed trying to press and hold the gauze against Nate's check long enough for it numb the side of his face. However, Nate had finally had enough and began yelling, thrashing, and crying. I tried to calm and reassure him, while also keeping the anesthetic soaked gauze in place.

Suddenly, two firemen dressed in full fireman gear and helmets pulled back our curtain and stepped up to the bed that Nate was lying on. They'd obviously come to the hospital after a call and had dirt or smoke smudges on their faces. They looked huge, like superheroes. Nate and I were both startled by their sudden appearance. In fact, Nate was so surprised that he stopped screaming and just gaped wide eyed at them.

One of the firemen asked, "What's going on little buddy?" Nate just stared, whimpering quietly. I briefly replied that my son was getting ready for a few stitches. Still looking at Nate, the fireman said, "If you promise to be brave, we have a special present for you." Nate nodded and stared with huge eyes as one of the fireman walked away. The fireman soon returned with a firetruck and handed it to Nate. The truck was about 2 feet long, complete with a battery powered ladder that went up, down, rotated and extended. It also had flashing lights and a siren. Nate loved trucks and this was by far the coolest toy truck he or I had ever seen. Nate was mesmerized and clutched the truck to his chest. I looked at the firemen with tears of gratitude spilling from my eyes and said, "Thank you so much. Merry Christmas."

The doctor gave Nate four small stitches and as promised, Nate was brave while clutching the fire truck to his chest. It was just after midnight by the time we left the hospital. Overcome from exhaustion, Nate almost immediately fell asleep in his car seat, still holding his amazing fire truck on his lap. As I drove back home on mostly deserted streets, I came around a bend before the incline of an overpass. Just as I drove up the hill, I noticed for the first time the full moon and the millions of stars in the clear sky in front of me. Suddenly it crossed my mind that it was Christmas Eve. As I looked at the sky and glanced in the rearview mirror to see my son safely asleep in the backseat with a band aid covering the stitches on his check, I was filled with a profound sense of gratitude and peace. I sent up a silent prayer to thank God. For the rest of the drive to my dad's house to get Jack, I was overwhelmed with love for my sons and a sense of surety that I'd made the right choice in creating my wonderful family.

As a footnote, Nate's fire truck had a prominent place on his dresser for the next 10-12 years until he entered high school. He still has the truck, though safely packed away on a shelf in his closet.

Traditions and adventures are a chance to strengthen family bonds, build memories and create a sense of continuity over time. Adventures may also include vacations. Similar to our nearby adventures, I chose vacation destinations that would be fun and meaningful for the kids and present us with the chance to share discoveries together. During summers we might rent a house or cabin near a lake for swimming and exploring. Most of our vacations tended to be 1-4 days over a weekend. We also took day trips to explore caves, ride horses, go to Santa's Village, visit nature centers or children's museums, experience historic re-enactments, ride antique trains, and experience other kid friendly activities. One year we traveled to a wild animal reserve in central IL and spent the night in a caboose that had been converted into a living space complete with bunk beds, a very small bathroom, and a kitchenette. Being able to sleep in the nature park – especially in a caboose - and have the ability to explore the nature park and watch the herd animals migrate was an amazing experience that we all enjoyed. Living near the Wisconsin border, we also visited the Dells for many years during a fall or winter weekend to play in the indoor waterparks and stay overnight during the cheaper off-season.

What makes an outing into an adventure is really just that it's special, different, and something that we planned and looked forward to experiencing together. We typically didn't spend a lot of money but did have a great time and our conversations during our drive home and subsequent dinner times helped cement the experiences and memories.

My objective for our vacations was always for us to learn or discover something new, expand our world and not leave me completely exhausted. Growing up, I'd had the chance to go camping with my best friend's family and during the Peace Corps had also gone backpacking/camping. When they were little, I'd imagined how cool it would be to teach my children the joy of camping and being in nature. However, I soon realized that maintaining a campsite with young kids on my own was just more work than I could manage, so we limited our "camping" expeditions to occasionally sleeping in our tent in the backyard. But I did try to get my children into nature regularly. Before I had kids, every weekend, 52 weeks a year, my dog Ripely and I hiked in one of the nearby state parks. For me, being in nature is both physical and spiritual. It calms me, grounds me and it makes me feel connected in a fundamental way to the earth, to this world. Nature is my church. While I wasn't up to teaching my children the fun of camping on my own, through many of our adventures, they each developed a love of nature, and all have embraced hiking and exploring state and national parks with friends.

Other than a wonderful trip to NYC to visit my Peace Corps friend Patrick for a kid friendly exploration of NYC when the kids were 8, 5 ½ and 3, our early vacations were limited to places we could reach driving. I'd find a place to stay that had a couple of bedrooms and a kitchen so I could keep the kids fueled with good nutritious food. Even on vacation, I tried to keep some semblance of our regular routines to help prevent the kids from becoming stressed or overtired. Not eating out for every meal also meant that I could spend more money on activities without breaking our budget. The more varied or unusual the activities the better. Our vacations were always adventurous and fun.

As discussed in the Empathy section, I wanted to give my kids the world. I also wanted them to appreciate and experience international travel. When Avery was 14 or 15, I applied for passports for all my kids. Starting in 2019 and roughly every other year since, some or all of my kids and I have taken an amazing vacation together. Typically, I find a range of dates during the summer that work for all of us. We agree on a destination and then we all contribute to developing a terrific itinerary that is both detailed and maintains flexibility. We buy advance tickets for "must have" experiences to save time and we limit our luggage to carry-on only. Nothing gives me greater pleasure than to share these trips with my grown children. I hope to continue this tradition as long as possible. It's even more enjoyable for me to travel with my grown children as once we're on the ground at our destination, they tend to take the lead and I just get to relish the experiences, our time together and take out my credit card as needed.

I am also elated that my children have completed international and domestic travel with friends. They truly see the world without limits. Having traveled together, I have noted that their objectives with travel almost always include efforts to understand and appreciate the local culture, embrace the outdoors, enjoy the local food, and strive to understand the history, traditions, and engage with local people. When my kids travel, they stay in youth hostels if possible and find ways to connect with others. We all actively engage with people on trains, in the market and other sites. I'm elated that my children don't travel to get "Instagram moments," rather, they travel to learn, challenge themselves, grow, appreciate, and expand their perceptions and understanding of the world, and hopefully make connections with others like themselves from other parts of the country or world.

A key aspect of traditions and adventures is that your family is all focused on the same activity. These activities matter because you all temporarily set aside the other distractions in your lives and come together to do or experience something together. Adventures don't have to be profound, just enjoyable, and hopefully different in some way that is intriguing or interesting. If they are repeatable, such as something related to a holiday or other periodic event, they can evolve into traditions – something that you all look forward to that both strengthens prior memories and creates new ones. As detailed above and below in Tales from the Front, we participated in many annual activities sponsored by our town and Park District. At the end of the day, it's just something enjoyable that you can do together, and if it's repeatable, it can become a tradition. For that period of time, family is front and center with each of you. Try to use that time to reinforce the joy of being together and the fun of new discoveries or favorite activities. Those experiences and memories reinforce your love and connection and strengthen your family bonds.

Tales from the Homefront:

Nightly family time in the pool. Installing an above ground swimming pool in our yard when my children were young was a fabulous decision. Our house sits on a small hill which enabled me to design a solution that incorporated a patio, a deck, and an above ground pool with the feel of an in-ground pool. I also purchased an outdoor shower which was really just a wooden platform, piping and a showerhead with an on/off handle that was connected to a garden hose – but the kids loved it. As we live in northern IL, I also installed a gas heater to extend the season for our pool.

I loved our pool for several reasons. First the kids became fearless of water and good swimmers. At the time of installation, while Nate could touch bottom with his head above water, for Jack and Avery, the water was over their heads. As a result of our pool, all three learned to swim. We started with life jackets, progressed to floaties and soon, they were all swimming. While they all had fun wearing goggles or snorkeling masks to search for toys at the bottom of the pool, by the second season, all my kids were opening their eyes under water and splashing each other in the face.

What I loved most though was that on summer evenings after dinner, we generally swam and played in the pool. I'd wash the dinner dishes and clean up the kitchen while the kids put on their swimsuits. We'd pull off the solar cover and while I ran into the house to put on my bathing suit, the kids would throw the blow up toys into the pool. Then we'd all jump in the pool together. As a single working mother with a management position, three kids and two dogs, I was never not busy. But the pool gave me 30-45 minutes each summer evening to just set everything aside and play with and enjoy my children. Blow up toys are cheap, and we had ride on inflatables for battles, pool rings, and beach balls. We made whirlpools, competed to see who could make the biggest splash, stood, or walked on our hands, did summersaults, played volleyball, basketball, etc. Pure unadulterated fun and a chance each night to unwind and laugh together.

Afterwards, the kids might take a quick outdoor shower, shrieking at the cold water. After putting the solar cover back on the pool and drying ourselves off, we'd head inside. While the kids were pre-pubescent, when we came into the house, they stripped in the kitchen, dumped their bathing suits into the kitchen sink and raced naked through the house up the stairs to their bedrooms. The "naked run" was all good clean fun and another treat as my streaking children screamed and laughed while dashing upstairs to put on their pajamas. I used the time to hang up the wet bathing suits on the clothesline in the basement and load the damp pool towels into the dryer. By the time I got out of my suit and had put on my pajamas, the kids had brushed their teeth and were ready for story time and bed. A delightful way for us all to wind down our summer evenings. Those are such fond memories.

Christmas family photo: As a single parent, especially before smart phones became ubiquitous, I was rarely in family pictures as I was generally the person behind the camera. However, I love photography and treasure old pictures of me and my extended family from when I was growing up. A Christmas family picture was a tradition I implemented after Nate was born. Up until 2006, the kids and I would go to J.C. Penney's or Sears (whoever had the best deal) to have a family photo professionally taken. However, after we adopted our puppies, Anthony and Murray, we all agreed that our puppies were part of the family and had to be in our Christmas picture too.

I own a Canon T-50, 35mm camera and tripod, so each year, I'd set up a location in our sunroom, the living room, the backyard, etc. for our annual family photo. I mounted the camera on the tripod, arranged additional lighting and used the self-timer. I pushed the button and then ran around behind my kids and the puppies. The first year was complete, utter pandemonium! Puppies squirming, kids laughing and misbehaving, puppies falling off the ottoman, kids and puppies wrestling or not looking at the camera . . . the outtakes from the 24 pictures taken that day still make me belly laugh. While our subsequent annual photo shoots became progressively less chaotic as the kids and dogs got older, I rarely got more than a couple decent shots to choose from as our "official" Christmas photo that was sent out with our holiday cards. Those pictures and outtakes are priceless to me, and I expect as my kids get older, they too will be grateful for those memories and pictures.

The Cardboard Boat Regatta: In June 1974, Crystal Lake IL had its first annual Cardboard Boat Race. Over the years, the event grew into a Regatta with participants from all over the world coming to compete to be the fastest boat in each category as well as vying for dozens of trophies (many trophies are made of cardboard) in other categories to encourage creativity and add to the fun of the event. Well it might seem that boats made of cardboard would dissolve or fall apart once exposed to water, multiple layers of cardboard and structural braces made of several layers of carboard taped together make the boats sturdy. Multiple coats of marine varnish or polyurethane make the cardboard boats waterproof. It just takes time, a large workspace, a good design and patience.

I always loved watching the Regatta and took my kids. The first time I was laid off unexpectedly in 2006, I was supported by a good severance package and decided that I'd use my extra free time between job searching that summer to build a boat so our family could enter the competition. My children were 8, 5 ½ and 2 ½ that summer.

Using instructions I found on the event website and large sheets of industrial grade carboard obtained from the Park District, I used our driveway as a workspace to construct two, two-seater cardboard kayaks that were 16' long and just over 2' wide that became the hulls of a catamaran. At that time, my boys were fascinated with Godzilla. I'd grown up loving Godzilla and had purchased many low quality Godzilla movies on VHS for the kids. Based on their love of all things Godzilla, I decided to incorporate Godzilla into our boat. I cut out and painted a 7' tall carboard Godzilla to straddle our catamaran. While I was proud of our entry and thought it was pretty amazing, the creativity that is on display at this annual event is truly astonishing. A quick internet search for "Crystal Lake cardboard regatta" can provide a sampling.

It took several months of measuring, drawing, cutting, folding, and assembling the boats on our driveway, plus another week to paint and add the multiple coats of marine varnish. To keep it cheap, we went to one of the local paint stores and purchased the tinting errors paint that was available for around $1 a quart, selecting colors that were close enough to what we wanted for Godzilla. The kids loved watching and learning as our craft came together, and virtually everyone in the neighborhood made a point of stopping by multiple times during construction to visit and watch how our boats were coming together. Neighbors and friends also helped me get the boat to the Lake for final assembly. Together our friends and neighbors formed a very substantial cheering section for us at the Regatta when we launched the "SOS Godzilla."

We entered the Regatta three times over the years, and while we didn't win any trophies in 2006, as we prepared to launch, the local tv news station, WGN, featured our boat in their news report – so we were on tv. I think the design and my three kids all in life preservers and sunglasses made a cute feature for the news. In 2009, I constructed a pirate ship of my own design, but the boat was too short and despite our efforts, we just spun in circles as we paddled and had to be propelled by two lifeguards to complete the course. Humiliation!

Our final entry, and first winning boat was in 2014, when Nate was 16, Jack 13 ½ and Avery 10 ½. I returned to our original catamaran structure, this time creating a 5' tall female zombie to straddle the kayaks and named our boat "The Rowing Dead." At the time, the boys and I were avid viewers of *The Walking Dead* – me for the moral challenges, they for the zombies. The boys agreed to participate, but only if they could do so with their friends rather than us as a family – in other words, Avery and I wouldn't be in the crew. I understood their feelings, and for me it was really about not having our embarrassing effort in 2009 be our final remembrance of the Regatta. My pleasure came from being part of the event and I derived satisfaction in building a great boat so that my boys and their friends could compete in this annual event.

Unfortunately, the evening before the race, Charlie (one of the crew) stopped by to see the boat and confirm plans for the morning. I had the kayaks on drop clothes in the living room and was just applying the final coat of marine varnish. I was also doing laundry and had to run to the basement to move laundry from the washer to the dryer. I told Charlie he could help if he wanted and showed him where I'd left off applying the varnish. When I returned, I found that Charlie had poured the rest of the varnish into the seats of one of the kayaks in the thought that more was better. Three layers of carboard were saturated with varnish – effectively destroying one of the kayaks! I was aghast. Stunned. There was nothing I could do. The damage was done. While I realized that Charlie had just destroyed the integrity of that kayak by saturating vs. sealing the cardboard, I held my tongue. There was no way I could undo the damage. My choice was either to acknowledge that Charlie had just destroyed months of work and pull out of tomorrow's event or feign ignorance. I didn't want to crucify Charlie for effectively ruining our boat, nor did I want to cancel our participation. I thanked Charlie for his "help" and sent him home reminding him to come to our house early the next day to help transport the kayaks and zombie to the beach for final assembly of the catamaran. I said nothing to my children about what had happened.

While I knew our boat was essentially ruined, I also knew that the Lake racecourse was in 4-5 foot deep water and ran parallel to the beach. While I fully expected the seats of one side of the catamaran to quickly disintegrate, I knew the boys wouldn't drown as they'd be wearing life preservers, the water wouldn't be over their heads, and they could all swim.

As it neared time four our boat to launch, Avery and I helped the boys carry the catamaran to chute. The boys climbed in, and Avery and I trotted down the beach through the crowds towards the finish line to follow their progress. Not long after launch, the seats in the damaged kayak disintegrated and the two boys on that side dropped into the water. However, they were not giving up. The boys started to run in the chest high water to propel the craft forward while the other two paddled furiously in the intact kayak. Due to the difference in speeds of the two kayaks, steering was challenging. In addition, the zombie in the middle blocked eye contact between the boys in the water and the boys in the boat. The emotions of the unexpected issue made communication among the crew even more challenging. In the heat of the competition, the boys accidentally slammed the intact part of the boat into a buoy. The force of the impact caused the intact kayak to be crushed. Suddenly, all four boys were in the water. However, they were still not giving up! They grabbed what was left of the boat and ran/swam to propel it across the finish line.

While we failed to win for speed, our boat earned the trophy for "Ugliest Boat" due to my hideous zombie, and the kids all had their names printed in the local newspaper. I was delighted that despite all the calamities, we were able to end with such a memorable, victorious result. To this day, our trophy for Ugliest Boat is proudly on display in our living room.

Adventures in nature: Weekends were always busy as we had errands, yardwork, and housecleaning. As the kids got older, youth sports also factored in. While time was limited, we typically carved out a couple hours during the weekend to visit one of the nearby state parks to walk the trails or find time to visit a playground when they were younger. My objective was to find something that we could all do together that was fun and got us out into nature. My children saw it as a chance not only to spot, but to capture wildlife - frogs, turtles, toads, snakes, butterflies or insects. They all came armed with shoe boxes, bug cages and nets.

My rule was to let any captured creature live at our house – in a fish tank, bug cage or kiddie pool on the front porch – for one week. As part of our home remodel, we had added a big wraparound front porch, so our creatures were in an adequately sheltered location. After one week, we had to return our creature guests to the wild so they could go back to their families. I figured that most creatures could survive for a week under our inexpert care without dying. I also didn't want any other pets except our dogs and the ability to interact with various creatures for a week or less (many toads escaped and took up residence in our yard under the pool deck) was a compromise that satisfied the kids and hopefully didn't harm these amazing wild creatures.

We all learned a lot from our wildlife interactions. One of my favorites was when Nate caught a praying mantis late in the fall. We kept "Praynee" in a large empty pretzel jar stocked with sticks and leaves. All of us used bug nets to catch insects – crickets, flies, moths, fireflies - that we could add to the jar. Once an insect or two had been added to the jar, our entire family would literally sit around the table staring at Praynee waiting for her to snatch one of the insects and eat it. We'd all exclaim with awe whenever Praynee stuck. It was truly captivating. Our own nature documentary. Our own reality tv.

Weekend Excursions: I wanted my kids to be curious tourists even nearby. Our house is located roughly 55 miles NW of Chicago, and we made many visits to the Field Museum, Shedd Aquarium, Museum of Science and Industry, the Art Institute, Lincoln Park and Brookfield Zoos, Peggy Notebaert Museum, the Indiana Dunes, and multiple Children's Museums. We also explored flea markets, county fairs, Santa's Village, and professional as well as local high school live theater productions.

For us, weekend excursions were almost like mini vacations due to their impact. We planned for them and always got up early so we could get to our destination near opening time and spend a full day. We were totally focused on the activity and each other. I always took lots of pictures and generally let the kids browse the gift shop to see if they found something they wished to buy with their money (I suspended the wait one week rule) or occasionally I'd make a family purchase (using my money) to commemorate our visit.

After every weekend adventure during our drive home before they fell asleep and over the coming days, each of us shared what we liked best and least about the day. Similar to our "high, low, medium, cool at school" discussions over dinner, this helped solidify the experience as well as expand our perspectives as each of us appreciated the unique details that others had enjoyed most. For me, it was insightful to observe the differences in what each of my kids focused on, and by sharing our individual observations each of us truly found the experience even richer.

Laugh loudly and often.

Rainy days are perfect for building blanket forts.

If you introduce your kids to The Far Side and Calvin & Hobbes, don't be surprised when you have a dozen angry, psychotic snowmen on your front lawn.

There's a reason some creatures eat their young.

Jigsaw puzzles are food for your children's brains and a fun family activity.

Let your kids be kids for as long as possible.

VALUES SUMMARY

As detailed herein, I recommend that you consciously identify your fundamental values and beliefs as you think about how you'll parent, nurture and create experiences to support your child(ren) and help them become the best version of themselves. Whether you have three, five, seven, or some other number of values is immaterial, what is important is that you use your core values to guide you and keep you on track as you navigate your role and responsibilities as a parent.

Good kids or bad kids don't just happen. All of us are the product of our environment, our experiences, our choices, and the people who impacted our lives. By modeling and teaching your kids your fundamental values, I believe that your children have a better chance of becoming responsible, confident, caring, independent young adults.

I hope that you've found the ideas and examples in this book beneficial to help you to think about and identify the values, principles, and lessons you'll strive to share with your child(ren). I've shown my values again below. Whether you and I embrace similar values or not, doesn't really matter. What matters is that you (and your partner) agree on which principles are most important to you and then lean into those values as you parent your kids.

Sally's Core Values and Guiding Principles:

- Consistency and Expectations

- Honesty and Transparency

- Empathy

- Consequences and Responsibility

- Delayed gratification, plus understanding money and credit

- Strategic thinking

- Family Adventures and Traditions

Being a parent can be overwhelming at times. There are so many things that you won't be able to control, and unexpected things will occur that you'll need to address on the fly. To strengthen your hand and reduce your stress, I encourage you to maintain a solid understanding of your values and guiding principles. They can serve as your roadmap as you consider opportunities and experiences to teach your child(ren) or help you determine how to deal with problems as they arise. Leaning into your values can create calm in the eye of the storm when the unexpected occurs to help you focus and move forward. As your child(ren) grow and develop, you'll be able to see examples that demonstrate your success in teaching those values. You'll also note when more work is needed; for example, if, like me, one of your teenagers finds lying expedient.

Knowing your values and guiding principles can also serve as a report card or yardstick against which you can evaluate all the ways you're succeeding as a parent while also highlighting areas that require more attention for all or perhaps only some of your children. I think it's safe to say that we all want our children to be healthy, well behaved, well liked, smart, talented, successful, etc. But, again, that doesn't just happen. It's your responsibility as their parent to teach and support them so that they can become their best selves. It's your job to fill their toolboxes with knowledge, skills, and the ability to make thoughtful choices. Just as it takes conscious effort and patience to obedience train a dog, so it takes conscious effort and patience to support your children so they can learn and develop into great people. I've encountered unruly, unpleasant kids and untrained dogs. It always makes me feel sad because I believe that they didn't have to be that way. With the right support, love and attention, they could have been so much better and had much happier, more fulfilling lives.

I encourage you and your partner to define your values and the kinds of experiences you'll strive to share with your child(ren). Decide what environment and atmosphere you want to try to create in your home to support your child(ren). Then act on those plans. Use some of the strategies I've outlined in this book to engage with your child(ren). Modify the strategies to be consistent with your values and develop other strategies that work for you and your family. So much of success in parenting comes from being mindful and being present. Mindful of what you're modeling for your child(ren) and mindful of how you're engaging with them. I think it's challenging to be successful without some kind of plan and difficult to be mindful without knowing your values and what you hope to achieve.

Once you've determined your values, think about the routines, the rituals, and the activities that you can incorporate into your lives to teach and reinforce those values for your kids. This book outlines the strategies, behaviors and routines I used to support my parenting values. Modify them to fit support your values. For example, if religion was one of your key values, you'd likely attend services regularly, have rituals around holy days and/or age milestones, you'd read the foundational book(s) and share stories that support the lessons and teachings of your faith. Likewise as you navigate life and have disputes, setbacks or achievements, use those incidences and connect those occurrences back to your religious beliefs and teachings. Similarly, if protecting the environment was a key value, you might involve your kids in planting and maintaining a garden, use alternative energy, actively avoid waste, avoid single use items, etc. and you'd explain both the benefits of these actions and help your children to adopt those planet friendly habits. Then you'd develop routines and behaviors to support those activities longer term. Whatever values you select, to model your values, think about the little actions, the choices and the behaviors that underpin them. Weave them into the fabric of your and your children's lives through your practices, your conversations and your activities.

As you embark or continue on your journey as parents, never forget that you and your partner are the most important resources for your child(ren). You are their first teachers. You are their protectors. Everything you do has the ability to nurture their souls, their minds, their imaginations, and their developing bodies. Or not. Without knowing your parenting goals and objectives, you're at risk of missing opportunities to positively influence your children and help them to flourish, vs. just survive. Invest in your children throughout their lives with time and encouragement. Help them discover and develop their passions and goals. Help them to learn to understand others and navigate the world. Help support them as they carve out their own life paths. Lead them and guide them as they blossom into their amazing selves.

Knowing, living, and teaching your values will help put you on the path to being a better parent, which should generate better outcomes for your child(ren). Your success is their success is everyone's success. We truly can make the world better one person at a time.

Dancing is good for the soul. Share the joy and fun of dancing with your children.

Build traditions.

A kiss makes an "owie" or "booboo" feel better.

I can't give you what I don't have.

I don't know when I've laughed so hard, been more tired or had such fun.

I'd walk through fire for any of my children.

TEENS

When my children were born, the internet was in its nascent stages and iPhones hadn't yet been invented. As mentioned, I was fine with my flip phone and my kids did not get smart phones until they were in high school. I believe that this positively benefited us in our family journey.

In high school my teens did use Snapchat and Instagram, but none of us were on Facebook. Until writing this book and creating an author website, my kids and I had limited our social media presence to LinkedIn. In addition because they were athletic, outgoing, and involved in multiple sports and clubs at school, most of my children's communication with friends was face-to-face while growing up, with their social media usage limited to texting and seeing who could have the longest streak on Instagram.

While my sons and I butted heads on occasion during their teen years, there was far less drama with my boys than with my daughter. Most of the arguments with my boys were over curfews or parties that I wouldn't let them attend. Nate and I also had a simmering feud over his decision to take what I felt were too many AP classes during his senior year of high school. My concern was that his extremely heavy class load risked ruining his GPA which could impact college scholarships. However, Nate took my concern as lack of confidence in his abilities.

My sons and I didn't argue about dating. They were fine waiting until they were 17 or older. Instead, we talked about college and used their junior and senior years to make visits to potential universities.

Strategy: *Teach your teens healthy skepticism and the importance of knowing the source and reliability of information.*

As your children and teens learn to safely navigate the internet, help them learn how to gather information and news from reliable, trusted sources.

The internet is both the wild west and a source of amazing information and opportunity. Teach your children to not accept information at face value and not to repost items without fully reading them and making an assessment as to their accuracy. We need to equip our kids with the ability and habit of examining sources of information to determine if there are biases or agendas that skew the information being presented. We need to instill in our children the ability to recognize when they are being presented with misinformation, false information, or biased information.

Provide you teens with the names of historically reliable news sources. Teach them to question, identify and understand any bias or agenda in the information that they ingest. Encourage them to read beyond the sound bite and understand information before sharing it. Equip them with the ability to see "the man behind the curtain" as they form their own opinions.

As your young adults begin forming opinions, are able to vote in elections, and take stances on political issues, engage with them. Share your thoughts about important issues and your rationale for the candidates you plan to support. Help your young adults to understand our institutions and processes. Guide them to reliable sources of information so they can gather factual information to form their own opinions. Whether your teens agree with you politically or not is less important than whether they are making decisions based on reliable, factual information or misinformation. Protect your young adults from being led astray by charlatans. Help them to see the world as it really exists, not as someone with an agenda tells them it is.

As with all stages of parenting, I had a plan and some strategies for the teenage years, but until you start to try to implement your strategies, there is always some uncertainty about how everything will play out. The criticism my sons regularly gave me as teens was not giving them more freedom. My sons were right, they were great kids, clearly responsible, and doing well in school. I had concerns about a few of their friends and recognizing that my influence was waning, I think I was trying to protect my boys a bit more than they needed.

But I also knew that each year of the teen years can be a massive increase in maturity for a child and I didn't want their futures derailed by doing something stupid urged on by one of their friends. It was also my perception observing my sons that group IQ can drop rapidly as more teens are together when trying to have fun. Not unlike "mob mentality," due to peer pressure and wanting to get along, the decision making process of a group of teens can quickly fall to the lowest common denominator of what might be deemed acceptable.

I'd also suggest that your ability to guide you children changes dramatically during the teenage years. By the age of 15 or 16, I realized that I could only lead my kids from behind. I could encourage and suggest, punish and hold them accountable, but really, they needed to step up and take the lead for their scholastic and future success. You can kick them in the ass all you want, but without their effort, trying to push your teens in a direction they don't want to go will likely have little impact other than to sour your relationship.

As you think about parenting teenagers, I would suggest that you keep two thoughts in the front of your mind at all times when trying to support your budding young adults and determine how best to support them:

1. **Teens don't have years of perspective and knowledge to fall back on.** As a result, things can take on greater significance, sometimes to levels that may seem irrational to you. Peer's opinions, embarrassment, heartbreak, can feel overwhelming and life shattering for your teen. Teens may be facing new emotions, issues, and experiences for the first time without the benefit of personal past history. They have no reason to assume that things will be ok after a negative experience. When they don't do well, feel foolish or embarrassed in front of their peers, it can feel devasting to them. Those emotions are real. Don't dismiss them or try minimize them, rather offer your support, and try to help your teen gain some perspective. Reassure them that they are loved and valued by you, your partner and their friends.

   Teens may become ultra self-conscious as they try to get comfortable with all the changes in their bodies and new additional hygiene routines. Even if they have older siblings and had Sex Ed in school, it's still all new to them. The changes may be frightening, embarrassing, and/or confusing. They also don't care about your experiences as a teen. For all they care, you lived when dinosaurs roamed the earth, and your experiences have nothing whatsoever in common with what they are experiencing. In some ways they're right, in others wrong. Do your best to be available and support them. Keep reaching out to engage with your teenagers even if they push you away.

2. **Teens are caterpillars in the process of turning (hopefully) into butterflies.** Puberty truly is a radical change. Everything about their bodies is changing. Their bodies are full of raging hormones and new emotions that teenagers are trying to understand and likely can't control. Wet dreams, menstruation, acne, hair in new places, body odors . . . teens can be walking wrecks trying to figure out how to control and respond to all these new things; and puberty's changes aren't consistent or predictable. Some days your teen will be faced with a raging five-alarm fire, other days will be smooth sailing, and others a yo-yo of emotions that change throughout the day. What makes it even more challenging is that neither they nor you know what kind of day it's going to be.

In addition, as part of the push/pull of this stage of their lives, your teens are being reminded by teachers and us that they need to make decisions about whether and where to go to college, and what to study if they go. Essentially, teenagers are being encouraged and pushed to make decisions and plans that can impact the rest of the lives. Is it any wonder that they can become stressed or feel overwhelmed at times? Try to be kind and patient with your teenagers. Which by the way will not always be easy.

Parenting my daughter as a teenager was vastly different from parenting my teenage boys. Like her brothers, Avery was, and is, very smart, talented, outgoing, and has lots of friends. However Avery tries to avoid confrontations if possible. If my teenage boys had an issue with me or my rules, they might raise the topic politely or throw it in my face, and we discussed it or argued but found a solution. If Avery felt I would object to something, she withheld that information and presented a request that I might agree to even if it was not completely accurate. While my sons were fairly open and communicative – even if our voices sometimes got loud - Avery tended to share information on a need-to-know basis and had no compunction about lying or withholding information to get what she wanted. I'd modeled honesty and my sons had rarely lied, so it took me a while to fully recognize Avery's behavior for what it was. Shame on me for being complacent and thinking that all three of my kids had fully embraced all my values.

As a parent, don't assume that reality is what you hope it is. Reality is reality, and it's our job as parents to recognize that. I could offer excuses and say that I was distracted by stresses at work, that I was overconfident from working through teen issues with my sons, and honestly, was exhausted from getting both my boys successfully off to college. However, I'd been a hellion as a teenager. Due to all the dysfunction and challenges following my parents' divorce, I had regularly lied to my mother and spent as much time as I could away from our house, so I really had no excuse for not anticipating and immediately recognizing Avery's behavior. I took my eye off the ball and inadvertently demonstrated to Avery that her strategies could work. My daughter got away with some things before I realized what was going on. As a result, my complacency taught Avery that her strategies worked and had put myself in the position of being reactive vs. proactive as a parent.

As I recognized these behaviors, I would ask my daughter more questions to ensure I had sufficient information before deciding if some requested activity was ok. I also occasionally told Avery that we'd have to discuss the matter later, especially when she presented requests to me while I was working at home and engrossed in work or meetings. While these tactics improved my understanding of the situations, they frustrated Avery and often resulted in more tension in our relationship. Occasionally, when I'd repeatedly said no to a request and provided my rationale, Avery would yell that she couldn't stand to be in the same house with me and would storm out.

When Avery stormed out of the house in anger after one of our many confrontations, I didn't let her take the car. While she typically reached out to a friend at those times, I didn't want my daughter behind the wheel when she was angry and frustrated with me. I also considered that someone storming out of the house as being similar to a 2-3 year old throwing a tantrum – flopping on the floor, kicking, and screaming. As a result, whatever Avery had been requesting before storming out became an absolute "No." She'd sealed her fate by her childishness. While that typically only added more fuel to the fire that was raging between us, I felt I had to enforce my authority as her parent and put an end to this toxic, childish behavior that was further damaging our relationship and our ability to communicate.

When my daughter periodically yelled in anger that she was 18, an adult and could do whatever she wanted, I'd remind her that as long as she lived in our house, she needed to respect me, our family rules, and my expectations. Depending on the tone of the conversation and my level of frustration, I occasional shot back that she was welcome to move out whenever she wanted and suggested that she not "let the door hit her on the ass on her way out." Parenting teens is not easy. As much as I knew I had to be rational and retain tight control of my emotions, at times my daughter just infuriated me.

Recognizing that we were in dangerous territory at those times, alarm bells typically rang in my head. I was generally able to rein it in a bit and in a more normal tone of voice say that while I wished Avery to stay, if she preferred to move out, she could take everything from her bedroom. Then I'd calmly tell her that while she'd always be welcome to come home no matter what, if she moved out in anger, I would not be paying for her college education nor would I provide further financial support. She'd be on her own. She'd need to get a job and support herself. Her choice. In some ways, I was calling her bluff and yet I always made sure to keep the door open. I was trying to remind Avery that her words and actions and decisions could have very negative and dire consequences, but that I would always love her.

Leaning into tough love generally enabled me to get my raging emotions – typically anger and frustration – under control. At those times, I always strove to make it perfectly clear that the ball was in my daughter's court. I wasn't trying to control her; I was giving her choices. While I was willing to state hard truths, I always tried to leave Avery a face saving way to step off the ledge. In my ultimatums, I communicated to my daughter that she'd always be welcome home – as long as she abided by our family rules and my expectations. Again, tough love. Not easy. But sometimes necessary.

The teen years were not the best of times, but due to my complacency, I needed to re-teach my daughter acceptable vs. unacceptable behavior, remind her of family expectations and re-establish civility in our relationship. I never wanted to push my daughter onto the streets. Likewise I refused to let my child live under my roof while acting in ways that violated our family values and disrespected me.

I've said many times that a key aspect of being a parent is working ourselves out of a job. From my teens' perspectives, they would've been fine if I just let them do whatever they wanted. In their estimation, they were completely capable of dealing with anything that came their way and were able to make all decisions on their own. It's cliché to say that teens often feel invincible, but it's true. On the one hand they can be exceedingly insecure, but when you offer advice, they may act as if they know everything. My experience suggested that the teen years are the time when our kids need more precision in our efforts to support their independence. We need to be prepared to answer any question and encourage them to have a more holistic understanding of situations as they start navigating adulthood on their own.

Strategy: *Recognize and diffuse destructive behaviors. Engage with professionals if necessary.*

Whether it's vaping, smoking, experimenting with drugs, alcohol, or sex, eating disorders or other harmful activities, as a parent, you need to be vigilant and respond to signs or changes in behavior that could be indicative that your child needs extra help and support.

Parenting teenagers can be exhausting. This is the time that as parents we need to be super attentive to recognize and respond proactively and positively to bad behavior or calls for help from our kids. Never forget that while they're growing into their new bodies, they're still your kids trying to find their way. If your teen's actions or behavior exceeds your abilities to cope and respond positively, engage with a counselor, the school, your doctor, whoever might be able to guide you to the resources that can help support your teen and your family to get back on track.

*Ask questions. Listen. Engage. Be tough. Your children will try to get away with things to please their peer group and demonstrate their growing independence. However, your kids are counting on you to be the "bad guy," to keep them out of situations that they're really not ready to handle. Lean into love. Lean into your values and support your teenagers even as they rage and rail against you. **Never forget, you're not their friend, you're their parent.** You need to be their loving parent who sometimes has to be willing to let them hate you so you can keep them safe and get them the support they need during this transitory time.*

Your teen may look like the person you've known and loved since birth, but he or she is becoming a new person. They want to be treated like adults and have hopefully gained lots of knowledge in their formative years, but puberty and transitioning from childhood to adulthood can be a rocky road. One of the lessons I learned from our experiences is that you really need to keep control of your own emotions when engaging with teens. Defer discussions if necessary to a time when you can be fully attentive and remain emotionally neutral. Don't just assume everything's ok. Ask questions. Be on the lookout for changes in personality or behaviors that might indicate a serious issue. Stay engaged in their lives even when seemingly the simplest things can set off an explosion.

As parents, we're the grown-ups in the relationship. We need to keep it together even when our teens are pushing all of our buttons or reeling from their own internal turmoil or their frustration with us. Strive to be empathic and patient, not judgmental and angry. Candidly, I often failed in that goal. When I failed and got angry, and sometimes yelled, I apologized and tried to keep facing forward with the aim of doing better next time. For better or worse, there were <u>lots</u> of next times.

As noted, my daughter periodically lied to me when she was a teenager. Her lying and the punishments I gave as a result drove a wedge into our relationship. Avery was as headstrong and determined as me; something I was proud of but frequently frustrated by. Many times I suggested that we see a counselor to help us improve our relationship and hopefully give us both tools to have better communication and interactions. Avery refused. Perhaps I should have insisted, but I didn't. While I was frustrated and disappointed in myself, I still recognized that Avery was a great kid with solid friendships and doing well in school. I didn't see or suspect any issues with drugs, self-harm, depression, or anything remotely similar so I didn't want to risk impairing our relationship even future by dragging her to a counselor against her will.

I think the greatest challenge as a parent of teens is giving them more freedom while still holding them accountable to your family values. This concept was perfectly captured by Persian poet Jalal ad-Din Muhammad ar-Rumi, who wrote: "Life is a balance between holding on and letting go." That beautifully sums up the fundamental goal of parenting teenagers. Find the right balance for each of your children. Lead from behind. Permit them to both succeed or fail by their own choices, while trying to ensure that they have the maturity to handle the consequences of either outcome. That said, always be ready to give them guidance and another chance. Remind your teens that you are always available listen or be a source of advice. Make sure they know that while you hold them accountable and responsible for their actions, you will always be in their corner; there to help them get through any situation.

Strategy: *Create bridges by creating space*

I've emphasized repeatedly how important it is to have family dinners together. However, I realized that with teens, especially angry teens, sometimes it was better to share a space together and just be present.

There were many times when my teenage daughter and I were upset with each other. As it was just the two of us in the house when her brothers were in college, I found that having dinner together while watching a movie or a Netflix show was better than trying to sit across the kitchen table from each other and make conversation. Watching a show gave us the chance to share a meal and if we talked, it was about what we were watching. Avery and I inhabited a neutral space, could make conversation about what we were watching and enabled us to set aside whatever we were angry about. It allowed us to act normally together and be polite to each other while sharing an experience.

Anger and resentment can create long silences and a vast space between people. Just sitting on the couch together regularly helped us keep the gulf in our relationship from growing too great, the silences too long.

Given the tension in our relationship, I should have reached out more to my daughter to try to connect on neutral topics. Daily, I wished Avery a good day at school and said, "I love you," as she walked out the door each day as she left for high school, but I didn't try hard enough to make conversation. Honestly, many days I was just relieved we weren't yelling at each other and thus kept the peace. I could have and should have done better. I encourage you to ask your teen if they want to talk and be prepared to accept when they say no. But make sure your teen knows that you love them and are available at any time to talk to them about any topic. There is so much push/pull during the teen years. At times you may want to give up. I wanted to. But you can't. You're the grown-up, you're the parent, and it's your responsibility to keep trying. Set your ego and your emotions aside and keep trying. Even when your teen yells at you, defies you or ignores you, they do still rely on the love, support, and boundaries that you provide.

My decision to not let my teens date until they were 17 years old had the objective of giving them more time to gain an understanding of their new bodies and new emotions before experiencing the supercharged emotions and sensations related to sex. I didn't expect my children to remain celibate until marriage, I just wanted them to be more prepared before adding sexual experiences to their lives. I recalled hearing about a study that found that rats would not cross an electrified floor for food, but the rats would cross an electrified floor for sex.

Growing up, I'd seen too many of my teenage friends confuse sex with love. The emotions – positive and negative – that can be experienced from engaging in sexual activity can overwhelm, confuse, or mislead teens as all those feelings and emotions are new to them and may be very powerful. I believed that it was important to give my children the space and time to find some semblance of equilibrium in their changing bodies without the additional confusion of sex. Despite that, one of the gifts I gave Nate for his 16th birthday was a box of condoms. I reiterated that I thought it would be best if Nate waited to have sex until he was older, but if he did, then I wanted him to be safe. I also told Nate that I'd purchased the large economy sized box so he could share the condoms with his friends if he wanted.

I believe conversations like that are important for teens. I was sharing my guidance and expectations yet was trying to keep him safe if Nate chose to act differently. Similarly, when Avery repeatedly defied me by dating at 16, I frequently raised the topics of birth control, pregnancy, and abortion. I encouraged Avery to let me take her to my gynecologist to be evaluated so she could start taking the pill. At the time Avery refused to consider it, yet as noted in her letter on lying that I shared in our Tales from the Homefront, clearly, she had heard and remembered these conversations.

As Avery chafed at my rule regarding dating and occasionally lied about her whereabouts and actions, it seemed to set the stage to disagree about everything. That period of our lives was exhausting and frustrating for me as I'm sure it was for her too. I reached out to many of my friends for advice and suggestions on what I might try or how I could do better. I got a lot of commensuration, but not much useful advice as friends who had their own teenagers at home were having comparable experiences. It was hugely frustrating for me, especially as I'd managed to successfully navigate the teens years with both my sons. Granted, my boys and I had fights and disagreements, and infrequent periods of intense anger, but on balance, my sons and I had managed to generally maintain mutual respect and had avoided the vitriol that seemed to characterize the relationship between my daughter and me.

Strategy: *Tap into the knowledge and strengths of your family to support each other and drive better outcomes.*

Some teenagers are more prepared than others to make decisions about college majors and choose the college that might be best for them. While my sons and I worked collaboratively and effectively to access potential areas of study and collages for them, Avery needed the influence and support of her older brothers in her decision and evaluation process.

Especially as a single parent, I strove to nurture and strengthen the relationships between my children. Despite having been exposed to the college selection process twice, Avery focused on interesting states to live in vs college programs or affordability. She also refused to engage with me at all. Her approach provoked me as I saw her behavior as spoiled and entitled – fully expecting me to pay for college but unwilling to approach the process in a rational manner. I was soon at my wit's end.

Given all the challenges that Avery and I had communicating about anything, I engaged with her brothers, Nate and Jack, to get involved in helping their little sister make choices and provide guidance during this critical stage of her life.

My sons and I used the spreadsheets that we'd used in their searches. We had family FaceTime conversations with all four of us. Ultimately, we generated a list of target universities for Avery and I to visit.

Helping Avery to land at the right university in programs that built upon her strengths and talents while providing several viable career options was truly a family effort. Her brothers knew her as well as I did. They also had more recent experience in college, and they used that knowledge and their love for their sister to help get her launched successfully.

As teens, each of my children felt I was being too strict about their social lives, while I believed I had the correct parameters for them. The parties that my sons and daughter missed in no way impacted their relationships with their friends – it just made me seem like a strict, caring parent. I firmly believed that waiting until junior year in high school was early enough to start dating. While Avery and I clashed about dating, I still think it was the right call. When Avery was 17 and a junior, she began a relationship with a boy that lasted for their last two years of high school. I was very supportive and welcoming. Avery went to both Homecoming and Prom with her high school boyfriend, learned a great deal about relationships and had a robust social life.

I repeatedly vocalized expectations and reminded my teenagers about the importance of honesty, accountability and continuing to meet family expectations. If they acted disrespectfully or missed curfews, I reminded them that if they wanted more freedom, they needed to demonstrate their ability to be responsible. I highlighted that defying me was evidence of childishness, not maturity. I countered their anger with tough love. My rationale was that I wanted to drive home all the lessons and values that they'd demonstrated that they understood while growing up. I wanted to make sure that my teenagers understood that those lessons and values were even more important as they gained greater independence and moved into adulthood.

Getting a driver's license is a big milestone for teenagers. I was also pleased that in the state of IL were we lived, that new drivers had to log 50 hours of drive time with a parent or adult before getting their license (that wasn't a requirement when I got my license). Not only was it a good way to ensure teenagers were decent drivers, but it also provided time for us to be together and talk about whatever they wanted. Just like mealtimes, I've always thought of drive times as a chance to talk. Whoever's in the vehicle is captive for the duration of the ride, so it can be a great time for conversations.

Many of my kids' friends received their own vehicles from their parents. That just wasn't an option I could realistically consider, and honestly, I didn't see it as necessary or desirable. Once Nate had his license and Jack was in Driver's Ed, I did buy a used Camry for the kids to share. But based on the great location of our home, the Camry often sat in our driveway unused. In addition, friends with their own vehicles were always happy to pick up my kids and drive. It wasn't until my teens started working that having the Camry for transportation became truly valuable.

Summer jobs can provide teens with so many great life lessons. Despite that, I discouraged my kids from working until the summer before college. I had several reasons. First, they didn't need to work for financial reasons. My children each had demonstrated good work ethics in how they approached schoolwork, sports, and personal responsibilities. In addition, each of my kids participated in several sports and our high school had athletic camps and training programs over the summer. I felt it was a better use of their time to be physically active and with friends than working a summer gig making minimum wage. But mostly, I wanted to extend their childhoods as long as possible. My children had 40 years of work ahead of them and I saw no reason for them to start before they had to.

As I look back over their lives thus far, it seems that at times teenagers can be similar to their 2-3 year old selves. As toddlers gain mobility and greater communication abilities, they are eager to explore the world. Toddlers are fearless. Everything is exciting and new. As they are learning to walk, they literally fall on their faces and yet get up and try again. But toddlers can get frustrated easily as they still lack a lot of skills, are still building their language abilities and have limited understanding about how the world works. Toddlers also haven't quite learned that they are not the center of the universe. Teens are similar. Like a toddler, teens are learning how to control their new and changing bodies. They have difficulty understanding and controlling their emotions. Relationships are changing and taking on new meanings. While they feel invincible and up to anything, they can also feel insecure and need to learn new skills to successfully navigate their expanding world. With all these changes, teenagers can become uber focused on themselves and like their former toddler selves, may become very self-centered and seem insensitive about their family, their siblings, and/or their parents.

Having raised three children, I believe the teen years were by far the most difficult. As noted earlier, I never wanted to risk crushing my children's spirits, but I was likewise unwilling to give them free rein or permit them to treat me like a doormat or be disrespectful. In addition, I'd experienced many negative situations during my teen years that had been devastating to me, and I wanted to protect my children from similar harm. No matter how difficult, I believe that it continues to be our job as parents to support and guide our teenagers through this important, transitional stage of their lives even when daily life seems unpleasant. Again, in hindsight, I recall many times that I think I could've done better. Although I didn't always succeed in being empathic and patient with my teenagers, I held tight to my values and always tried to communicate my love for them. While it was rarely easy, we all survived.

When talking about parenting my teens, I often say that due to their age spacing, for seven years there was always at least one person in our household who was actively angry with me. While that's an exaggeration, it often felt that way to me. Getting through my children's teen years was one of the most exhausting, challenging times of our lives. I was blessed to have friends and work colleagues who gave me strength, lifted me up and shared comparable frustrations and concerns about their own teenagers. Regardless of how difficult it was, I always tried to make the decisions and take the actions that I thought were best for my children despite any negative blowback that might result.

The proof that I found the right (or close enough) balance during their teenage years came from my kids themselves. During the first ride home from college, before Thanksgiving, first Nate, then Jack, and then Avery each told me that they were glad I'd been so tough on them growing up. Each time, it was only the two of us in the vehicle for the 3-6 hour ride home, so we had time for a wide ranging conversation. Each of my new college students talked almost non-stop about their experiences, their new friends at college and shared many stories. At some point during the drive, each of them independently raised the subject about how grateful they were for what they'd learned from me, despite being angry with me at the time. They each shared stories of other kids they'd met at school and their struggles and cluelessness. My kids talked about how the lessons they'd learned as part of our family left them better prepared and helped ease some of the transitions to living on their own. They talked about their friends from high school who were making what seemed to my children to be dumb choices. Nate encouraged me to continue to be tough on Jack and Avery. Jack encouraged me to continue to be tough on Avery. Avery too told me she finally understood and appreciated what I had been trying to do.

I can think of no greater complement than the approval of my children affirming the positive impact that my parenting has had on their lives. I took our Thanksgiving drive home conversations as confirmation that they each saw the "man behind the curtain" and realized that all the levers I'd been pulling had somehow achieved the goal of giving them the tools and abilities to help them succeed in their independent lives. Never forget that our job as parents is to work ourselves out of a job. If we succeed, we earn the right and the ability to enjoy our children as equals and friends.

Tales from the Homefront:

Managing through a pandemic: Avery was a sophomore in high school, Jack a college sophomore, when COVID shutdowns occurred. My children and I each got vaccinated. Avery and I were also boosted. Once our high school moved from remote to asynchronous learning, I made our house available to Avery and her friends to support connectivity and normalcy.

Our house is located three doors away from the high school. During the pandemic, while schools provided lunches for students who needed them, the school cafeterias were closed, and students needed to find a place outside of the school to eat. For Avery and her friends, our house was that place.

After removing our swimming pool, Nate, Avery, and I had built a circular stone patio and stone bench that served as an area for a fire pit. I added six Adirondack chairs. Our backyard was extra deep and once Avery made the volleyball team, I had put up a volleyball net in our backyard so she could practice. Our entire family had fun playing and we used the net for both volleyball and badminton games. There was never a shortage of competition or a desire to practice in our family.

During the warm months during the pandemic winddown, Avery and 6-10 of her friends made the daily trek to our backyard during lunch break. They relaxed, ate lunch, laughed, and talked on our new patio. Then they played volleyball until it was time to go back to school. Visits from the kids were a daily delight for me. I was working remotely and had a desk in our sunroom which faced the backyard. While I didn't engage with the kids, I anticipated their daily visit. I was glad that these kids had a chance to unwind and have fun together. Their presence and laughter were a welcome diversion for me, and my spirits were always lifted by seeing them. I was glad I could contribute to their happiness though our hospitality. Later, my neighbors also told me that they too looked forward to the daily visits by Avery and her friends.

On rainy days, Avery and her friends gathered on our big wrap around front porch which had a patio table, chairs and plenty of seating for all. Once the weather became too cold to be outside, I let Avery, and her friends hang out in our living room. The additional advantage of having the kids on the porch or in our living room was that I was able to hear their conversations. Their conversations reinforced that these were good kids, with good heads on their shoulders, who relied on each other for advice and guidance, and friends to help navigate their expanding world. Despite all the challenges that Avery and I wrestled with in our relationship, I was relieved and comforted to know that she had the support of such good friends. I was likewise heartened to hear that the advice Avery gave to her friends frequently echoed guidance I'd given to her and her brothers.

Recognizing when more is needed: Virtually every teenager gets pimples. It can be even worse if they're playing sports that require helmets or other gear that can trap dirt and sweat against their skin. As the oldest, Nate was the first to experience pimples. As part of the enhanced hygiene that comes with puberty, I helped Nate find the products that worked for him to clear up his skin and soon pimples were an infrequent occurrence. Avery likewise got pimples, and she too was able to use over-the-counter products and good hygiene to keep her skin looking good.

Unfortunately for Jack, he inherited the bad acne gene. My dad's younger brother had had horrible acne growing up and as an adult had acne scars on his face. Growing up, I'd wondered why my uncle Danny looked a bit different, but we loved him and his wild stories, so none of us ever gave it much thought. Growing up, my siblings and I had all had pimples as teens, but nothing crazy, just the normal teenage pimples.

When Jack started getting pimples, I just assumed that like Nate, this was just a phase, and his skin would clear up soon. I was wrong. Poor Jack. We tried many over-the-counter products, but nothing worked. It took Jack actively requesting that I take him to a dermatologist before I realized how serious his condition was. It wasn't that I didn't look at my son every day, I just looked past the acne and saw the essence of my son. Ultimately, Jack's acne required both oral and topical prescription medication that he used for several years.

It wasn't until we saw the dermatologist that I understood the difference between severe acne requiring medical attention and normal pimples. It took that interaction with the dermatologist to make the connection to my uncle. I wish I hadn't let Jack's acne languish untreated for so long. Not long after he started treatment, we began seeing results. Soon, it was almost completely under control and he only experienced periodic breakouts.

It was so unnecessary for Jack to suffer with acne. It just didn't occur to me that acne was a medical condition. As his mom, I wish I'd been more aware and recognized that medical intervention was required.

As you parent your children, try to be aware that you may have blind spots. Strive to be sensitive to your teen's needs and make sure you're doing everything you can to address issues that are negatively impacting them or their psyche.

Don't try to live vicariously through your kids. Instead, nurture and appreciate their thoughts, their dreams, and their desires.

Heartbreak is part of life.

Dreams are fragile. Nurture them.

Give your kids the latitude to be who they want to be. Love them no matter what.

Imagination fuels dreams and ideas.

No one said this was going to be easy.

INDEX OF STRATEGIES

Use of Timeouts	36
Two Bite Rule	38
Importance of Routines	40
Two Minute Warning	42
Handling New Situations	45
Empowering Kids to Make Choices	46
Setting Expectations and Milestones	49
High, Low, Medium for communication	65
Encouraging Kids to Write	69
Teaching that Winning Isn't Everything	71
High, Low, Medium to Support Empathy	87
Managing Transitions	92
Reading the Books Your Kids Read	94
Letting your Kids Select Gifts	96
Teach Negotiation and Problem Resolution	108
Understanding Privileges aren't Rights	117
Teaching Time Management	119
Goals of Allowance	127
Wait a Week Before Buying	128

Opportunity Cost   132

Teaching Money and Finance   137

Benefits of Public Libraries   156

Use Dinnertime to Reenforce Family Bonds   160

Build Traditions   162

Reliable Information Sources   184

Address Destructive Behaviors   189

Create Bridges with Angry Teens   191

Harness the Power of Your Children   193

Managing Money and Credit   215

APPENDICES

Sample Budget 203

- Evaluating Expenses 253
- Savings Strategies and Using Credit 257

Paying for College 215

Daycare 227

Sample Daycare Contract 237

Sample Daycare Information Sheet 241

Insemination 243

Wills and Insurance 309

Acknowledgements and Footnotes 259

About the Author 261

SAMPLE BUDGET

An Excel file is attached at the end of this section with contents of the file shown below. If you'd like a live file, email me or complete the form on my website: **www.SallyMunn.com**

A few comments re file:

- Fields shown in **green** require your input.

- Fields shown in **blue** automatically calculate or move data from Tab 1 to Tab 2.

- If you wish to add more lines to the worksheet, I recommend doing so in the middle of a section as all totals correctly use the SUM function.

- You can also change the headings of line items to make them more meaningful to you.

- Note that the budget contains a field labeled "Date prepared." As mentioned, every time I considered having another child, I updated my budget. I would encourage you to save multiple copies of your budget. Just rename the file, update the date, and preserve a record of how your budget changes over time.

Finally, please read the footnotes for each tab as they provide guidance and hopefully will assist you in accurately completing the worksheet.

Please note that there are two tabs in the spreadsheet:

- Tab 1 - Current Earnings & Expenses

- Tab 2 - Estimated Budget with Child(ren)

I used Microsoft Excel and inserted calculations to let the spreadsheet do all the math. To use the spreadsheet, just **enter data in the green shaded cells**. A few comments:

- I set up the spreadsheet so all the income and expenses from Tab 1 automatically populate into Tab 2. If you or your partner will work less or one of you will quit working, just enter your updated income info on Tab 2 by typing over the auto-populated values.

- If this is your first child, you only need to use one of the columns on Tab 2 for new estimated child related expenses and leave the second column blank.

- If this is a subsequent child, I recommend using both columns.

- If it's your third or more child, I would recommend just using the first column for all current expenses and the second column for the anticipated new expenses.

Remember the purpose of your budget is to give you information. Be honest, be thorough. Use your budget to help you identify expenses that you may need to reduce. Use your budget to help you make decisions about your ability to afford a child or an additional child.

While you may discover from your budget that you have to wait until you pay off a car loan (for example) until you can afford to have a child, that's good information. While it may be disappointing, it gives you a path forward, an action plan. Trying to successfully parent without sufficient financial capacity is a situation that unfortunately many people experience. To the extent you're able, use your budget to affirm whether you have the financial capacity to be the wonderful parent you aspire to be.

Tab 1: Current Earnings & Expenses:

Monthly Budget   Date prepared:

Income[1]

	Name monthly	Name monthly	Total Montly		NET EXCESS OR SHORTFALL:	$	-
Net **after tax, post deduction** earnings[2]			$	-			
bonus (if received annually, divide amount by 12)			$	-			
tax refunds (divide amount by 12)			$	-			
tips or gig work not included above			$	-			
government support			$	-			
alimony / child support			$	-			
pensions or other			$	-			
other income/earnings			$	-			
other income/earnings			$	-			
TOTAL	$ -	$ -	$ -				

Expenses[3]   monthly

Housing (mortgage or rent)
Homeowners Association Fees (if not included above)
Property taxes (if not included above)
homeowner's or renter's insurance (if not included above)
Regular services: maid, lawn/landscasping, snow plow, etc.
Vehicle loan payments
Student debt payments
Other debt payments
Auto Insurance
Health insurance (if not already deducted from net income)
Medical out of pocket costs: co-pays, prescriptions, etc.
Natural gas
Electric
Phone
Cable / Internet / streaming
Water & sewer
Garbage / trash collection

Groceries
Other food (coffee bought away from home, eating out, etc.)
Entertainment not already captured above
Gasoline, parking, tolls
Subscriptions
Sports / health club / other
Savings
Other (specify)
Other (specify)
Other (specify)
Miscellaneous (suggest 5-10% of total expenses)

$ -

(1)   List all sources of earnings or cash received. If your income varies, use your best estimate of an average per month.
      If two people are completing the income info, use both columns. If only one person's income is used, use either column.
(2)   If you receive a paycheck, use the amount of money that is after all deductions and taxes; i.e., the net amount deposited into your bank account or received in your paycheck
(3)   For expenses like groceries, it may be easier to estimate an average weekly cost and multiple by 4 to get the estimated monthly amount spent
      For expenses paid annually, semi-annually or quarterly, divide by 12, 6 or 3, respectively, to determine the monthly cost. Even though the payment isn't made monthly,
      your budget should include these costs.

Tab 2: Estimated Budget with Child(ren):

Estimated Monthly Budget with Child(ren) Date prepared:

Income[1]	Name monthly		Name monthly		Total Monthly		NET EXCESS OR SHORTFALL:	$	-
Net **after tax, post deduction** earnings	$	-	$	-	$	-			
bonus (if received annually, divide amount by 12)	$	-	$	-	$	-			
tax refunds (divide amount by 12)	$	-	$	-	$	-			
tips or gig work not included above	$	-	$	-	$	-			
government support	$	-	$	-	$	-			
alimony / child support	$	-	$	-	$	-			
pensions or other	$	-	$	-	$	-			
other income/earnings	$	-	$	-	$	-			
other income/earnings	$	-	$	-	$	-			
TOTAL	$	-	$	-	$	-			

Expenses[2]							Current Expenses		
Total expenses from Current Budget							$	-	*This will auto fill from the first tab*
Note any regular expenses that will be reduced or eliminated[3]									
- List expense to be reduced and amount of savings vs. Tab 1									
- List expense to be reduced and amount of savings vs. Tab 1									
- List expense to be reduced and amount of savings vs. Tab 1									
- List expense to be reduced and amount of savings vs. Tab 1									
					$	-	$	-	*Total modified current expenses*

NEW Expenses	Existing Child(ren) Expenses		New Child Expenses		Total Children Related Expenses	
Daycare	$	-	$	-	$	-
Diapers + wipes	$	-	$	-	$	-
Formula / Food	$	-	$	-	$	-
Baby clothes	$	-	$	-	$	-
Babysitting (other than normal daycare)	$	-	$	-	$	-
Doctors appointments	$	-	$	-	$	-
Medicine	$	-	$	-	$	-
Other (specify)	$	-	$	-	$	-
Other (specify)	$	-	$	-	$	-
Other (specify)	$	-	$	-	$	-
Other (specify)	$	-	$	-	$	-
Other (specify)	$	-	$	-	$	-
Miscellaneous (suggest 5-10% of total NEW expenses)	$	-	$	-	$	-
			Total new expenses	$	-	

(1) *The spreadsheet automatically copies information from your current budget (tab 1). If you or your partner's income will change after having a child, change it on this tab. I also recommend changing the color or the text or highlighting it so you remember that you manually changed the amount.*

(2) *New expenses EXCLUDE the cost of baby gear - nursery furnishings, car seats, strollers, play pens, etc. While you will need to buy or otherwise obtain them, your budget should only include regular, on-going monthly expenses. You MAY wish to use one of the "Other" lines for baby toys and updated baby gear.*

(3) *Example, if one partner will work part time, costs related to gasoline, parking, etc. may be lower. If these costs reduced from say $100/month reported on tab 1 to $40 enter $60 above and change the comment in Column B to something like "Savings on gasoline expense"*

Budget%20sample.xl
SX

EVALUATING EXPENSES

A s you begin to examine all the places and ways you're spending money, you might be surprised. Building a detailed budget gives you a chance to identify spending that you might be able to reduce or eliminate. As a current or future parent, reducing expenses can be a valuable source of building savings. Common areas where people may spend more money than they realize include:

- Meals and snacks eaten away from home. Eating breakfast at home is likely both cheaper and healthier. Can you pack lunch? Keep a box of granola bars or healthy snacks at work rather than buying items from a vending machine? Make coffee at home? I regularly made tasty, nutritious dinners for the four of us for $20 or less. Eating out can cost many times that amount and quickly add up over the course of a month.

- Cable/streaming/subscription services. Do you really need all those channels and services? Do you have subscriptions that you're paying for and not even using the services? Cancel them. In addition to books, magazines and internet access, public libraries offer movies, music and videogames for free.

- Heating and cooling costs can be expensive, I kept our thermostat set to the edge of comfort. In the winter, I had it set at 65-66 and in the summer heat, I held off on the A/C as long as possible and generally didn't cool it below 75-76 degrees. I also closed and opened window shades as the sun moved through the sky to avoid using or stressing the A/C and to help reduce indoor heat in the summer. You might consider adjusting your thermostat to reduce energy costs. Likewise, having a programable thermostat permits you to adjust your thermostat by 3-4 degrees daily if no one will be home during working/school hours. All these little actions save money. At $10, $15 or $20 a month, savings can add up to $120 - $240 a year or more.

- Store brands and generics. I only buy generic medicines, use many store brand toiletries, and regularly try store brand food items. For quality and taste, I actually prefer many store brands over name brand food products; the cost savings is just another benefit, but each of these choices lowers my weekly grocery bill.

- Memberships and subscriptions. Are you using them enough to justify the cost? The subscription business model is one that companies love. Why? Because most users pay much more than the value they get. What's worse is if you're on autopay that money gets charged to your credit card or taken from your account every month like clockwork. Unless you balance your bank statements and credit card statements monthly (something I still always do), it's easy to forget about these payments. That's something else companies love about autopay. They're willing to give you a small cost reduction to get your account on autopay because it will take effort on your part to stop it. They count on our laziness and forgetfulness to keep taking our money.

Again, I have no issue with the subscription business model, and I understand the convenience of autopay, but you need to be aware of your expenses and ensure you're spending wisely. If the personal value you're getting is below the cost you're paying, why continue to pay or overpay? Eliminating or adjusting these subscriptions to better align with your needs and usage can save you tens or hundreds of dollars a month. Multiple that by 12 and it may become hundreds or thousands of dollars. Especially as a working parent, it would be so much better to have that money going into your savings account. Never forget, reducing your expenses, reducing spending results in more money in your pocket or your bank account. More money to address bad things if they occur and more money to enable you to do things that you want to do, perhaps even pay for your kids' college education.

- Services such as lawn care, snow removal, house cleaning, salon treatments, dog grooming, etc. Could you consider doing these activities yourself? Then save the money you would've spent to boost your rainy day fund.

- Shopping for recreation or because you're bored. This is just a bad idea. Examine your spending and eliminate impulsive or non-essential purchases. Do you really need more clothing? Or another gadget? My daughter and her friends love thrifting for clothes. I got lots of secondhand baby clothes from friends, church sales and my daycare providers. Don't sabotage your financial well-being by unnecessary spending.

- Gifts. Can you reduce or eliminate these purchases? Spend time together, offer to help with chores, invite friends and family over for a meal at your home or find other ways to give of yourself and share experiences vs. spending money on an item that may end up at the back of their closet or re-gifted.

Never forget how hard you work to earn your income. Don't waste it. If you really take the time and are honest with yourself, I expect you can find savings opportunities in your budget. Finding expenses that you can reduce or eliminate may be the difference between being able to afford a child or not. Knowledge is power. Try to think about changing your spending habits as something that is positive, perhaps a way to support your decision to become a parent and potentially build savings.

A budget gives you the ability to understand where your money is going and identify the areas where you have the power and ability to make changes. If your morning coffee purchased from your preferred coffee shop is important to you, so be it. Just account for it as a line item in your budget. I'd also suggest you note how much your daily coffee costs over the course of a month and compare it to other monthly costs for context. At the end of the day, it's your money, your choice. A detailed budget provides the information you need so you can potentially make changes. As parents, we have to make lots of tough choices. Ideally you can use your budget as a tool to align your spending with your financial and life priorities in a manner that enables you to meet all your family's needs.

SAVINGS STRATEGIES
AND USING CREDIT

I t is so rewarding to watch your savings grow. Once my savings grew to over $10 thousand, I felt proud and relieved. I'd created a safety net for me and my kids. While an unexpected car repair or medical bill might put a dent in your savings, having those funds vs. taking on debt when you have that unexpected bill or emergency is a massive stress reducer, especially as a working parent. The upside is that if you don't have those unexpected expenses, your savings can grow and continue to be the source of opportunities – vacations, a new car or covering all or part of college costs for your kids.

I saved vigorously all my life and have been debt free for roughly nine years. Aggressive savings combined with elimination of debt enabled me to put all three of my kids through college debt free. Doing so was a personal goal of mine since the time I decided to have kids on my own. That said, I didn't offer my children a blank check. I required my kids to find good schools that were strong in their chosen major and within my cost parameters. I also required the kids to vie for scholarships, to work during summers, earn As and Bs in college and also never take on even $1 of debt. My deal was if they took on any debt, they would get zero money from me for college.

My sons are both college graduates and have great jobs. The fact that they have no student debt has given them a huge financial advantage vs their peers who have student loans. My boys have both travelled domestically and internationally, are contributing to 401(K) accounts, and are likewise building savings. My daughter will be starting her junior year of college this fall and is on track to follow her brothers' lead.

A few thoughts regarding credit cards. I've heard many people over the years say that they have no discipline when it comes to credit cards. They quickly and repeatedly have used up their available credit lines and find themselves carrying credit card balances that they cannot pay off. As discussed in the section Delayed Gratification, plus Understanding Money and Credit, being able to manage and use credit appropriately is an important life skill. While those I spoke with generally switched to debit cards and avoided further use of credit cards, my guidance has always been and will continue to be that that they need to learn to use credit cards wisely. With no credit history and only a history of credit write-offs or bankruptcy, they are condemning themselves to a future with no access, limited access or only very expensive access to mortgages, car loans, etc. They were also giving up all the protections that credit cards can provide such as dispute resolution, fraud protection, insurance, expense tracking and potentially, rewards.

I currently use credit cards for virtually all my purchases and regular payments unless there is a fee charged by the merchant. While I like the convenience of autopay, I hate making it too easy for people or companies to take my money. I also don't want to lose sight of my spending. Each month, I review my credit card and bank statements and always pay my credit card balance in full every month.

As a parent, you'll want to teach your children the basics of money. Think how much better those lessons will be if you can show your kids how you are able to manage to your budget, consistently save even small sums and create a safety net that supports your family. Ideally you are both teaching and living your values. While I might suggest that financial health is both a value and a necessity, hopefully the desire to be even more fiscally responsible for the sake of your child(ren) can strengthen your saving discipline and lead to even better spending choices.

Strategy: *To improve visibility of credit card spending and avoid overspending, pay off your balance daily or weekly or track spending in your check book.*

I had always paid for groceries using a check until the first time a clerk took my check then after processing it, handed it back to me. The realization that the merchant had just taken my money immediately from my bank account as I stood in the grocery line caused me to switch to using a credit card. I never wanted to be exposed to the risk of a mis-keyed amount or lack of available funds that could generate overdraft or other bank fees.

However, when my children were young, my budget was super tight. I also didn't want to lose sight of the amount of money I was spending on my credit card. I don't use on-line banking, so to avoid overspending, after completing our errands each weekend, I would use my receipts from our purchases, enter each amount into my checkbook and deduct the funds as if I'd written a check. I'd then use a highlighter to highlight the amount in my checkbook and, on the line, next to it, I would write "Visa – groceries" or something similar. This procedure enabled me to know exactly how much I had left in my bank account at all times. I used credit cards for safety and convenience. <u>I never spent more on my credit card than the amount I had in my checking account</u>.

At the end of each month when it was time to pay my credit card bill, I'd total all the highlighted amounts, add them back to my running bank balance and then write a check for 100% of my credit card bill. Then I'd start the process again.

This manual process mirrored the way a debit card works. However, this strategy enabled me to retain the discipline of a debit card while gaining all the benefits of using a credit card. But by actually using a credit card, I gained all the protections and benefits provided by using credit vs. debit or cash. This also helped me to build an excellent credit history and an exceptional FICO score.

Tip: **Using credit cards AND carrying a balance for basics such as groceries puts you on the road to financial ruin. If you're in this situation, you HAVE to find a way to cut expenses, earn more income or both. Go back to your budget and find expenses you can cut. Do it for your children and yourself.**

PAYING FOR COLLEGE

Similar to my comments at the end of the Introduction to this book when I suggested several of my personal truths about parenting, I'd like you to consider several strongly held beliefs about obtaining a college education.

1. **College is not for every child.** I am fully aware of the findings that average earnings of college graduates are higher compared to average earnings of those without degrees. But those are averages. Each child is unique, and children have different strengths, talents, and capabilities. In addition to four year universities, there are vocational schools, trade schools, apprentice programs, etc. A young adult may grow in an early job that they enjoy and follow a path that leads to greater leadership or managerial opportunities. Likewise community colleges offer programs to assist students to obtain certifications as medical technicians, get HVAC training, or skills related to becoming an electrician. Trades offer many opportunities to develop skills that can be foundational to a well-paying satisfying job and even used as a launching pad to establish their own business. Other paths might include developing products and/or services for their own business, working in a family business, or finding other ways to earn a living. Just keep in mind that college is not a one size fits all proposition. The worst outcome is to spend tens or hundreds of thousands of dollars only to discover that college was a bad choice. It would be even more devastating if you or your child has college debt afterwards.

2. **No one is entitled to the "college experience."** The cost I paid for my kids per year just for a dorm room and meal plan at college was approx. $10-14 thousand per year. That was just the cost of living at college so they could have what I'm calling the "college experience." This was before the cost of tuition, fees, books, etc. or the laptop, mini fridge, and other items we had to buy to use in their room and in their studies. To save costs, you and your child may wish to consider the pros/cons of your child living at home and commuting to a nearby college or university. Likewise consider the possibility of your child taking a year or two of community college courses to complete the basic Gen Ed requirements or preliminary courses. Remember, a college degree is issued by the university where students complete their senior year and that fulfills the school's graduation requirements regardless of how many years they actually attend.

Not long after I started my sophomore year of college, my mother called to tell me that she was getting divorced again and would no longer be able to give me any financial support. I was 19 ½ at the time, had no income and had approximately $13 thousand in student loan debt. At the end of the semester, I left school. I went to Chicago and found a job and an apartment the same day. I worked full time during the day and in the fall started university full time at night. Virtually everyone in night school was working too. Students' ages in night school ranged from my age to people in their 50s and 60s. I left my Chicago apartment each weekday around 6:30 a.m. to catch the "L" to get to work and school in the Loop and didn't get back until 9:30/10:00 p.m. four nights per week. I ate dinner in the college cafeteria. I lived paycheck to paycheck but managed to pay my bills and get by without adding any more college debt. It was not easy, nor was it the "college experience," I'd hoped for, but I earned my bachelor's degree and years later, my MBA.

3. **Student loan debt is like a bad car loan. Avoid it if at all possible.** To me, it is borderline criminal that virtually all college web sites include debt as part of their "affordability" calculators. If you or your student need to take on debt to "afford" a college or university, find another school, find another way. Student loan debt will be an albatross around your child's neck crushing their financial health for years, even decades to come. It will be even worse if they don't graduate or work in a field with low to moderate salaries. Likewise, I strongly urge parents not to forgo your retirement savings or take on (or guarantee) college debt for your children. With very few exceptions, a debt financed college education is not worth

the price you have to pay.

Joining the Peace Corps after earning my bachelor's degree froze my student loan debt. However, 6 months after completing my service and returning to the US, I had to start making payments. My Sallie Mae loans had interest rates of 9-11% so I tried my best to pay them off as quickly as possible. It took me approximately 3 years to pay off my $13 thousand in student loan debt. I just remember feeling a huge amount of pressure to deal with the debt. At the time, my annual salary was just under $30 thousand. My monthly rent was around $600 and my debt repayment around $400 a month. Once again, I was back to living paycheck to paycheck.

4. **Your child's dream school may not be an option.** I built spreadsheets for each of my kids that we used to help us in the college selection process. To evaluate the potential universities, we considered 20-30 different factors including but not limited to:

- rankings of the school's programs for their desired major(s),

- student body size,

- average SAT & ACT scores compared to their own results,

- geographic location (as this would impact if we could drive or if they needed to fly),

- estimated costs using the net price calculators on the university websites and my income info, and

- info and impressions gathered during visits to their prospective schools.

Based on the above, some schools were not good potential fits or simply not in our price range. For a few schools, I paid the $40-60 application fee to see if my child might earn enough from scholarships to make it affordable, but if the free money wasn't sufficient to get total estimated costs within my parameters of what I was willing and able to pay, we moved on to consider other schools.

There are thousands and thousands of good colleges and universities in this country with price tags that run the gamut from reasonable to insanely expensive. It takes work and compromise, but your child can find a school that offers a quality education in their desired field of study, will be a good fit for them personally and will truly be financially affordable.

1. **Exercise caution in seeking college credit for AP (Advanced Placement) courses.** My kids grew up in a location that has strong school districts. Unfortunately, there was a period during which the school district pushed AP classes well beyond what I felt was appropriate, sometimes to the detriment of the students. From my perspective, too much effort was spent in AP classes on learning how to do well on the AP exams vs ensuring that the students thoroughly understood the course concepts.

   In promoting AP courses to students and parents the high schools emphasized the ability to earn college credit and save money. I will state emphatically that an AP course is no substitute for a good college course. I paid the fees for my kids to take AP exams that would enable them to clear some Gen Eds, but refused to let them take AP exams for classes that would support their likely majors in college. While I appreciated the increased rigor of AP classes, I believed it imperative that my kids not skip fundamental, foundational college courses that supported their major. It absolutely cost me more money to make my kids repeat material in college vs. comping out. But getting the college level instruction on top of the high school AP coursework helped my sons and daughter succeed. I'll also note that we saw several very smart talented friends flunk out of college after trying to start some courses at the sophomore level by using AP credits. How sad. Not money saved, rather money and time lost. Worse, those kids were left feeling the failure of their first attempt at college, some with college debt.

2. **If you make a bad decision, make another one.** My life is guided by this concept. It is also applicable to college. If despite all your and your child's best efforts, they find that the college that they're attending or that college in general is just not right for them, so be it. Call it what it is, a mistake. Learn from it and move on. To the extent possible, have them tough it out until the end of a semester. College itself is a big adjustment, and your young adults need sufficient time to be sure it's not for them. Likewise, finishing the semester will generate a clean end point and perhaps give them credits that could be transferred if they chose to attend another college in the future. Try to salvage something for all the money and effort you all spent.

   Then look to Plan B. Plan B might be a different college, community college, a gap year or something completely different. But if being at that college was the wrong decision, admit it and move on. Make a new plan. It is far too costly – in terms of money, mental health, and happiness. If they're on the wrong path, work with them to find a path better suited for them that will keep them heading towards achievement of their life goals.

To use or not use 529 College Savings Plans:

I'm a person who tends to read the fine print. Not only am I naturally curious, but when I was first on my own and especially when I became a single, working parent, I was living without a material safety net for a long time. I couldn't afford to incur an unexpected fee or expense because I failed to understand the terms of my lease or how my health insurance worked. I might not always follow all the rules, but I tried to make sure I knew and understood them.

I'm also generally willing to forgo a modest benefit today if there might be conditions that could severely limit my future choices or create the risk of material issues down the road. That's how I viewed 529 College Saving Plans. The plans became extremely popular around the time my kids were little. Newspapers were full of articles praising the benefits of these plans. I chose **not** to use these plans as part of my college savings plan for three compelling reasons:

- Our financial situation was tight for the first 8-10 years of me being a single parent. Despite the potential tax benefits of 529 plans, I was not comfortable with not being able to access college savings in the event of an emergency. For instance, I once started a new job where the company paid employees only once a month. The cash flow impact of that resulted in me having to borrow money from my kids' savings accounts to pay the mortgage while I waited for my first paycheck. While I was able to fully replace the money in my kids' accounts once I finally got my first paycheck, I'm not sure what I would've done if I hadn't been able to access those funds.

- Early 529 plans seemed to indicate that funds could only be used in the state where the plan was based. That may've changed over time, but that was problematic for me. Only Jack went to college in IL, my other two kids went to out of state universities - Nate in IA and Avery in OH. What would've happened had all college savings been in an

IL plan? A current internet search suggests that while rollovers to other states' 529 plans are possible, there may be penalties, fees, and tax implications. I also highlight that the tax benefit of 529 plans is derived at the state vs. federal level. When my kids were little, the IL state income tax rate was around 3% and is currently around 5%. Lots of risk for a small tax benefit. No thanks.

- Most importantly, when colleges evaluate potential financial aid packages for applicants, I learned that the college or university would count money in a student applicant's 529 plan at 100% in evaluating the student's ability to pay – **thereby reducing potential free money dollar for dollar for every dollar in the 529 plan**. However, money in parents' bank accounts would be counted at a reduced percentage. Seemed a no brainer to me. I saved college money in my bank account.

As college costs or savings were ultimately all my money, I chose to save in a way that gave me maximum flexibility but skipped potential state tax savings. When my kids got closer to the time that I had to write big checks for their college expenses, I traded return on investment for principal preservation.

Take advantage of changes in your budget to drive savings:

So how did I save enough money as a single, working parent to write those big checks? My children were born over a period of 5 years. I really did use the budget tools I've shared in this book and while I always erred on the side of over estimating expenses and also included additional cushion in "Miscellaneous," I was confident in my abilities to make things work even when the unexpected occurred or a large expense had to be addressed. As mentioned previously, I had to trade in my SUV for a minivan when I had my daughter. Net of my trade-in, the minivan sucked up $16 thousand from my emergency/college fund. Ugh!

The four key mechanisms I used to drive savings were:

1. Always having a portion of my paycheck deposited directly into a separate savings account.

2. Whenever I got a raise, I increased the amount deposited to my savings account and also increased the amount that went into my 401K.

3. Ferociously managing my expenses and not letting them grow as my salary increased.

4. **As my daycare costs declined, I increased my savings rate by an amount equal to the reduction. <u>This supercharged my savings.</u>**

In the main body of this book, I highlighted that my daycare costs – which were only slightly below my annual mortgage payments at their peak of roughly $18 thousand per year – were the primary vehicle that I utilized to ratchet up my savings. As the kids got older and spent less time in daycare, my daycare costs declined and eventually went away. As these costs declined, I allocated the funds previously given to my daycare provider to my savings. To illustrate, when my daycare costs reduced from $18 thousand to $15 thousand, I increased my annual savings by $3 thousand. So if I was already saving $100 per paycheck generating $2,400 in annual savings, I increased my auto-deposit, so that my annual savings were $5,400. By the time my kids were done with daycare, I was saving $25 thousand per year, or more than $2,000 per month.

Remember, if your budget could support the daycare expenses at their peak, unless you have a pay cut or job loss, you can continue to afford that expense – just put the money into your savings account rather than giving it to your daycare provider. All you need is the discipline to save these funds vs. letting them flow into your checking account where they can be spent.

Daycare is a great expense to use to drive savings, because even if it increases as a result of having more children, ultimately, it's going to decline and at some point, go away completely. Assuming daycare stops sometime in middle school, that gives you 5-7 years to sock away large sums of money for each child. Regardless of whether you follow my recommendations or not, I urge you to create a mechanism that causes you to increase your savings by a material amount each year in addition to any wage increases. The objective is to find ways that work for you to enable you to consistently increase your savings rate over time. For example, if you have a car loan and pay it off (first, yeah!), change your direct deposit allocation of your paycheck so that the money that used to go to your bank or finance company for your car loan gets deposited to your savings account. Similar to daycare payments, if you've managed without those funds, keep managing without them. Put them into savings. Remember, if you need or want those funds, they're there for you. As a parent, you can never have too much money saved.

Whenever I got a raise or a bonus, I increased both my pre-tax (401K retirement) and post-tax savings amounts. For raises, I'd calculate the amount that my paycheck would increase and then I took around 25% of the increase to allocate to after-tax savings. Then I increased my pre-tax savings by 1% (example from 6% to 7%) and let the balance flow to my checking account. Similar to the above, unless you have credit card debt, student loan debt or other personal debt, I strongly recommend allocating some of your new future earnings to both retirement and after-tax savings. Again, if you've managed to live without this money so far, even if your budget is tight, maintain your discipline. Drive your savings. For bonuses and tax returns, I generally took a relatively small amount of money to celebrate – perhaps a night out for dinner for me and the kids and/or some other fun activity – then I saved the rest.

As noted above, I've always ferociously managed my expenses. The thought is that keeping control of expenses, especially as earnings grow, is another way of saving. Spending less results in more money in your pocket or bank account. As detailed in the Budget sections, especially as a parent, you need to stay intimate with your expenses, keep a clear differentiation between wants and needs, and periodically update your budget.

Conceptually, I've never thought of saving as depriving myself. I've never felt that my self-esteem or status was increased by having a flashy car or a big house or wearing designer clothes or otherwise trying to keep up with the Jones. Between my lower middle class childhood, having to work my way through college and spending 25 months in the Peace Corps, the value of money has been ingrained into my DNA. Money doesn't bring happiness, but the lack of it can create substantial difficulties and unhappiness. I strive never to waste money.

It's also been my experience that as long as you have enough to get by and meet all your true needs, you can be happy and content without spending a lot of money. While the lack of sufficient money to meet basic needs can absolutely cause stress and unhappiness, money really can't buy happiness. For me, money is something that keeps me and my children safe, protects us against adversity and likewise enables us to capitalize on opportunities and fund our adventures. Growing up, my kids had everything they needed. I emphasize, not everything they wanted, but everything they needed. That reality was consistent with my values and helped them to appreciate what we had and our occasional splurges. We were wealthy, but not rich.

I'm proud of getting my kids through college debt free. It was a personal goal for me and one that I achieved both for myself and them. Each of my children did the hard work of learning and earning As & Bs which was part of our deal. As noted, I did not give them a blank check. Based on the amounts I was able to save and my salary, I determined that I could pay $25 – 30 thousand per year in college expenses for each of them. Due to their age spacing, there were four years when I knew I'd have two kids in college at the same time. I was afraid of those years as at the start of the school year during that time, I wrote checks totaling $57 thousand. That's a lot of after-tax money to spend every year for four years.

Fortunately, just about the time Nate was ready to head off to college, I paid off my mortgage. **With no debt, and no daycare expenses, I was able to save over $45 thousand in after tax earnings every year.** That sounds huge, and it was, but recall that was roughly equal to the amounts I'd been sending to the mortgage company and giving to my daycare providers. With those expenses gone, instead of giving that money to others, I had it directly deposited from my paycheck into my savings account. By putting it in a separate account, I didn't see it in my checking account as money available to spend, so I wasn't tempted. **Essentially, I had my savings deposits on autopay – to myself.** Try to imagine the sense of pride and accomplishment when my savings account exceeded $100 thousand. You can do it too; it just takes a process that works for you, a good understanding of your changing budget over time, a commitment, and the discipline to stick to it.

As mentioned earlier in this book, I deposited the checks for college expenses into my kids' bank accounts and made them manage the money and the actual payments to the university. I also encouraged them to use their credit cards for books and other costs as they knew they had the funds to pay off the bill in full. My reasons for doing it this way included ensuring the kids learned how to manage the university system, giving them practice in handling large sums of money, and continuing to build their personal credit histories and scores. I never worried that they'd take the money and blow it on something else, I trusted them, and they knew they wouldn't get another dime from me if they did that.

When my sons wanted to move off campus in their junior and senior years, to share apartments with friends, we agreed that I would not pay more, my check would be based on the cost of a shared dorm room and the level of meal plan they'd used the prior two years. If they could spend less, they were able to use the extra for groceries or other personal costs. I also read the leases and only supported arrangements where each renter was responsible only for his share of the rent. In other words, the lease had to be structured so that if one student couldn't pay or dropped out, my son's obligation was not impacted.

We also checked to see if the lease was for 9 months or 12 months. If it was 12 months, my sons knew that they might need to personally fund any shortfall relative to the money I would provide.

The management company who ran the apartment complex that Jack shared with 3 friends during his junior year asked for a parental guarantee for every student tenant. I refused. However Jack and I worked with the management company and learned that if Jack could show his bank statement with a balance covering the year's rent my guarantee wouldn't be necessary. Problem solved. I gave Jack his full college payment early and no personal guarantee was needed.

In addition to covering the known college costs plus an estimate for textbooks, I deposited $100 each month into each of my kid's bank accounts as allowance during the time that they were at school. Any money for activities, entertainment, etc. that was above that my children needed to cover from the money they'd earned during the prior summer. While my salary was too high for need based aid, each of the kids earned some level of academic scholarships and they all attended great universities with excellent programs for their areas of study. Each hustled, joined clubs and groups related to their field of study, played intermural sports and earned paying internships during their college careers. The internships, research opportunities, co-ops and other activities helped build their resumes and give them real world experience in their fields before they graduated.

Paying for college and getting the kids through school debt free was a driving personal goal for me. I can't forget how my modest $13 thousand in student debt required personal sacrifice to pay back. It was hard. Despite a college degree, when I first started out, I still had small salary. As noted, it took me approximately 3 years to repay my student debt. I shudder at the sums that some students and/or their parents are signing up for. It's like agreeing to pay a mortgage level payment but not getting the house. However, as I've outlined, by planning ahead and always understanding how your budget changes over time you can build savings to pay for some or all of your child(ren)'s college hopefully without needing to make major changes to your household budget.

Financial professionals will talk about the power of compound interest, dividend reinvestment, diversification, and balancing risk vs. return. All are very important. However, when you're just building your savings, the most critical factor is to save something from every paycheck. Use your budget to determine how much you can allocate to savings. Treat that amount like an expense and ideally set it up for direct deposit to a separate account. Then, don't touch it unless it's truly an emergency. All the financial drivers or investment advice is meaningless if you don't have money saved.

My secret sauce to build college savings was recognizing early on that my ability to cover daycare expenses at their peak level could be a mechanism to super charge my savings as daycare costs declined. Getting the additional cashflow benefit of fully paying off my mortgage the year that Nate graduated high school and was heading off to college enabled me to divert those monies to savings too. I had been worried about the four year period when I'd need to cover two kids in college – essentially the four years when Jack was at college. Had I limited my savings just to $18 thousand per year tied to my former daycare costs, it would have been tough or perhaps impossible to save enough in time to pay for two kids in college at the same time. However, because I also deposited bonuses and tax refunds to my savings account, I knew it would be a close call but that I'd find a way.

The steps I've discussed above have enabled me to pay over $302 thousand in college expenses to date. My daughter Avery has two years to go. I have the money in the bank to cover her final two years. I was always clear that I was only paying for the first four years of college. If the kids wanted to pursue master's or other advanced degrees that was on them. However, I encouraged them to look at employer programs which might cover 50-100% of the cost. Nate is currently doing just that.

At the end of the day, you do not owe your child a free college education or even a partially funded one. College may not even be the best path for your child(ren). Regardless, building savings for safety or opportunity is something that I'd strongly recommend that you incorporate into your budget and lifestyle if you're a parent. Having a pile of money that you've accumulated over time is wonderful. It reduces stress, gives you more control and stability in your life and empowers you to make choices about how to use that money for you and/or your family. By making savings important and talking about it with your children, you can hopefully help them to model your behavior and incorporate savings and good money management into their lives as well.

DAYCARE

As a full time working parent, reliable, affordable daycare was essential. Even if they weren't with me, I wanted my kids to be together. Commercial daycare centers typically separated kids by age, which might have resulted in my kids being in the same building but apart all day. The commercial centers were extremely expensive, and would have severely strained my budget, so in addition to not being what I really wanted, they were not realistically a viable option for us.

Instead, I advertised in the local newspaper for daycare providers who would care for my kids in their home. I also responded to ads of providers offering their services. While this type of advertising has changed form, a quick internet search for "daycare provider ads," generated good results. Not sure how one goes about placing an ad to request services nowadays, but I'd expect it's comparable to how providers list their services.

Having my children in the daycare provider's home was less expensive than a nanny in my home as it gave women the chance be in their home to care for their own kids and to take in kids from other families as well if desired. It also meant that my kids and I would leave and return home together each day as I dropped them off on my way to work and picked them up from the daycare provider's house on my way home each day.

In Illinois, providers can be licensed or unlicensed. If licensed, the state would inspect their homes and presumably do a background check. I don't recall if it was an annual process or just once when they were applying for their license. Over the years, we had to make a lot of changes to our daycare providers. My experience was that I honestly didn't find that licensing resulted in better care or a safer environment. I found it best to rely on my own assessment while interviewing the provider in her home, and I always requested a minimum of three references and contacted all of them. For the providers we utilized, I also relied on feedback from my kids about any issues or concerns.

In our state, providers were limited to a maximum of 10 kids. My experience was that providers who had lots of kids truly considered their services as a business sometimes cut corners on the quality of food provided and/or found ways to incorporate additional costs for me like having to bring food or snacks weekly or requesting holiday and/or vacation pay. While I generally felt comfortable with my daycare choices, I didn't find that the care or relationship with my kids was any better with the providers who addressed it like a business than providers who just did it to earn extra income while working in their homes.

I'd also highlight that when you use private individuals, your situation can suddenly be thrown into chaos due to things beyond your control. Twice ladies quit with little notice, one due to health issues and a second due to struggles with menopause. Another time, I had a daycare provider who when I shared that I was starting my home remodel project, presented me with a letter demanding I pay her roughly double our agreed upon rate or I should use her letter as her two weeks' notice to quit. Linda said that if I could afford to improve my home, I could afford to pay her more. I was stunned by her actions and told her that while it was none of her business, I was paying for our remodel by reducing the amount I was putting in my 401(K). She held her ground. On the last day of her notice period, I picked up my sons and told her that I'd found alternative care. She clearly didn't have the character of someone I wanted to influence my children.

I had other challenges that caused me to leave a sitter. One I left because she allowed parents to bring sick kids to her home and invariably my kids caught the illness which resulted in doctor visits and me using vacation time to be home with my sick children. In addition, because I always paid my providers when my kids were sick, I was effectively paying her despite her creating an environment that contributed to my child becoming ill. I left another provider who was having marital difficulties and became distracted and a little unhinged. I just didn't feel safe having infant Nate with her. Another we left after several weeks as she just seemed to disregard any comments I made about expectations for my children's care.

When I left a daycare provider, depending on the circumstances, I may or may not have given her a final check payment for one week. But once I communicated that I was ending our relationship, I never left my kids with her again. After I fired the woman who completely disregarded my comments, she showed up at our house several times to yell at me and give me angry hate filled letters berating me for my decision. Very scary. Scarier still was that I'd entrusted her with the care of my children for several weeks.

Before my kids entered kindergarten, I used some daycare providers in our town, and others closer to work. The company I worked for when my kids were young didn't have onsite daycare, but I believe more companies are offering these types of benefits. There are advantages and disadvantages to all situations. I would encourage you to find the right balance of safety and well-being for your kids and the cost and convenience that works for you.

Some individual daycare providers declared their income for tax purposes and gave me their social security number so that I could take advantage of offsetting some of my daycare expenses when filing my federal income taxes. Others did not. When all three of my kids were in daycare, I was paying approximately $18 thousand per year in daycare costs. While getting a modest tax benefit was very much appreciated, my longest provider was a woman who did not claim the income, but she was a wonderful solution for my kids. When it came to my kids, and I expect yours too, the most important factors were knowing that my children were safe and happy and that I could trust and rely on my daycare provider. Thankfully, while the tax benefit was a nice thing to get, it wasn't a must have. My budget worked even without the tax savings.

Given our inconsistent experiences with daycare, when Nate and Jack were in elementary school and Avery a toddler, our daycare solution evolved to maintain two primary providers at all times. I learned that that the ideal daycare solution was moms with kids similar to my children's age who attended the same elementary and middle schools. When I advertised for providers, I mentioned the names of our schools. To ease the burden and ensure I always had back-up care, our best daycare situation was to split our daycare needs between two moms each with their own kids. Generally one worked 3 days and the other 2 days, while for another pair we split 4 days and 1 day. As long as my children were happy and my daycare providers were satisfied, I was happy and made the situation work.

We had long relationships with two ladies, one a mom who just wanted to earn a little income on the side and had two young daughters, the other a mom who was educated in child education but was taking time off from working outside the home to care for her own three daughters. When one of the families was on vacation or had a sick kid, my providers were awesome and almost always stepped up to provide back-up coverage 5 days a week. The arrangement provided flexibility for them and us. One provider was even generous enough to provide overnight care – for an agreed upon additional cost – when I had to take infrequent business trips out of state.

The other wonderful benefit to having my children in another family's home was that my sitters' kids became like cousins to my children. They formed bonds like family, played together, sometimes bickered, and rode the bus to school together. We had some turnover with daycare providers, but ultimately, I found several that lasted for many years. Our kids literally grew up together. My daughter even got hand-me-down clothing as my sitters' daughters outgrew some of their beautiful outfits. The whole situation was truly better than I could have hoped.

As you consider daycare for your child or children, think about how they'll be spending their day and the people who'll be shaping and affecting their day. I loved that my kids had a change of scenery and different toys than ours. In addition, Avery had two brothers, but my long-term daycare providers each had only daughters, so Avery got the benefit of playing with five girls of various ages who were like older sisters to her. My sitters' kids likewise benefited from having boys in the house, giving their daughters the chance to have surrogate brothers.

As noted at the outset of this book, I completed a current and expected future budget before attempting to get pregnant. I researched the potential range of additional expenses including the various options for childcare. It was hard to maintain good, consistent private care, but it was critical to make our life work. Infrequently, I found I needed to move away from a provider and on occasion, providers quit. Whenever these situations arose, I did whatever I could to ease the transition and arrange the next hopefully permanent solution. It wasn't always easy and on occasion, I had to use vacation time and once the internet became more reliable, rely on the kindness and support of my manager, Michelle, to give me flexibility to work remotely periodically.

Children are a part of your heart living outside your body. Making decisions about who will care for your child(ren) while you are working or traveling is a vitally important task that will be impacted by what you can afford, what you want for your kids, and the logistics of making it all work each and every workday.

As you develop your daycare solution, recognize that as your child(ren) get older you may need or want to make changes in their care. Things you may wish to consider as you evaluate potential daycare solutions:

- <u>Cost</u>: When completing your budget (ideally before you're pregnant like I did) research current costs for the various daycare options. I'd encourage you to incorporate the expenses for the highest cost option that you'd like to consider. If your budget supports those costs, wonderful, if it doesn't then you'll have to find a way to generate more income, make permanent cuts to your other expenses or consider lower cost daycare options.

- <u>In home or other location</u>:
  - If your home. Live in or come daily?
  - Commercial daycare centers.
  - Preschools.
  - Private homes. Licensed or unlicensed?
  - Before / after school care at the school.

    I couldn't afford a private nanny or commercial daycare centers. I also wanted my kids to have the opportunity to engage with other kids, different toys, and different environments. I choose to use care outside of our home. I liked the fact that the kids and I left together and came home together each day.

    Once my sons reached middle school, I switched to daycare for them only before school and let them be home alone after school. In the winter I paid for my boys to ride the bus home, and in the other months let them walk home with our neighbor Cameron who was Nate's age. It gave them a sense of pride, confidence, and accomplishment to be trusted at home until I came home after work with their younger sibling(s). They had to lock the door and call me when they arrived home and other than Cam were not allowed to have other kids over unless I was home. Nate had roughly a year when he was able to be home alone for several hours. Nate told me years later that he absolutely loved that time and relished having the whole house to himself.

- <u>Socialization</u>: Especially if you have only one child, daycare can be a great opportunity to expose your child to other kids and give your child the chance to build their social skills. Due to their years in daycare outside of our home, acclimating to elementary school was seamless for my children. They were used to listening to and obeying directions from other adults, they had learned how to engage with other kids of various ages, and they had learned good self-control.

I'd also encourage you to investigate area institutions for other learning opportunities. Our local high school district had an amazing program for high schoolers who planned to go into education. In spring each year, the lab part of the high school program enrolled preschoolers from the neighborhood for two, two-hour long programs each week for 15 weeks. The high schoolers had the chance to engage with real children under the guidance of their teacher and the children had the chance to get one-on-one attention from their student "teachers" in a preschool environment. Super cheap and wonderful for all. My daycare providers loved it as they got to drop off my kids for 2 hours twice a week and still get paid for that time. One provider asked me if I was willing to do it a second year for Jack as the experience had been so beneficial for her young, introverted son. I readily agreed.

- Environment:

  o Is it safe and stimulating? If your child(ren) are there for 8-10 hours each day, will they have a good experience?

  o What areas of the home (or center) will they play in? Will they be limited to only certain rooms in the home or center? What does the outside play area look like? Is there a playset, trampoline, or other items that will stimulate and entertain the kids? Is the yard fenced?

  o Will pets, other adults or older kids be engaging with your child?

  o Are there any concerning elements at the location or house? Examples might include a second story deck, a pool or pond, a busy road, etc. that are sufficiently mitigated, or should you reject this location?

  o Are you comfortable with the number of kids that your provider or the center is caring for? Will your children receive sufficient attention and care?

  o Understand how the provider disciplines kids.

- o How does the provider manage sick kids? As noted, I had to leave a provider who was too flexible in permitting sick kids to come as my kids got sick from other children and I'd end up taking time off to take my kids to the doctor and then miss additional work to care for them.

- Commercial vs. private care:
  - o While commercial care tends to be more reliable, it's also typically more expensive.
  - o Commercial care may result in your kids being in separate rooms all day.
  - o As detailed above, private care can be unreliable or suddenly need to be replaced.
  - o Private care can be more flexible that commercial care. As mentioned, I infrequently had to travel and was able to arrange overnight care with one of my providers.
  - o My best, final solution was always having two providers who lived in our school districts watching my and their own kids in their homes.

- Convenience to work and/or school. Our town has two commuter train stations. My two best providers lived on the north side of town, and I had to cross the train tracks twice each morning and night during my commute as we lived south of the tracks and work was to the south and east. This made my commute a bit more challenging as I needed to be aware of the train schedules to avoid getting stuck waiting at a train crossing. I learned the train schedule and did my best to keep us on time.

- Reliability. Just like when your child is sick, if your daycare is unexpectedly unavailable, it impacts your ability to go to work.

- References. Whether using commercial or private care, I strongly urge you to speak to several references and ask probing questions. I asked about discipline, sick kids, other people who came and went in the house, etc. I asked why they left the provider. I asked if they had any issues or concerns during the time they used the provider's services and how those issues were resolved.

We had various situations and arrangements throughout the years and as indicated above evolved into employing two separate moms who had their own kids similar in age to mine, who lived in our school district and generally only watched my kids and occasionally those from 1-2 other families. They each had a vehicle that could accommodate all the kids – theirs and mine – but also lived either within walking distance of the school or were on the bus route. Several keys to our success:

- I had an agreement with my daycare providers that we both signed (see below for a sample). The agreement outlined hours, holidays, illness, meals, vacation, late fees, etc. During the interview process, we agreed on details together - always with the objective of fairness. Some providers had their own agreements and if acceptable, I used their agreement or modified mine to our mutual satisfaction.

- In addition to our agreement, I provided one page of written info about the kinds of foods my kids did and did not like, and guidance on other relevant issues.

- When my kids were infants, I provided a schedule of feeding and sleeping times to help ensure the daycare providers and I maintained a consistent schedule. We both updated the schedule as it changed.

- I also provided a sheet containing contact info for me, our emergency contacts, the other provider's contact information, our pediatrician's name and contact info. and our preferred hospital.

- I also created and signed a medical release form so that in the event of a serious injury or accident that required paramedics or other immediate care, my provider had my authorization to get emergency care for my kids if needed and not delay as I traveled from work.

- I always paid my daycare providers weekly, in advance.

- I paid the provider if my child was sick and staying home with me. It just seemed fair. Likewise, I generally didn't pay if the provider was sick or on vacation and I had to pay someone else to watch my kids.

- I did everything in my power to always maintain regular hours and never arrive late to pick up my kids. If I knew I'd be late, I always phoned and if I was going to be extremely late, I collaborated with my provider to find a solution (perhaps dropping my kids at our house or permitting another adult to stay with them in her home) that kept the kids safe and was fair to the provider. I also always offered to pay them extra, but this was rarely required. My providers knew how much I valued them; my being late was highly unusual, and my track record was of always treating them with respect and fairness.

- We maintained open communication and I demonstrated trust in their decision making. I also always expressed gratitude for their feedback – even when it was something negative about my kids or me – and asked for their guidance when appropriate.

- I also strove to ensure my providers felt respected and appreciated. I wanted them to like my kids and me and never feel like I was taking advantage of them.

- When I took vacation days to complete house projects like painting and had the kids at the daycare provider's home or had partial vacation days for doctor's/dentist or other appointments for my kids, I paid my providers for a full day and also strove to collect all my kids early to give my sitters extra time back. I relished the additional time with my family and wanted my daycare providers to enjoy the paid free time.

- The providers' kids became like cousins.

- The benefits of using two providers included:

  o Enabled each provider to make sufficient income without having to watch my kids all week.

  o Provided variability for my kids as they got to go to two different homes.

  o Built in back up coverage and flexibility for when providers took vacations, needed to adjust days for appointments, had a sick child or when I or they decided we would end our arrangement.

I've provided several daycare templates that I use, if you'd like an electronic copy of either or both, email me or complete the form on my website: **www.SallyMunn.com**

DAYCARE AGREEMENT

---·)·❦⟨◇⟩❦·(·---

Regular Days of Attendance [1]: _____ **Start Date**: _____

Hours[2]: _____

Tuition:

- Tuition will be paid on a weekly basis on the first scheduled regular day of attendance. The provider will retain the right to charge a late fee (up to $5/day) for late payment and may charge a fee (up to $25) for a returned check.
- Overtime, vacation, and sick days will be paid at the rates noted below.
- Emergency or back-up daycare provided during regular, weekday hours will be charged at the regular tuition rate. The provider will notify parent whether daycare will be provided to cover the given emergency or back-up situation.
- Care requested outside of regular weekday hours will be mutually negotiated on a case-by-case basis.
- Providers will not be expected to provide daycare on holidays (see footnote #1 below) and will not be paid for holidays.

Regular Tuition:

- $xx /day for xx kids on non-school days; reducing by $xx / day for each child who's in school full time (1st grade & above).
- Provider will notify parent of SS# for income tax purposes.

Overtime Tuition: $5 for each 30 minutes.

Provider Sick or Vacation Days: $0. Advance notice of vacation days will be given to the extent possible so that alternate care can be arranged.

Parent or Child Sick Days or Vacation Days: Regular tuition rate.

Parent or Child Partial Days: Regular tuition rate.

Supplies:
- Parent will provide diapers, wipes, and extra clothing for kids.
- The provider will give any soiled clothes to parent at end of day for replacement.
- The provider will notify parent when supplies need to be replenished or altered.
- Lunch plus morning and afternoon snacks will be supplied by the provider.

Illness:
- Child(ren) will not be admitted to daycare if he/she has an unexplained fever over 101 degrees, has diarrhea or vomiting, or if he/she has a contagious illness. However, the child(ren) may be accepted if he/she has been taking medication for at least 24 hours and the physician asserts that there is no risk of infection.
- The provider will notify parent (with as much notice as is possible) if other children in the provider's family or care are ill or if provider is sick.

Medication:

- Provider will not administer medication to child(ren) without the prior consent of parent except for Orajel or Tylenol for teething (provided by parent).
- In the event child(ren) requires medication, provider will administer medication per parent's or doctor's instructions, or with the advance verbal consent of parent, in accordance with the written instructions on OTC infant/child medication.
- Provider will contact doctor and parent should child(ren) experience an adverse reaction to any medication.

(1) Holidays: New Year's Day, Martin Luther King Day, Presidents' Day, Memorial Day, Independence Day, Labor Day, Columbus Day, Veterans' Day, Thanksgiving and Christmas Day, or the dates on which these holidays are celebrated.
(2) Full day, regular tuition rate will be paid for any partial days.

Provider Signature: _____

Date: _____

Parent Signature: _____

Date: _____

DAYCARE PROVIDER INFORMATION

—•⟨❊⟩•—

Name: _____

Social Security # _____

Address: _____

_____

Phone #: _____

Alternative # _____

Spouse Name: _____

Children:

_____

_____

Others regularly

in your home:

_____

_____

Back-up Provider (if any): _____

Planned Vacation Dates (if known)   _____

Other Important Info:

_____

_____

_____

_____

_____

INSEMINATION

Whether you may be considering using artificial insemination due to infertility issues or like me plan to use it because you lack a male partner, it's important to use a reputable facility. You'll also want to educate yourself on the process and all the factors you may wish to consider when selecting the donor.

Resources and selection:

There are many statistics on success rates which vary if you're using fresh or frozen sperm. Success will also be impacted if you have any fertility issues. My options when I decided I wanted to have children on my own were essentially:

1. finding a male friend willing to help me and all the complications that that might entail.

2. trying to get pregnant on the sly by some guy and either tell him or not tell him about the baby.

artificial insemination.

I've read articles about co-parenting, surrogacy, and open adoptions - and applaud all those striving to make those relationships work, ideally in the best interests of the child. Those weren't options for me.

The idea of insemination was suggested by my dear friend, Kathyrn, who I'd met while we were both volunteers in the Peace Corps. Kathryn lived in Orange County, CA and suggested the Sperm Bank of California, a non-profit organization. In the pre-internet age, I had no idea how to find information, so I followed my friend's advice and contacted the Sperm Bank of California and was very impressed. The organization is a non-profit, hugely supportive, full of information and provided ample guidance that helped me navigate this new territory with confidence. For people in the area, the organization offered classes, sessions, and lots of support. I also liked that they were located just over a mile from the University of California, Berkeley, which in my mind at least increased the likelihood that donors might be students attending the university.

I was pleased and relieved to learn that the Sperm Bank conducted medical tests on the donors to ensure that there were no health concerns. They also evaluated the motility of the sperm and gathered extensive medical information on the donors and each donor's family – siblings, parents, and grandparents. While it added complexity for me, the Sperm Bank also required a copy of the medical license of my OB/GYN and his/her signature on every order form for a shipment of sperm. While they were willing to ship sperm to my home or the doctor's office, shipments of sperm were considered human tissue and needed to be under the supervision of a physician.

At the Sperm Bank, all sperm donors were paid. Donors were also offered the option of being identity release or non-identity release donors. The difference was that if a child conceived by sperm from the non-profit contacted the Sperm Bank at or after the age of 18, the Sperm Bank would automatically give the child contact information for identity release donors. If the organization was contacted by an adult child who'd been conceived using sperm from a non-identity release donor, the Sperm Bank indicated that they would try to contact the donor to see if the donor had changed his view over time and would be agreeable to have his contact information shared. If not, no further information would be provided. I'd highlight that only the adult child(ren) could reach out, not the women themselves who'd used the services to conceive the child. I liked that as it felt right.

The Sperm Bank tracked the number of live pregnancies from its donors to ensure that no one donor exceeded their threshold of 10 children. They also had a policy that ended up being a wonderful benefit for me. Once a donor was no longer actively donating, the Sperm Bank limited use of the donor's remaining inventory of sperm solely to women who had already conceived and delivered a child using that donor's sperm. At the time the donor I used stopped donating (I presume graduated), the Sperm Bank contacted me and asked if I wished to purchase inventory in advance to reserve it solely for my use. While the Sperm Bank wouldn't destroy the donor's inventory if I elected not to buy it, there were no guarantees that his sperm wouldn't be used by either of the two other women who had also conceived children using his sperm. While I always knew that I wanted to have at least one more child, at the time, I didn't have the room in my budget to commit to the purchase and storage costs. Gratefully, there was sufficient remaining inventory that enabled me to conceive both Jack and Avery over the next five years.

As a side note, at the time I chose artificial insemination, medical insurance only covered insemination in cases of confirmed fertility issues. My medical insurance refused to cover my costs for insemination as I wasn't infertile, I just lacked a partner. However, insurance would cover my pregnancy and delivery even if I had to resort to being promiscuous and having a one-night stand. Seriously? I believe this has changed over the years and that insurance coverage has significantly improved and might cover costs for women in situations similar to mine. I was just grateful that as a non-profit, the Sperm Bank of California offered their services at very reasonable rates that I could afford and pay for even without the use of insurance benefits.

To assist in donor selection, the Sperm Bank sent me information about their current available donors and a price list. Free information included donor details such as height, weight, hair and eye color, race, and ethnicity. They also provided free, detailed information about donors that I wished to consider. This information included the donor's health info, medical test results and answers to open ended questions about the donor which provided insight into why he was donating, why he'd selected to be identity release or non-release and a bit about his personality, interests, hobbies, etc. Finally, for a small fee, the Sperm Bank offered a multi-page packet of detailed information about the donor and his family including general info, education, type of work and medical history about his siblings, parents, and grandparents.

The Sperm Bank also offered a service where women could submit a picture of themselves, and the Sperm Bank would try to match them with a donor who looked similar. I did not use that option. Instead, I focused on clean medical history, physical traits, and ethnicity to create a short list. Next, I requested and reviewed the detailed information on each of these donors. Finally, I purchased the full packages of information on each donor that I hadn't eliminated in the prior steps.

At the time I was going through this process, I took a commuter train to work each day to my job in downtown Chicago. During my commute and walks across downtown to work, I'd look at people and try to guess their ethnicity to try to create mental pictures of what the donors I was considering might look like. Finally I made my decision. I selected a donor who had a clean medical history, characteristics I liked, who came from a professional educated family and was identity non-release.

My mother and her brother (separate genetic mothers) had both been adopted by my grandparents in closed adoptions in the 1940's. I'd also had a serious relationship with a boyfriend who'd been adopted. I felt that my mother and Mike struggled with many issues regarding their identity and the reasons around why they might've been placed for adoption. Over the years, I've also known adoptees who've connected with their genetic mothers or parents. Feelings were mixed. I think the key is managing expectations. This can be challenging given the profound impact that adoption has on the lives of all those involved. Rightly or wrongly, I chose an identity non-release volunteer to make the decision for my children and close that door. I also believed that by having more than one child using the same donor, my children would know themselves better through their sibling relationships. Having conceived them via artificial insemination, my children could never doubt that they were both planned and wanted.

The Sperm Bank offered two methods for shipping sperm – a tank filled with liquid nitrogen, or a Styrofoam cooler filled with dry ice. The guidance was that the dry ice would last approximately 3 days, while the liquid nitrogen tank lasted much longer. However, the tank was more costly and also required payment for return shipment expenses. Due to cost factors, I choose the cooler vs. the tank. Only once (due to a holiday weekend), did I ever need to purchase additional dry ice to keep the sperm frozen until my perceived best conception time. I was able to buy dry ice from a local ice cream parlor for $25. My children were conceived with sperm sent cross country from CA in a cooler of dry ice delivered via FedEx priority overnight. No stork stories in our house!

Getting pregnant:

I will share what I did to determine when I thought was the best time for me to inseminate and the strategies I used to derive that window. My results far exceeded the average statistics provided by the Sperm Bank. I achieved three successful pregnancies over seven cycles and 21 insemination attempts (three each cycle). That said, I'd highlight that I had no infertility issues, and my menstrual cycle was very regular. I just lacked a male partner. The Sperm Bank and your doctor are the best sources of information to assist you and your specific circumstances.

At least six months before trying to get pregnant, I started tracking three things to estimate my ovulation pattern:

- Menstruation days. Ovulation generally occurs roughly halfway through a 28-day cycle.

- Daily basal temperature. This is your temperature when you wake up in the morning before getting out of bed. It may rise slightly (up to 1 degree) after ovulation.

- Consistency or change in daily mucus. It may also change several days before ovulation.

It was my understanding that frozen sperm that was thawed prior to insemination had a life cycle of a couple days at best. This compared to fresh sperm which could live in a woman's body for up to five days. It was also my understanding that women had a better chance of conceiving if they had sex (or insemination) a day or two before ovulation.

While I was fortunate to have a regular menstrual cycle, the changes in my basal temperature were measured in tenths of degrees and the changes in mucus very subtle. I strove to get intimately in tune with my body and the very subtle changes that might signal ovulation. Given the shorter lifecycle of previously frozen sperm, I also decided that for each attempt to get pregnant, I would purchase three vials of sperm and inseminate over 3 consecutive days starting on the date I estimated to be 2 days prior to ovulation and ending on my estimated day of ovulation.

It was also my understanding that having an orgasm in conjunction with insemination increased the chances of pregnancy as orgasm would move the sperm further into my body. Therefore, I chose to have sperm delivered to my home (vs. my doctor's office). That decision enabled me to relax in the comfort of my own bed and after the insemination process achieve orgasm. To further assist in the process, I remained in bed for 30-45 minutes after insemination with my hips elevated to get the benefit of gravity moving the sperm in the right direction.

Insemination considerations:

Having decided to have children as a single parent and having concluded that insemination was the safest and best way to create a family in my situation, I decided that I would be completely open and honest with my child(ren) and everyone else about how my child(ren) were conceived. The Sperm Bank provided great newsletters covering many topics including tips to improve the chances of getting pregnant and how to talk about the process. I read and saved every newsletter in my files for future reference. While I was trying to get pregnant, I only shared my decision with two close Peace Corps friends, Katheryn and Pat. Until or unless I became pregnant, I saw no upside in sharing my decision with my family or others. I correctly anticipated that their feedback would be less than supportive, so I chose to face the emotional journey of getting pregnant mostly on my own and share my news of being pregnant only if and when I was successful.

It was a lonely and very emotional time. When my first try at insemination failed, I was anguished, sobbed uncontrollably, and believed that God was punishing me for prior life choices. However, I had to hide my sadness and go about work and life as though everything was normal. Gratefully, the second month of insemination was successful, and I became pregnant with Nate. A pregnancy test confirmed I had a new life growing inside me. Joy, excitement, and fear flooded me. However, I decided that I wouldn't share the news until after the first trimester. I also realized that there was the possibility that others wouldn't share my feelings of joy, and I wanted to treasure those feelings before I had to defend my choice of deciding to become a single parent.

Embracing the pure delight of my pregnancy, I committed to myself and my unborn child that:

- If my child was healthy, I would try to conceive at least one more child using the same donor. I believed that by getting to know each other, my kids would know themselves better. In addition, having deprived my children of a dad by my decision, I wanted to give my child as much of a family as possible.

- I would be completely open and honest with my child(ren) and everyone else about how my kids were conceived. As outlined in this book, honesty is a core value for me. Honesty is foundational to my strength, my identity. I'm proud of who and what I am, and while not everyone likes me or agrees with my choices, I can abide those opinions if they're based on an honest assessment of me, not some lie or fiction.

- I would ensure my child(ren) knew that they were wanted. When they were younger, I compared sperm donation to blood donation, as something men might do to help couples and women like me who wanted children but couldn't do it without their help. By virtue of the way they were conceived, my children could never doubt that they were wanted.

- I would provide my child(ren) with all that information I had about the donor and the process. I hoped that full disclosure would help them to feel comfortable with who they were and how they came to be.

Tactical issues:

- Select a reputable agency. The Sperm Bank of California is a non-profit and I felt comfortable with their reviews and approach. I also had confidence in their medical screening and liked the option of using both the free two-page donor profiles as well as the ability to pay a small fee to obtain a detailed family background and medical history of the donor. Another option that appealed to me was the ability to reserve sperm for a fee, for future use. As it happened, the donor I used moved away, so his inventory was only made available to me and women who'd already conceived children using his sperm, so I was able to conceive all three of my kids from the same donor, making my children full genetic siblings.

- The Sperm Bank required me to provide a copy of my OB/GYN's license but gave me the option of having the sperm sent to my home or doctor's office. I chose home delivery because for each attempt I inseminated three times over three consecutive days in the belief that the strategy would improve my chances of success.

- Volumes of information are available about how to track and predict ovulation. As noted, I used a calendar and tracked my menstruation, basal temperature, and my mucus for at least six months prior to each attempt to get pregnant. As frozen/thawed sperm have shorter life cycles than fresh sperm, I ordered three samples each attempt to cover a wider time frame to sync with actual ovulation.

- Shipment options were nitrogen tank (had to be shipped back) or

Styrofoam cooler with dry ice. I chose the cooler due to lower costs and the avoidance of the cost of return shipping.

- Artificial insemination is the "turkey baster method." The sperm arrived via FedEx overnight on dry ice. I thawed it by rubbing/twirling the vial between my hands for several minutes (similar to the motion of making a snake out of clay). When thawed and warm, I inserted and waited at least 30-45 minutes with my hips elevated before getting up.

- The literature also suggested that having an orgasm helped move the sperm up higher into my body potentially aiding in the goal of conception. This was another consideration when I decided to inseminate at home. It also eliminated the need to schedule multiple, consecutive doctor's visits.

Talking to others about using artificial insemination:

Other than my Peace Corps friends, Kathryn and Pat, the first person in my family that I shared the news of my pregnancy with was my brother. Although my brother is ten years younger than me, we'd been close growing up. He was cautiously supportive, and echoed my concerns about how the family would react.

When I got pregnant with Nate in 1997, I worked for one of the top three banks in the US in the middle market commercial lending division at their office in downtown Chicago. I was stunned to learn that I had no short-term disability insurance coverage. While I was eligible under the Family Medical Leave Act ("FMLA") for job protection, I would receive zero income during my maturity leave. I was completely blindsided. Working for such a massive corporation, it never even occurred to me to verify my short term disability insurance coverage.

The second issue arose as I had a male manager at the time. Although Steve was married, had children, and we'd had a very good relationship prior to my getting pregnant, he made it abundantly clear that he was not happy with my decision to get pregnant. He repeatedly told me that I should not expect any special treatment. The last three months of my pregnancy with Nate became a tortuous experience as Steve made my work life increasingly difficult. While I've never requested special treatment and had always striven to take the high road, I fought back with doctor's notes. Due to the long commute to the city and lack of support from my employer, I knew without any doubt that I'd need to use my maturity leave to find another job. While I didn't receive any income during maternity leave, job protection under FMLA ensured I retained medical insurance coverage for my delivery and hospital stay as well as coverage for Nate and his initial visits and vaccinations.

While my misogynistic manager made my situation difficult, I was completely surprised by the number of professional women at the bank who told me they admired my courage and wished they'd had a child on their own. They were all successful and accomplished in their careers but had never married or had children. Their kindness and moral support helped me more than they realized. The entire experience revealed to me how little women were supported in our society. It left me saddened but more determined. While I'd known women who had unplanned pregnancies and became single moms, I'd never met anyone who'd deliberately chosen single parenthood like me. The vote of confidence from these women whom I respected and admired was priceless.

As previously noted, I told my neighbors how I'd become pregnant and left it to them to determine how and what they wished to communicate to their children. I was friendly with all my neighbors and their kids. I considered my neighbors as friends, and none of them ever expressed any concerns about my choices and were always welcoming and helpful. They never made me feel different or strange and my kids were welcomed by all of them. What a blessing. As indicated, the wonderful people in my neighborhood were a key factor in my decision to remodel and build an addition on our house vs. moving.

My family was not happy with my decision to be a single parent. In fairness, I think part was due to worry about my ability to manage on my own, and part due to my decision essentially making the man superfluous. As mentioned, my parents' divorce was very ugly and over 20 years later old resentments still existed. I think my life choice aggravated those feelings.

While they never volunteered to help out or babysit, my dad agreed to drive me to the hospital when I went into labor and he and his wife were present when Nate was born. On balance, they accepted Nate and then Jack as part of the family. My siblings, stepsiblings and their spouses were polite at family gatherings at my dad's house but otherwise displayed only passing interest in my life or the lives of my children. As noted earlier, once my dad died and the family heard that I was pregnant with Avery, they openly disparaged and criticized my children and me. Knowing that their toxicity was not beneficial for me or my children, I stopped contact with my stepfamily and moved on with our lives without them. I maintained largely superficial relationships with my own siblings for many years.

I found and started a new job 8-10 weeks after Nate was born and had a wonderful woman manager who I reported to for nine years. When I decided to try for a second child and learned I was pregnant with Jack, I shared the details of my pregnancy and full story with my manager, Michelle, including that I used the same donor for both children. Michelle was utterly delighted with my story, my success in getting pregnant again and supportive of my decision. She completely understood and trusted me when I promised that I obviously wanted to continue to work after the baby was born. Michelle was equally and consistently supportive during the hospitalization and ultimate death of my dad as well as my subsequent pregnancy and maternity leave with Avery. What a different experience from my first pregnancy!

Michelle and I were part of the corporate Credit team. It was important to me to communicate my decision to our corporate leader, Chris. There were several unmarried women at the company who had children, and to the best of my knowledge, all were treated no differently than any other employee. However, most of these women had one child and for whatever reason had not married the father. As a credit professional and someone on the management track, it was important for me to ensure that executive leadership, including Chris, understood that my single parenthood and pregnancies were not an accident, but rather a conscious decision.

My conversation with Chris was actually fairly comical. He and I had a good working relationship, and I asked if he had 15 minutes for a conversation with me. He agreed and in my open, honest fashion, I told him that I wanted to share the exciting news that I was pregnant. Then I asked Chris if he knew anything about how I'd conceived my son, Nate. Chris was caught off guard and was flustered by my unexpected question. He stammered, blushed and was clearly uncomfortable, so I just told him I'd wanted a family, had no partner so I'd gone the route of artificial insemination. I assured him that both of my pregnancies were completely planned. I told Chris that both my children were conceived from the same donor so that they were full genetic siblings. I apologized for over sharing but explained that it was important to me that Chris knew the truth. I told him that I didn't want him to think I was careless or had accidentally gotten pregnant twice. I wrapped the conversation by saying as a single parent of two kids, I was very committed to my job. I don't recall that Chris had much to say, perhaps "congratulations," but I never felt a change in our relationship and always felt I had Chris' support.

Talking to my children about their conception via artificial insemination:

The key aspects that I enforced with my kids over the years when we discussed the topic were:

- They all came from the same donor. So while they didn't have a dad, they were all full genetic siblings.

- They should never doubt that they were wanted and loved. I sought to address and avoid the types of thoughts that may plague adoptive children.

- The donor was not their dad. He was a donor and did a wonderful thing that enabled them to be created, but while they had a genetic link to him, he was not a dad, not a father to them.

While we occasionally joked about "Imaginary Dad," I saw that as their comfort or acceptance of their reality. Over the years, my kids periodically shared stories of conversations with classmates who insisted that everyone had to have a mom and dad and what my kids said in return. Nothing I heard suggested that my kids had concerns that needed to be addressed.

During the year that Nate turned 18, I gave each of my kids a folder filled with information. I included information from the Sperm Bank – copies of order forms related to their conception, the 2-page summary sheet for the donor I'd used which included 10-12 open ended questions he'd answered that provided a sense of his personality and why he'd elected to be a donor as well as his 15-page detailed family information. The folders also included copies of all the newsletters and information I saved from the Sperm Bank. In addition, I included a family genealogy prepared by my dad's oldest sister, Martha, and photos from my childhood with our extended family that hopefully provided my children with a richer sense of connection. I reaffirmed that while the donor I'd selected had chosen to be a non-identity release donor, that if they were interested, they could contact the Sperm Bank and ask if he'd changed his mind over the years. I made it clear that their decision to seek information or not about the donor was totally up to them and that it would not make me feel bad, mad, sad or anything. I would love them with all my heart as long as I had breath in my body.

The only cautionary advice I gave to my children was that I suggested that whatever they chose regarding a decision to contact the Sperm Bank or not, I wanted them to consider their expectations and understand their objectives in seeking to learn more about or potentially meeting the donor. I suggested that they think about what they might hope for if they sought contact. Was it just curiosity? Did they hope for a relationship? I reminded them that I'd had all three of them in the hopes that they'd each know themselves better through their relationships with each other. I also suggested that they all likely had some image in their heads about the donor and that mental images were rarely reflective of reality. I suggested that they think of all the fathers of their friends that they knew and how they'd feel if the donor was like one of them. I reaffirmed that I'd given them all the information I had because I wanted them to know everything that I knew, including our family history that my aunt had amassed. I told them whatever they decided, I'd support them. My sole concern was that I didn't want them to be disappointed or hurt.

My youngest, Avery, is now 20 years old. To the best of my knowledge, none of my kids ever contacted the Sperm Bank to request contact information about the donor. Whenever the topic came up, I always assured my kids that I had no objection to them making contact and only cautioned them that if they choose that route to manage and understand their own expectations. While their "Imaginary Dad" was a concept that periodically arose over the years, a real person is someone who likely would not align with their preconceived ideas. Whether for better or worse, the reality of the donor would likely to be different.

Thank you:

I am eternally grateful to the donor who gave me the opportunity to conceive my amazing, beautiful, wonderful children and to the Sperm Bank of California for making the process safe and reliable. While I regularly gave blood during my 20s and am an organ donor upon my death, I cannot fathom the generosity of the men who've helped so many women like me. Thank you. Thank you.

WILLS AND LIFE INSURANCE

The glorious moment when you first become a parent, you (and your partner) become fully responsible for the life of another human being. As anticlimactic and unpleasant as it may seem, something that I encourage you to address is what will happen to this wonderful, amazing new little person if you die.

As a single parent, I was acutely aware of the need to make decisions about who would care for my son, and ultimately all three of my children if something happened to me. Financial decisions are relatively easy. Selecting a guardian for your children is much more challenging. The easy answer is to select a family member. While this may seem a simple, logical answer it may not always be the best choice.

My recommendation for selecting a guardian is to find someone whose values align with yours. Someone who cares about and understands, at least in part, the essence of what makes you special and your partner special. If you're lucky, there will be several people in your life – family and friends – who might fit these basic criteria. Once you and your partner have a short list of candidates, talk with these people. Ask them if they'd be willing to take on this huge obligation, emphasizing that ideally this is an obligation that they will never need to fulfill.

I also suggest that you reaffirm this willingness regularly. Originally, my brother agreed to be the guardian for my sons, but after my family grew to three children and he and his wife had been devastated by miscarriages, my brother informed me that the risk of taking on three children, albeit remote, was an obligation he no longer felt he could support. While I was deeply hurt by this information, I also understood and empathized. I made other arrangements.

The other two key things you need to address are:

1. Who will be the executor of your will? Essentially the person who will ensure your desires are carried out.

2. How much money will your children and their guardian need to support them, minimally until they are legally adults?

Your executor could be a lawyer or someone you trust, who will likely engage a lawyer. I suggest the latter. Select a friend or family member who you trust and then have faith that they will engage professionals as needed to help them carry out your desires to the best of their ability.

Regarding money to support your family, I am a strong proponent of term life insurance as a means to get the biggest bang for your buck. I maintained at least $1.5 million in term insurance plus several times term coverage of my salary through my employer's medical plan while my children were young. I needed to ensure that there would be sufficient funds to cover the costs of raising my kids, as well as covering college costs as that was also a goal of mine. As they got older, I decreased my coverage and currently maintain $500 thousand in coverage. Once Avery finishes her college degree and is also working, I'll likely drop my life insurance coverage to $250 thousand or completely eliminate it.

There are many options to create a will. You can engage a lawyer, use an online tool, or some combination thereof. Whichever avenue you take, my recommendation is to ensure that your will lay out the most fundamentally important concepts that are important to you. That said, don't try to rule from the grave. If you've made good choices regarding your guardian and executor, trust them to make decisions on your behalf. Trust them to do what they think is best. Give them maximum flexibility in executing the terms of your will based on the high level parameters included about your goals for your children.

Finally, in addition to writing a will, I strongly recommend creating a document which outlines all your assets including all the relevant information about those assets. Assets include bank accounts, retirement accounts, pensions, brokerage accounts, Social Security, life insurance, real estate, titles to vehicles and other investments. To hopefully simplify the transfer of assets,

I've also executed POD documents – "Pay on Death" – so that most of my monetary assets can directly transfer to my children without having to go through probate.

Your will needs to address what you want to happen to your child(ren) and your assets if, god forbid, you should die prematurely. It is something for which you must plan. While it's something that none of us wish to contemplate, as a parent, it's something you really should address. As a single parent, it was imperative for me to complete these steps.

When Nate was 16 years old, Jack 14 and Avery 11, I had a job that required me to travel roughly quarterly to Toronto. Whenever I got ready to leave for a trip to Canada, I pulled out all my files and laid them at the bottom of my bed. My files contained a copy of my will (original in my safe), a listing of my assets, investment and life insurance information and contact information for my guardian, executor, and other critical people. As awful as it seems, I needed to ensure that in the unlikely event my plane crashed or some adverse circumstances befell me, my children would have all the information at their fingertips to initiate the process. My kids eventually took it in stride.

FOOTNOTES AND ACKNOWLEDGEMENTS

Footnotes:

(1) *https://mission-statement.com/disney/*
(2) *https://thewaltdisneycompany.com/app/uploads/2022/11/TWDC-Standards-of-Business-Conduct-Nov-2022.pdf*
(3) *The Random House College Dictionary, Revised Edition.*
(4) *https://kidshealth.org/* **How Toddlers Communicate** *Between the ages of 2 and 3, toddlers have a huge jump in language skills:*

- **At age 2,** *most kids say at least 2 words together. By 30 months, they are saying 50 words or more and are understood about half of the time. They are using words like "I," "me," or "we." By 30 months, most kids can follow 2-step instructions, like "Pick up the ball and bring it to Daddy."*
- **By age 3,** *a toddler's vocabulary is usually more than 200 words. Kids can string together 2- or 3-word sentences. They can talk with you in a conversation that has at least 2 back-and-forth exchanges. Other people can understand your toddler most of the time.*

Acknowledgements:

A special thanks to Jill Kelsey, Editor/Publisher, *First Time Parent Magazine.* Jill provided my first pre-publication review for my book and also published my article "Why Choose Artificial Insemination?" in *First Time Parent Magazine (1/18/2025).*

ABOUT THE AUTHOR

Sally is a retired credit professional. During her 40+ year career, Sally served in leadership positions for 19 years and believes that being a parent made her a better manager and being a manager helped make her a better parent. As an avid saver, Sally chose to retire early when faced with an unpleasant work situation and Return To Office mandates post-COVID. Her first major project was writing "***Raising Kids Training Dogs and Living the Life You Dare to Lead***," which outlines her parenting philosophies while sharing her unique journey into parenthood. Her main goals in writing the book were to create a legacy for her own kids and to share her approach, strategies and ideas to help others raise amazing kids too.

Sally continues to reside in the 100+ year old house in northern Illinois where she raised her family. She's an avid DIYer, dedicated gardener, and voracious reader. Sally makes time to take long walks in nature, attend plays/musicals, play pickleball, research and plan future trips, and explore other creative pursuits.

www.ingramcontent.com/pod-product-compliance
Lightning Source LLC
Chambersburg PA
CBHW071718120626
46550CB00001B/289